His Perfect Imperfection

By award-winning author

Natasza Waters

Natasza Waters

His Perfect Imperfection
Copyright © 2015 Natasza Waters
Print ISBN: 978-0-9947772-2-5
E-book ISBN: 978-0-9947772-1-8

First E-book Publication: July 2015
First Print Publication: December 2015

Cover design by Dawné Dominique
Edited by Write Right Edits

<u>Dedication</u>

Our emotional stature, to a large part, is a complicated mix of how we see ourselves; how we see others, and how we think others see us. Physical imperfections challenge us to look deeper for the beautiful person inside. Our emotional maturity is measured when we look upon a perceived physical flaw, and can see beyond skin deep. In truth, you are not just a body. You are a perfect being.

When two people love each other, they don't love a part; they love the whole person. Love is truly blinded when it sees the soul shining from within. Love brings out the best in people. Never doubt yourself. We are all a perfect imperfection.

I'd like to dedicate this book to my gorgeous "shiny" wife, and all those who are living with a challenge that makes them unique, not flawed.

Ken Leonard (Natasza's HB)

Natasza Waters

Acknowledgment

It is an odd fact that grief can be a powerful creator, and with Dawné Dominque's amazing talent, she brought to life the adage, "A picture is worth a thousand words." After the death of her brother, she created the image which would become the cover of His Perfect Imperfection. My condolences and deepest thanks to Dawné.

Diana Barrios Tan, you were my first official fan. We've had a lot of fun on Waters' Warriors (our street team) and Diana came up with a pet name for HB: Hot Buns! Hope you'll be around for another few books Diana!

A big thank you to my beta readers, Sheri Fredricks, a talented author herself. Tonya Gibbons Smalley, Chief Coordinator at InD'Tale magazine, and the captain of Waters' Warriors, Kimberly Hickey.

Lee Macdonald (Fraser), an officer and a lady. Thank you for explaining what it's like to run the Good Life Marathon.

Prologue

Beneath this skin lives a soul within.

A flurry of fingers that point and eyes that gawk.

Amongst you all, I must walk.

With a shield of silver scales the mirror reflects a grotesque

tale.

A dragon's heart, I have not.

I am more than lesions, cracks and spots.

See my soul beyond its mottled case.

I shed no tears, nor hide my face.

I am the perfect imperfection

Natasza Waters

.

His Perfect Imperfection
Natasza Waters
Copyright © 2015
Chapter One

Sitting at a small table sipping coffee in her favorite Sidney hangout, Mika ignored the couples drifting by the window, smiling at the sights and one another. Being single wasn't her biggest concern. At the ripe old age of twenty-nine, she was on the verge of becoming homeless.

As the steam curled from her cup and the death of a thousand coffee beans scented the air, she read the tiny ads in the Victoria Times newspaper. Numbingly similar, one looked the same as the next. She needed a two bedroom place by next month or move back in with her mother. She loved her mom, but she'd rather be dragged across Georgia Strait by a pod of killer whales than show up at her front door.

Her best friend, Dinky, a name she'd gotten when they were in grade one and before any of them even knew what a dinky was, had accepted her boyfriend's proposal. Mika couldn't afford the small house they'd rented for the last ten years on her own. The time had come to fly solo.

1

She sipped on her Americano and crossed out the ads, searching for a place closer to Esquimalt, where she worked. The murmur of café conversation drifted like white noise in the background as she crossed yet another ad off the page, due to the price. Her pen hovered over the next one. Less descriptive than the others, it had two bedrooms and a reference number. The price sat at the top end of her budget, but what piqued her attention was the area. Living her whole life on Vancouver Island, mainly Victoria, she knew where the wealthy people resided on large waterfront estates. She circled the ad and picked up her iPad, searching for the listing on Craigslist. There wasn't much more information. She responded with an email.

Hello, I'm interested in the two bedroom you have available. I'm single, no pets, although I like dogs, and I have a full time job at the base. I'm quiet, don't smoke, and my roommate is getting married. I need a place quickly. If your rental is still available, please call (604)555-8282 Mika.

She leaned back in her chair, cupping the weighty porcelain mug in both hands. Many of the properties on the eastern shore of Victoria had carriage houses, and the owners would either rent them out for the summer or in this case, long-term. At least, she hoped it was long-term.

She asked the barista for a takeout cup and transferred her coffee, snapping on the lid, and walked the one block to her house, dodging the tourists headed toward the waterfront pier.

Sidney by the Sea's population bloomed in the spring. An eclectic mix of coffee shops, restaurants, boutiques boasting pillows with embroidered sea shells and all the marine trinkets tourists loved, nudged together to create the quaint main drag.

She shucked her light jacket and slung it over the hook near the front door. Stretching out on her couch, she faced another Saturday with nothing to do but skim the television channels. Dinky spent most nights over at Jeff's since he'd popped the question. Maybe she'd call one of the other gals in her close-knit group of friends.

Everyone was married now, except for her and Jennifer. Cyn, Sarah, Kate, and now Dinky, had found their true loves. Jen would probably never get married. She had an image of the kind of man she wanted—rich, handsome, sweet and sexy all rolled into one guy. *Good luck with that.* Mika snorted. In the meantime, Jen test drove any guy who asked her for a date, unlike herself, who never dated. She exercised, ate reasonably well, and had a pretty good figure for five-foot-eight. Nope, the reason she didn't date was far more menacing, but now that she was in remission, maybe she could take a test drive.

Her phone sang out with Bon Jovi's ringtone, *It's my life.*
"Hello?"

"Mika, I'm Cain Sallas. You emailed about the two bedroom?" He pronounced her name Mike-ah.

Her brows rose. Some woman had one helluva hunky-sounding husband. He also had an accent. It was slight, but it was there.

"Yes, but it's actually Mee-ka. Is it still available?" She crossed her fingers and clenched her teeth.

"It is. I'm home today. Can you come by in an hour?"

"Yes, and I can bring a reference from my current landlord. My friend and I have rented this house for several years."

"Fine."

He gave her the address while she bounced up and down on the couch trying to write at the same time. "Thank you, Mr. Sallas. I'll leave now."

****

She almost missed the driveway. Only two brick pillars marked either side of the entrance. A line of Douglas firs and Arbutus trees, with their fawn colored bark, hid the property located on the infamous Ten Mile Point. She backed up a few feet and turned in. The road wound its way through the thick, green forest then broke from the tree line.

"Wow," she said, as she slowed down to look at the expansive property.

Perched near the cliff's edge, the two-level building sat nobly with floor-to-ceiling windows instead of walls, offering a three hundred and sixty degree view, surrounded by pristine landscaping. A hexagonal-shaped tower grew from the center, reminding her of a lighthouse. A unique mix of Victorian and

4

contemporary. She slowed down as she passed a separate garage with five bay doors. The deep green, perfectly trimmed lawn had to be an acre in size. Flower beds with spring bulbs popped their heads from the rich soil, coloring the mounds of rocks and dirt. Amazing! They had to be a very well-to-do family.

She stopped her heap of a Toyota at the end of the driveway. Old Tess burped once then coughed before shutting down. Only a few months to go and she could finally afford a new car. She liked doing it the old-fashioned way. Cash in hand. No debt or credit cards for her.

Plucking her purse from the passenger seat, she shimmied from the car. Stepping up to the massive glass doors, she blew out a breath and rang the doorbell.

"I'll be down in a second," a deep voice came from the speaker next to the entrance.

She backed away and waited. Less than a minute later, the door opened and a big German Shepherd bounded out.

"Hey," she said, squatting down. The dog sniffed her legs, then sat on its haunches, sweeping the walkway with its tail.

"That's saying something if she likes you," he said.

Mika's gaze started from the bottom of his jeans and climbed up the man standing in the doorway. Her gaze skittered up long legs to a taut waist, clambered over the ribbed contours of his tight t-shirt fitted across the molded muscle on his upper arms, and landed on a face that shoved her nerve endings into

5

high gear. Scruff! Shit! He had scruff covering the hard angles of his jaw. Blue eyes, so dark they almost seemed black, with infinite depth, accentuated his swarthy features. She gave the dog a scrub behind her ears.

"Your dog is beautiful. Shepherds are my favorite." As if she understood, the dog gave a short bark, making Mika laugh. "And you're smart."

"This is Breeze, and I'm Cain Sallas." He held out his hand.

"Nice to meet you, sir." She looked at the garden beds lining the cobblestoned walkway leading in both directions from the house.

"I'm renting the cottage." There wasn't a lot of warmth in his gravelly voice or his harsh expression, which was intensified by two dark slashes of eyebrows. "Follow me."

Breeze ran ahead of them. "You have a beautiful home."

He nodded. "I travel a lot. I'm hoping whoever rents the cottage, will look after Breeze when I'm gone." He whistled and Breeze's ears perked up. When Cain revealed a tennis ball, she started to jump up on her hind legs. His muscled arm drew back, and he sent a homer across the massive lawn. Breeze charged after the ball at full-speed.

"I wouldn't mind taking care of Breeze at all. I work eight to four."

"Good."

Cain walked to the end of the right wing of the house, and Mika looked over her shoulder. The back of the house faced the

6

ocean, and the front was designed for entertaining. He and his wife must have a lot of parties.

"Did you build this house?"

"No, I bought it a couple years ago."

The front yard was a mix of concrete and lush green landscaping. A large outdoor living area with a fireplace and a circular cement table for at least twelve people hovered in the middle. A large Jacuzzi sat near a wooden pergola with vines growing around the beams. During the summer months, they would be in full bloom. Metal tiki torches surrounded the entire patio.

Talk about party central, Mika thought.

Breeze returned with the ball and dropped it at her master's feet. Cain sent it flying again as they crossed the immaculate lawn toward a cozy-looking cottage. Whitewashed with a splash of color from the red door and a tiny side yard laid with patio tiles, it would make a painter's mouth drool.

Cain stuck his hand in his jeans pocket and pulled out a set of keys. She opened the screen and held it for him while he unlocked the door. Letting her enter first, she took a peek as she brushed by. Leaping up and down with joy as she scanned the cozy cottage wouldn't be the most mature thing to do, but she sure felt like it. An island in the kitchen separated it from the small living room and dining area. Large windows brightened the space. Sunlight splashed across rich wood floors and built-in shelves.

"The bedroom is down that hallway," he said, pointing to their left.

Plank flooring infused the cottage with warmth. She pushed the first door on the left open to reveal the bathroom and shook her head. Beautiful. Why wasn't he asking an arm and a leg for this place? Cottages like this in Victoria were usually rented on a nightly basis to tourists. Or used as a guest house for family and friends. The marble counters and deep Jacuzzi tub sat next to a two-person shower. It was large by her standards. Normally, she had to leave her bathroom to change her mind. She carried on down the hallway and found a sizeable bedroom with a small, walk-in closet.

The second bedroom across the hall was smaller, but just as nice. When she returned to the living room, she noted his domineering presence.

"Was there a misprint in the ad?" She should have shut her mouth, but if there had been a mistake, she needed to know now before she dropped to her knees and begged him to let her rent this place.

"Misprint?" he asked, and angled his cut jaw.

"Yes, I mean the ad said a thousand dollars a month. Did you forget to put a two or a three in front of the rent?"

Although he didn't smile, his expression softened. "No, but if the tenant is willing to take care of Breeze and they're responsible, then I'm satisfied." He paused. "What do you do on the base?"

"I'm a technical writer. Policies and procedures mainly, but I create equipment guides as well. Nothing earth-shattering by any stretch."

"How long have you worked there?" he asked, pulling aside a curtain to let more light in.

"After I earned my bachelors from UVIC, I landed the job about seven years ago. I'm not military, I'm a civilian employee."

He nodded and surveyed her. "Are you moving in here alone or do you have someone else coming with you?"

"It's just me. My best friend is getting married. I can't afford the house we rent alone, and I'd rather avoid having a roommate who's a stranger."

She wondered what he did for a living. Probably some executive in a bank or some high-flying company she'd never heard of. His looks were so rugged and sexy, she imagined his secretary thought she was the luckiest girl on the planet, never mind his wife. Speaking of which, if he wanted her to look after Breeze, where was the wife and kids?

She rummaged around in her brain cells to convince him.

"I'm sure you have several people to choose from, but I promise I'm long past frat parties." She held up her finger. "I have to admit my friends celebrate everything from birthdays to

9

their kids getting a new front tooth, but we don't swing from chandeliers anymore." She tipped her head back to look at the ceiling. "See, no chandelier. We're good."

His brooding expression lightened, and he nodded with a hint of a smile on his lips. "Okay, that's honest enough." He stepped toward the front door, and she followed. "Can you move in by the first? That's only two weeks away."

Did she dare to hope? "Yes. I have a month's rent and the damage deposit." Patting her purse, she'd come prepared.

Cain opened the screen door and she followed him. "The first month's rent is fine. I trust you'll stay away from the light fixtures and avoid burning the place down."

With an inner sigh he couldn't see, she added a smile that he could and dug in her purse, pulling out an envelope with the money. "Here." *Please, please take it.*

This cottage was a godsend, and she couldn't ever imagine moving away. He'd have to kick her out.

"What do you think, Breeze?"

Breeze lifted her nose in the air and barked. "Guess she approves." He politely accepted the envelope from her.

"Thank you." She tipped onto her toes and back down again. She thrust out her hand and ignored the zip of excitement when his warm fingers clasped her hand for a cordial shake. "Would it be all right if I started moving things in this week? I'll wait until the last weekend to bribe my friends' husbands to help me move the big stuff."

He nodded. "That would be acceptable."

He escorted Mika to her car. "Thank you so much, Mr. Sallas." Surprisingly, he opened the driver's door for her. It yielded with a loud squeak. She didn't miss the somewhat disapproving glance he tossed at Old Tess. "It runs," she spouted. "I'm just saving up for a new one."

He offered her the keys to the cottage. "I'll have the tenancy agreement prepared the next time you come by. We'll see you soon, Mika, and I'm Cain, not Mr. Sallas."

Faster than a cartoon character, she took the keys from him. They were warm from his large palm. Breeze ran up with her tongue lolling out of her mouth, and sat beside her master.

"Bye, Breeze." She gave the dog a quick rub between her ears.

Driving down the paved roadway, she strayed a look in the rearview mirror. Cain stood where she'd left him. He was probably taking note of her license plate to hand it over to a friend in the RCMP to check on her. She didn't mind. The only thing on her record was a picture and an entry that said pathetically single, but a hard worker and a good friend.

As soon as she got home, she called Dinky. With excited squeals, she told her about the new place. Dinky hurried home. They did what two best friends would do—they found the property on Google Earth and zoomed in so Dinky could whistle at her lucky find.

11

They stared at the semi-clear image from the satellite. The property was huge, probably four acres or so. Dinky stood behind the chair and wrapped her arms around Mika. "I'm going to miss you, girlfriend."

"Naw, you won't. You'll be too busy with all that wedded bliss and hot sex."

Dinky sat down on the corner of their scuffed desk and covered Mika's hand. She wore her hair in braids, and the freckles on Dinky's face made her look younger than twenty-nine. "I love you, and no matter whether or not I'm getting married, you're still my number-one bestie." She grinned at her. "I want you to remember that while I'm having wild monkey sex with Jeff."

Mika burst out laughing. "You are such a bitch."

"I know." Dinky bobbed her head and shifted to the couch. She slid one of the million wedding magazines that littered their house onto the middle of the living room table and waved for Mika to join her. "Okay, we need to plan."

Mika groaned. Since Jeff asked for her hand, they'd done nothing else. "Let's order pizza before that," she suggested. "I feel like celebrating."

Dinky smirked at her. "Don't think they make a carrot, hummus, and cucumber pizza."

"Psst, very funny. I mean the cheese and pepperoni, greasy kind."

Later, as they gnawed on pizza, Mika described Cain.

"Where's the missus?" Dinky asked.

She shrugged, pulling a long string of cheese from the pizza, and bridging it to her mouth. "He didn't say, and I didn't ask. By the looks of him, I'd guess she's tall, slender, model material with big blues and legs up to her eyeballs."

Dinky swallowed her mouthful. "You saying this guy is hot?"

Mika fanned herself. "Nope, I'm saying he's jaw-dropping, make a girl sweat, and squeeze her thighs together, hot."

"Whoa, I'm helping you move in."

Mika smiled. And that—she thought, was how you conned your best friend into moving heavy boxes.

Chapter Two

Mika clipped the bungee cord to the trunk lid and found a notch under the bumper to secure the other end. She stood back and appraised her work. Everyone driving behind her would laugh, seeing the boxes stuffed into her old Toyota. Packing was not one of her strong suits, but at least they wouldn't land on the highway on her way to the cottage. Cain's place was situated on the eastern shore of Victoria.

The Friday night traffic going into the city rolled along bumper to bumper. Tourists flooded in as she merged with the ferry dump from Swartz Bay headed southbound. It took her forty-five minutes on the Pat Bay Highway to reach Cain's winding driveway at 7:30 pm. Light beamed from one end of his home. The curtain-less floor-to-ceiling windows revealed everything inside. She slowed down as she passed the main house, and saw Cain rise from the couch.

He gave a short wave back when she stuck her arm out. Mika didn't want to interrupt him and his family at this hour. Breeze could be out and about, so she reduced her speed and came to a rolling stop in front of the cottage. Flicking the living room lights on after fiddling with the front door, she smiled. She hadn't been dreaming.

14

This place rocked! Unloading the boxes, mostly pictures, bedding and books, she found a place on the built-in shelving units in the living room for her favorite hardcover books. Dinky liked to collect stuff. Without a roommate, Mika would keep the cottage an airy uncluttered space. Unzipping a leather case, she yarded her laptop out and flashed it up. An external speaker boosted the sound, and she found her favorite playlist, then turned up the volume.

With her arms full of bath towels, she strode down the hallway and tucked them neatly on the open shelving unit next to the shower. Technically, she wasn't a renter yet, so she couldn't fill up the huge tub with bubbles. Soon, she grinned. Very soon.

Balancing another box on her hip, she pushed open the door to her bedroom. The guys would help her with her queen size bed, but for now, she plopped the box of bed sheets and pillow cases in the corner.

It took thirteen steps to get from one end of the hallway to the other. She rounded the corner, humming to the music. Alanis Morissette streamed from her speaker. She put a little bounce in her step headed toward the remaining boxes. As Alanis's alt-rock angst filled the air, Mika couldn't help getting her groove on to *You Oughta Know*. With a sway of her hips and a twirl, she rounded the kitchen table. Hands on her waist, she shook her hips, swinging it like a good thing. Throwing her arms into the air, she booked it with a sexy move no one in the free world would ever see.

****

Sitting on his couch with his nose in a new political thriller, Cain's eyes strayed to Breeze when her ears perked and she whined from her blanket near the fireplace. As Mika's old Toyota passed by, he gave her a quick wave. He told her she could drop off a few things before the start of the month, and the woman seemed to follow through. He read another page, and Breeze whined again.

"What's the matter with you?"

Breeze padded to the door.

"You want to see her, don't you?"

Breeze turned once and barked at him.

He sighed and rose to his feet. "Let's go, then. We'll make sure everything is working."

As they neared the cottage, he saw Mika, illuminated by the light through the screen door. A song poured from a speaker attached to a laptop. He watched as she twirled and swayed her hips, a huge smile beaming on her face. Breeze cocked her head.

"Think she likes the place, girl."

Breeze trotted ahead of him, and he continued to watch Mika twirling with abandon in the living room. A sloppy, loose sweater and baggy jeans cinched at the waist with a belt, hid a tall but curvy figure. The woman was definitely in her happy place. He gave a short whistle.

16

"Don't think we'll interrupt her tonight," he said, giving Breeze a few strokes when she returned to his side.

As he pet the Shepherd's soft coat, Cain appreciated the carefree nature of his new tenant. He found Mika's raw innocence refreshing. Her honest joy when he handed over the keys to the cottage was sincerely cute. In his profession, he didn't run across that very often.

****

Each night, exactly at 7:30, Mika drove in the yard with more boxes jammed in her trunk. On the seventh night, he took Breeze for a walk around the property and stopped at the cottage.

"Miss Makris."

"Oh, hey." She opened the door. "I'm not disturbing your family by coming at this hour, am I?"

He shot a look at Breeze and then back at Mika. A messy but very cute bundle of curls topped the woman's head, and small, gold hoops dangled from her lobes. She didn't wear much makeup. A natural beauty with big, dark eyes and narrow features hinted at something other than Caucasian. If there was one thing he knew about, it was women. Most used modern cosmetic miracles to help soften the rough edges, but Mika didn't need any. She'd been blessed with long dark lashes and blush cheeks.

"No, not at all." He scanned the cottage and saw the few personal items she'd brought to make the space her own.

17

"Come in. Hey, Breeze."

Breeze didn't wait for another invitation. She squeezed past his leg, trotted into the living room and flopped down on the rug as if she owned the place.

"I'm just filling up the kitchen cupboards," Mika said, sliding past him, and quickly placed the box she'd emptied onto a pile of flattened cardboard by the window.

"I have a recycle bin near the garage. Leave them on the porch, I'll get rid of those," he offered.

She nodded her thanks.

"I checked everything—oven, fridge—before listing the place. They should be working. If something isn't, let me know."

"It all works just fine. In fact, I've got juice and water in the fridge. Would you like something?" She paused after opening the cabinet.

"No, I'm fine, thanks."

He watched her stretch to her tippy toes and grasp a glass from the top shelf.

"I can't wait till this Saturday to finally move in. Think I've convinced most of my friends' husbands to help me get the heavy furniture over here."

He watched as she filled the glass with ice from the freezer and topped it up with water. "That's good. I've, uh, got to fly out on Monday. On the weekend I can show you where Breeze's food and bowls are. I'll give you the code to the main house." He didn't trust many people, mainly women, but something about Mika rang true, and maybe a little naive.

"Of course."

"Good."

"I don't want to disturb your family too early, so I'll come by around nine?"

He cleared his throat. She'd mentioned family a few times. He might as well clarify now. "I don't have a family."

Mika gazed at him for a second, allowing his comment to sink in. "You live in that enormous house by yourself?"

He jerked his shoulders. "Breeze and me."

She surveyed him with her intelligent eyes. He almost chuckled. It wasn't the first time he'd seen a questioning look like hers. She probably thought he was gay. Now *that* was funny.

Without a hitch she said, "I'll be over early Saturday with a load of boxes if that's all right, and then the guys will follow in the U-Haul I rented later on."

"That's fine." He called Breeze to his side and tossed a, "Good night," over his shoulder.

He liked his privacy. As long as Mika didn't invade his space, their arrangement would work.

****

Toweling his hair, he heard the rumble of an engine as someone drove past the house Saturday morning. Wandering to the bedroom window, he looked out to see Mika parking an old

19

pickup she must have borrowed. She released the tailgate and pulled a wood plank from the bed, settling it on the ground. With a couple bounds, she was inside the truck bed and returning with her arms filled.

Tossing the towel over the leather lounger, he walked into the massive walk-in closet. Half of it was empty, even though it held his suits and a varied selection of shirts and slacks. Fine wood cabinetry stored his cufflinks, socks and other clothes. He wouldn't pack for his job until Sunday night. The suits, he carried on to the plane. Image was everything in his profession, and this job had some unique qualities.

Technically, spending a week in Fiji with a British executive wouldn't be considered a hardship. He mixed business with pleasure as a matter of course, with a satisfying end for his clients. He finished dressing, and headed downstairs.

Settling in front of his computer, he searched for his client on the internet. He read magazine columns, news articles, and memorized the business mandate of the company she ran. Changing the search to images only, he typed in her name. Like a chameleon, she changed her appearance from top-ranking businesswoman to chic and graceful party attendee. Her family was well known in society, but she'd made a name for herself in the last few years. It would be an interesting week.

The next time he looked up it was one o'clock. Breeze whined and stood at the door, signaling she needed to go out. Time for a run. He changed into shorts and tied the laces on his running shoes. He headed out, nearing the cottage, Cain intended on passing by with only a wave. His pace slowed when he heard Mika cursing up a storm. The patio was littered with bits and pieces of what would become a barbeque.

Mika flipped a screwdriver back and forth between two fingers and held the instructions in her other hand. With a huge sigh, she picked up two pieces and tried to match them together. A growl emanated from her, telling him she'd done this a few times already without success. She didn't see him and with a frustrated shout, she hurled a side panel from her hands. He couldn't dodge it, but managed to grab the flying debris before the metal slammed into his chest.

Mika's hands flew to her mouth. "Oh God, I'm so sorry. I didn't see you there."

Again, he felt his lips curl with an uncommon smile. "Obviously. I'd hate to think you're trying to kill your landlord already."

"Are you okay?" she asked, stepping toward him.

He nodded and surveyed the mess.

"I know, I know." She flapped her arms. "It's embarrassing, don't ask."

"Trying to put this together?"

"Yes." She spat out, getting angry again. "I wanted to make everyone steaks for dinner. You know, to thank them."

"You write procedural manuals, don't you?"

21

Her eyes glared at him, and she shook the screwdriver. "I still have this to kill you with."

He chuckled and lifted both hands in peace. "As long as you promise not to cause bodily harm, I can give you a hand."

She read the instructions and handed him the parts as he put it together. In forty-five minutes, they hoisted the top piece with the burners onto the stand, and he bolted it down. Mika lifted the lid a couple times, then pressed the igniter.

"Now, why couldn't I do that myself?"

He swiped his hands and shrugged. "I'm sure given a few months, you would have." He watched her lips twitch, giving him a surprising amount of pleasure.

Mika narrowed her eyes. "Not funny. True, but not funny."

He handed her the screwdriver. "Come on, Breeze. Let's go."

A panel truck rambled down the roadway followed by four cars.

"Looks like the troops are here. Umm, you're very welcome to come for dinner. The ladies are making a ton of food, and they're all good cooks."

"Thanks for the invitation. I'll think about it." He ran toward the path leading through the tree line before any of her friends stepped out of their vehicles.

Did she think they'd become friends? Women weren't his friends, they were business. He had a few acquaintances and his brother, but he lived a solitary lifestyle outside of his contracts.

22

He ran at a medium pace, checking his heart rate on his Fitbit. After two rounds on the trail the community had hacked through the tree line, he jogged down to the public beach access. Once he'd passed onto his waterfront property, he took the stairs that led to the back of his house. Breeze, as usual, had made it home before him and lapped at her water bowl.

Pacing his back patio to cool down, he saw the group milling around Mika's cottage. The sound of laughter reached him. His stomach rumbled with hunger when the scent of steaks on the grill wafted through the air. If he joined them for dinner, he wouldn't have to cook for himself or go out. It wouldn't hurt to check out her friends. There were at least five ladies darting in and out of the cottage. One guy stood by the grill, as smoke curled into the air. The rest sat in lawn chairs around the permanent fire pit built into the brick patio stones.

Shower first, then he'd consider his options.

****

Mika caught a glimpse of Cain down on the beach. She waved, but he was intent on his jogging. He looked like a machine with taut, rhythmic steps. He'd been running for well over an hour.

Jen joined her and watched him run by.

"Look at that hot specimen of man-flesh," she purred.

"Jen, don't you get tired of the chase?"

With a *swoosh* of her blonde, thick ponytail, Jen gazed at her like she was nuts. "No. In fact, the first part of any relationship is the best. You should try it sometime."

"You know my reasons."

Dinky wandered up and strung her arms across their shoulders. "Whad'up, girlfriends?" She shifted her gaze. "Oh, I see. I mean, no I don't."

They all chuckled.

"Didn't you say you were going to start jogging?" Jen asked, her gaze never leaving Cain's body as he passed by below them.

Mika nodded. "I am. Tomorrow."

"Nice dog," Jeff said, wrapping his arms around Dinky.

The girls all murmured their assent.

Jeff chuckled. "You still looking for Mr. Perfect, babe?" He asked Dinky, then bit her neck.

"Nope, found him already," Dinky said, turning in her fiancé's arms.

Mika watched them with a tinge of jealousy. They were so in love. All her friends had found great guys.

Jen shot a look her way, and if not mistaken, there was a little jealousy in the blonde's eyes as well. What girl didn't want to find someone who adored her?

They milled around for another twenty minutes, the guys with cold beers in their hands and the ladies sipping their favorite beverages. Mika breathed in the warm spring air and looked out over the ocean. She might not have a guy who loved her, but she had this place to come home to every night, and she was happy about that.

"How is the chicken coming?" she asked Jeff, who was still kissing his soon-to-be wife. "Hey, you two, knock it off. The chicken's on fire."

Jeff broke the kiss slowly and stared with absolute adoration at Dinky, who flushed at his attention. "A little fire is good for the flesh." He winked at her. "We can take 'em off and start the steaks."

"'Kay, then I'll get inside and finish things off. I'm sorry I don't have a table. We'll just have to balance the plates on our laps."

"I have a sheet of plywood and a couple saw horses in the garage, if that would help?"

She turned, and so did her stomach. Cain stood there, freshly washed with a little scruff on his jaw. A comfortable pair of jeans hung low on his hips and a dark blue t-shirt was tucked into his taut waistband.

"Well, hello," Jennifer said, before Mika could find her tongue again.

Cain's gaze swerved up and down Jen with a glint of appreciation. "Afternoon," he said politely.

Mika immediately felt like hiding under a rock. A side-effect of the white elephant she dealt with played mind games with her. In school, all the guys gravitated toward Jennifer.

Being Jen's friend, she sometimes got a cursory glance. Funny that the prettiest girl in their group wasn't married to some rich businessman, but Jen always found fault and dumped everyone she'd dated.

Cain's gaze veered to Mika. "I'll get a couple of your friends to give me a hand."

"Hey!" Kate's husband, Tad, joined them. "You say you need a hand with something?"

Tad had a big, teddy bear heart, even if he was a salesman. Jeff, Dinky's heartthrob, wasn't far behind, and introduced himself.

Then Sam leaned in. "I'm Sarah's ball and chain," he said.

"Nice." Sarah threw over her shoulder.

Tad sized Cain up while Jennifer had shifted into her "see me" stance—tall, curvy and very wide-eyed to accentuate the blue.

"Thanks, Mr. Sall…" She paused not knowing what to call him. He'd told her to call him Cain. She could call him landlord, maybe Mr. Hot and Handsome. "Cain is my landlord," she said, introducing him to all of her friends.

Jeff nodded. "You've got a beautiful place here."

"Hey, I'm Mac and this is my wife, Cyn."

"Nice to meet you all," Cain said, gripping every hand with a firm shake. "The materials are in the garage."

"We're on it," Tad said. "Lead the way."

Mika and all five of her friends watched the guys head across the lawn.

"Melt butter on my ass and call it popcorn," Jen murmured. "That is the most exquisite man I have ever seen." She ribbed Mika with her elbow. "Why the hell didn't you say he was your landlord when we saw him earlier?" Her lips curled into a wicked grin.

Mika shrugged. She knew full well.

"Think I might hang out here a little more often," Jen teased.

****

After all the food had been consumed, Mika wandered into her kitchen to clean up the utensils and throw some glasses into the dishwasher.

"Interesting guy," Dinky said, coming in with a handful of cutlery. "He seems…well-traveled. A little dark and broody, but I don't think he's a serial killer."

She grinned. "I hope not."

"Don't worry about Jen. You know how she is."

"Not worried. They'd make a beautiful couple."

Cain had paid a lot of attention to Jennifer during supper and the half hour that had passed since then. He really didn't have a choice. Jen had squished herself next to him at the table and put all her charms to good use.

"Cain said he had a phone call he had to take and wanted to tell you thanks. He's gone back to the main house. Personally, I think it was to get away from her."

"He's a big boy. I'm sure he can fend for himself."

"No estranged wife or babies?" Dinky asked, cupping her chin in the palm of her hand.

"I don't know. Probably. I mean, what guy looks like him and isn't married at least once or four times."

Dinky snorted. "It's kinda mysterious, him living in that big house all by himself."

Mika shut the cupboard after putting the washed glasses away. "Maybe he's a serial killer." She popped her brows a couple times. Her voice dropped to a spooky tone. "He lures women with his exotic, rugged looks and enticing eyes back to a secret cave under his glass house and tortures them."

Dinky's brow rose. "You really should think about movie production."

"He'd make a sexy book villain."

"I've got a better story. He's a tortured soul, living with a deep, dark, painful secret, and along comes Mika to soothe his old wounds."

Now it was her turn to snort. "More like Beauty and the Beast, and I'm the beast."

Dinky grabbed the towel and dried a plate. "Why do you do that? You think humor and a sharp tongue will keep a guy who really falls for you away?"

"Nope." She gave Dinky her toothy smile. "Just have to be naked. They run away screaming all by themselves."

Dinky rolled her eyes. "You're stupid."

"Yeah, you're stupider, but I love you."

A short while later, she hugged her friends and watched them depart. Jeff took the U-Haul and would return it for her on their way home.

With her kitchen cleaned up, she dried her hands on the dish towel. The couch and TV were in place, but the rest of the cottage was a mess of boxes. Breeze bumped her nose against the screen door and sauntered in.

"Hey, girl."

She had to be fat and happy. Everyone had snuck her a piece of steak when Cain wasn't looking. She hoped like hell Breeze wouldn't erupt in hot spots with all the well-meaning love from her friends. Rounding the island, she plopped down on the couch and stared at the remote control. Television was such a time-waster, but when you didn't have anyone else to talk to.... She plucked up the remote. Breeze padded up and stared at her.

"Well, what are you waiting for?" she asked.

With a graceful bound, the dog settled on the couch and placed her head on Mika's lap.

The drone of the TV and warmth of Breeze's body lured her into a happy sleep.

"Sorry, I was looking for Breeze. Figured she'd be here."

Natasza Waters

Mika blinked her eyes open. Cain stood in the shadow of the room, his body a silhouette of alluring male—not a serial killer—a few feet away. Breeze had curled herself behind Mika's legs, eyeing her master, but in no hurry to move.

"Sorry, I dozed off." She pushed herself to a sitting position. "I should have brought Breeze back to your place."

"Teaching my dog bad manners," he said, without humor.

She swallowed and gave the dog a rub. "Hers are a lot better than mine," she joked. "I guess she's not allowed on the furniture."

Cain watched her with his dark, brooding look. "No, she isn't."

"Time to go home, Breeze." She gave her a little nudge and the dog begrudgingly jumped off the couch, hit the floor, arched her back in a big stretch, and gave her head a shake that worked itself all the way down her body.

Cain paused at the door. "Thank you for dinner. It was good, and your friends are decent people."

"Light fixtures are still intact, too."

"I see that. Good night," he said in his low timbre.

Yeah, he was just Jen's type, excruciatingly handsome and cold as an arctic blast.

Chapter Three

Sunday morning arrived with a brilliant blue sky and calm waters as she looked out her window. Mika stretched and smiled at her first glorious day in her new home. She'd made herself a promise and was going to keep it.

She pulled a pair of loose jogging pants from a box. All her clothes were on the loose side for a reason. As she sat down on the bed, she stared down at her legs. The battle she'd waged left scars, but she was winning, at least for now, and tugged on her pants and the rest of her running outfit. After chugging down a glass of orange juice, she wandered out her front door.

Breeze barked and ran across the lawn that separated her place from the main house. Mika followed the instructions she'd read online about doing several minutes of stretching before heading out on a jog. As she lunged forward, stretching her thigh muscles, a ball dropped at her feet. She laughed, picked it up and tossed it.

"You throw like a girl." She heard from behind her.

"That's odd," she said, squeezing her brow together. "My sex change was supposed to take care of that."

Cain's eyes widened.

31

"Course I throw like a girl. I am a girl."

He looked a little embarrassed even though his sexy dark features didn't shift all that much.

"You run?"

"Yes, but I'm a rookie."

Cain's running gear looked high end and fit his chiseled body like a professional athlete. "How long have you been running?" he asked, stretching out.

She pretended not to copy him, but she did. "Today," she said, peeking at what Cain did next. "Usually I work out on the base and use their facilities, or else I just take one big-ass, long walk."

He watched her while she tried to look less like a newbie and more like a serious athlete.

"Well, you're doing those wrong." He knelt with one knee beside her. His hand cupped the underside of her thigh and anchored her heel. "Now push forward."

"Whoa," she exclaimed, feeling the muscle stretch.

"Good," he said. "Other leg."

As she did it, he slowly let go and allowed her to get the feel without his hand putting resistance on her heel.

"Another one I use is this. It focuses on hips and glutes."

Watching him first, she then imitated his movements. She felt the pull and nodded.

"These are called the squat-thrust climbers. Stand with your arms at your sides. Squat to the ground with your knees close together. Place your hands flat on the ground, shoulder-width apart. Keep your abs tight, and jump your legs back to assume the pushup position."

Mika kinda forgot what she was doing because as soon as he tightened his abs and assumed the position, as he called it, his upper arms clenched with muscle and her abs tightened all by themselves. He slowly turned his sharp jaw toward her, waiting.

She scrambled down on all fours, but not nearly as elegantly as him. He jumped up and walked behind her.

"Up on your toes," he commanded. "Straighten your body out a bit more."

She blew out her breath, already feeling her arm muscles begin to yell at her. Man, she had a long way to go.

Cain's large hands gently grasped her hips. "I'm going to hold some of your weight, now run your legs under your chest, bringing your knees high and keep your hips low. Then jump your legs back to the squat position, stand and repeat."

Worried he might end up with a hernia if he held her ass up, she said, "Show me." Yeah, it was sneaky, but she had to shake her arms out.

Cain's strength made the exercise look easy. When he finished, he loosened his shoulders with a slow roll.

"Your turn."

"Crap. Can't I just run until I'm panting and then give up?"

A smile curled his lips. "I suppose, but if you're going to run, you should work the muscles like they need to be worked."

She groaned and did the squats and lunges. Cain whistled and Breeze came running. "Let's go," he said.

"What?" The blood drained from her face. "I can't run with you. You're like the Terminator."

This time he did chuckle. "I'll go at your pace and give you some pointers. If it gets too much, walk, but don't stop."

She blew her breath upward, and the bang that consistently found a place over her eye fluttered. "Okay."

They made it to the trail cutting through the forest, surrounding his property. Good effort, but her breathing was coming too fast.

"Walk," he commanded.

"This isn't very much of a work out for you."

He strolled beside her with a gait like a panther. Fit and sleek, he didn't have a slender runner's body, he had weight and muscle.

"Usually Breeze and I do ten kilometers a day."

"Ten?" Her eyes bugged out. "Think I'll be lucky if I make it to that tree down there."

"Run," he commanded.

Her breathing had slowed, and she put it into a trot. "You should run a marathon," she said. "You'd probably win."

"I don't run to prove anything. I set my own benchmarks." He turned and jogged, facing her. "You're breathing is too shallow."

"Gasping is all I got," she huffed out.

He placed his palm on his abs. "Breathe from the stomach. Running is one hundred percent mental as well. Concentrate and control your air."

Running on the treadmill at the gym seemed easier. Her legs weighed a ton. They walked, then they ran. After repeating the process three times, she figured out he was pacing her with a formula. "This isn't random, is it? The stopping and starting."

He shot a look across his shoulder. "There's a ratio."

At kilometer two, she stopped and bent over. Her eyesight was fuzzy, her lungs burned, and she wasn't sure she even had legs anymore. A warm hand palmed her back.

"You're doing really well, Mika." He curled his hands over her shoulders, urging her to straighten.

"Maybe this running thing isn't for me," she said, gulping air.

"It gets easier, and I expect you to run every day while I'm gone."

She took a step, but it was really a trip and a stagger. "I forgot you're leaving."

He nodded. "Let's take a shortcut." He headed through the trees, and she followed, hoping a big lake had formed

35

somewhere in the woods, so she could do a face plant like a Kool-Aid plunge.

They emerged near her cottage.

"Thank, blessed God." Breeze ran ahead of them, toward the main house. "Where's she going?"

"Her water bowl," he said, slowing to a walk.

"Think I'll join her." That's it, she was dead. The grass was green and cool. She dropped to her knees and rolled onto her back, doing a starfish imitation. Looking up into the blue sky, the sun beat down on her.

"Waiting for a migratory flock of Canada Geese?" he asked.

"Aww, nice," she drawled.

Cain sat down and crooked one knee with his arm. She closed her eyes, taking in deep gulps of sea air. She felt a drip first, and then a big, wet doggy kiss landed on her face.

When she squealed and lunged for Breeze, the dog jumped back and started to gallop like a puppy. She laughed at her antics. "How old is Breeze?"

"She's three," he said, throwing an arm around Breeze when she got her frisky under control and laid down beside him. "I brought her up here from the States."

"Is that where you lived before?" she asked.

"For a while." Cain stared off toward the tree line. "If you can walk, I'll show you where her food is."

That was a quick subject change. She rolled onto her knees and pushed herself up, thanking the heavens for the deep bathtub that awaited her in the cottage.

Cain stopped at his back door. "The code is five, eight, seven, eight," he said, pushing the buttons. "There's an alarm system in the house, but once you use the code, it won't go off unless you set it from the inside panel."

"Pretty straightforward," she said. They'd entered a back room with a line of closets. Dark, louvered doors offered plenty of storage space. Arches made of thick beams segregated the glass ceiling. If this was the mud room, she could imagine what the rest looked like.

Cain opened the first closet. "Her food is in here." After filling a small pail, he walked down the hallway into the kitchen, a big, open, austere kitchen. The honey-colored wood cabinets weren't enough to warm the cold chrome accents. Elegant, but maybe too much so. A massive hood sat over an eight-burner gas stove. He had two ovens, two fridges, two sinks and a wine cooling unit. Everything sparkled as if no one used them.

"Where's the French maid with the mini skirt?"

"Her bowls..." Cain paused, the comment obviously catching wind, and he raised a brow at her.

She shrugged good-naturedly.

"I keep her bowls over here," he said and filled one.

Natasza Waters

A spacious great room adjoined the kitchen. Expensive dark furnishings anchored the seating area in the center and a large stone fireplace rose up the wall. She panned a look around. "It's very…magazine-worthy."

He tilted his head at her. "You don't like it?"

"No," she spurted. "It's ah, pristine."

He chuckled. "Is that another way of saying cold and empty?"

"Err, maybe." She had a problem lying, so she became a master at avoidance until someone cornered her.

A grin crossed his features, and her heart skipped with an uneven beat. He drew out two glasses and filled them with ice and water, passing her one. She chugged it in three swallows. Before she could set it down, he took it and filled it up again.

"Drink plenty of this tonight to replenish what you lost."

"Think I'll do that through osmosis via a long soak in the bathtub."

His firm lips parted. He hesitated, but finished by saying, "You can use the Jacuzzi if you want."

"Thanks, but no. I don't do those."

His brows shot together. "Why not? I have it cleaned regularly."

"Oh, no," she spouted. "That's not what I mean." And she wasn't going to tell him what she meant either. A slip of the tongue. People with her disorder didn't do well in those things. All the chemicals played havoc with her skin. "My bath is good

38

enough, but thank you for the offer." She quickly looked for a diversion, and her eyes fell on the grand piano in the corner. Not a speck of dust, nor a fingerprint marred its polished perfection. "Do you play the piano?"

Cain leaned against the counter. The glass hovered at his lips. He lowered it slowly. "Used to."

"I always wanted to play, but I never got around to it. It's a beautiful piano."

He nodded vaguely, his gaze turning inward. Then he downed the water. "I'll be leaving early in the morning."

"Should I have your phone number in case something happens you need to know about?"

He hesitated again. "Sure." He scribbled it down on a pad of paper he snagged from an end table in the living room. "That's my personal number. Not my…business number."

"Okay." *Would it make a difference?* "I'm sure I won't need to call."

"I may not have cell service where I am. Leave a message. I'll check when I can."

"You hitchin' a dog team and doing the Iditarod?"

He shook his head and laughed. "No."

"Well, thanks for the pointers and have a good trip."

He led her to the front door. Cain grabbed Breeze's collar. "See you in seven days." He paused. "And, ah, think about getting some better running shoes and new running clothes. They wick away the moisture."

She gave Breeze a scratch on her chest getting a happy thump of her front paw on the floor. "I'll see how expensive it is, but I'll check it out."

"And...um...you might want to buy a good running bra." Her eyes popped open with surprise. "See ya." And he closed the door.

She instinctively palmed both boobs. What the hell did that mean? She looked down and then around. Were her boobs too big? Is that what he was implying? Shit, what a coarse, broody, no-filter-on-the-mouth kind of guy was he, anyway? She paused in front of his enormous windows, forgetting her breasts were still cupped in her hands.

Maybe he was chucking shit at her over her comment about his house? If that was the case, he had a sense of humor after all. One he hid for some reason. She could lob one-liners with the best of them. A skill she perfected to cover up her other fault.

Movement caught her eye. She turned on her heel just in time to catch Cain scrubbing his chin with a slow hand, hiding a huge smile as he moved out of her view. She dropped her hands instantly, realizing what she must look like supporting the sisters.

Oh yeah, next time her tongue would show no mercy.

****

At ten after nine, Cain walked to the window, and then the front door. He whistled. Breeze had gone for her nightly mission, but she didn't come for his call. He rolled his eyes, knowing where she must be. He slipped his shoes on and jogged over to the cottage. A dim light shone from the living room. He didn't see anyone through the open door, then knocked.

No answer.

Pulling on the screen, he entered. "Mika?" Maybe she was in the bathroom. "Hello?" he called out, walking down the hallway. A light shone from the end of the hallway. He felt a little weird just sauntering into her space. Probably a huge blunder in the Landlord-Tenant Act, but....Reaching the end of the hall, he stuck his head in the door.

His heartbeat hitched a little. Mika was fast asleep, her bedside light illuminating her peaceful features. The sheets were all twisted up around her legs, and her arm draped over Breeze. What a sight. Breeze's ears twitched.

"Stay, girl."

He motioned with his hand. Breeze sighed heavily and laid her head down on the pillow. He backed out quietly. About to switch the living room light off, he paused. The chaos of boxes had been unpacked. Her essence along with her belongings made the cottage a quaint, comfortable home.

With Breeze beside her, Cain didn't have to worry, but he still wished he had an extra key to lock up when he closed the front door. Dogs had a keen sense. Maybe Breeze sensed a need to stay close. Mika seemed anything but needy, with her fiery

41

personality and razor-sharp tongue. She definitely didn't have a boyfriend.

He wondered whether or not someone would show up when she moved in, but the moving party proved to him, aside from her loose girlfriend Jennifer, Mika was the odd woman out. The rest of her gal pals had their mates. He didn't really understand it. Mika had a great sense of humor. Maybe she was fussy, but nothing about her rang any alarm bells. Last night, her quick wit had the guys laughing at her jokes when she poked fun at them.

He opened the door to his house and turfed his shoes. Compared to the cottage, his place did seem cold. She'd teased him this afternoon. His home didn't appeal to her, but every time she stared at the cottage, her eyes sparkled. A seven million dollar home, and she preferred the little rustic cottage with whitewashed siding and gingerbread shingles. He caught himself smiling again and shook his head.

It was time to finish packing. He'd be on the seven o'clock plane out of Victoria. A change in Vancouver, a one-night stopover to visit his brother in LA, then continue on to meet his client in Fiji. As he zipped up his suit carrier, he paused with the overwhelming urge to unzip it and cancel. His reputation made him a wealthy man. Cancelling was out of the question.

Warmth ebbed from his heart. This is where he'd leave it, until he returned. The sound of the zipper sliding closed broke the silence, but not the chill of a stone-cold soul.

Chapter Four

Cain stared out at the crystal-clear sapphire water, his forearms resting on the bamboo railing of the hut built over the Fijian Sea. He turned a look over his shoulder. Carrie lay in the rumpled sheets of the bed. With a sobering feeling in his heart, he found his pants draped over the bedroom chair, pulled out the phone and escaped outside.

"Hello?"

"Hey, it's Cain. How are things going at home?"

"I'm spoiling your dog rotten," Mika teased.

He ran a hand through his hair and smiled. "I bet you are."

"I'm just kidding. She misses you."

"You're lying."

Silence and then a chuckle. "Well, yes, I am and she's lying on the sofa with me. Mine not yours, and we're eating popcorn and bacon strips."

He gazed at the ocean's white seabed, illuminated by underwater lights. Here he stood in paradise, where a man and a woman could indulge in romance and endless sensuality. He wondered if Mika would like it here.

"She's staying with you in the cottage, isn't she?"

"Hmm, maybe."

"Moved her dog food and dishes into your living room?"

"Possibly."

He laughed. "Do I get my dog back when I come home?"

"Doubtful," she drawled.

Grinning to the point his cheeks hurt, he shook his head. "And how about the running?"

"Hey, Mom," she said with a sassy tone. "Mind your own business."

He rubbed his chin. "I'll know if you haven't been." A set of slender, pale arms wrapped around his bare waist and a chill slithered down his spine, even with Carrie's warm cheek nestled against his back.

"I'm doing three kilometers a day, and I'm going to try for four tomorrow. Happy, slave driver?"

He unhinged Carrie's arm from his waist and stepped away from the wealthy executive. "You still have my number?"

Mika's voice cut in and out for a second. "Yes, why?"

"Just making sure."

"Don't worry. If I burn the place down, I'll make sure to call ya from a non-extradition country." She paused. "Business good?"

"Making progress." His pulse thrummed with the lie. "I...yeah, it'll get done."

"Awesome. Feel free to call again. If I don't answer, I'm either having a wild sex orgy in your fancy digs or mowing the lawn, but I'd put money on the lawn."

He muffled a laugh. "The gardener comes tomorrow. Don't go joy riding on the lawn mower," he threw back. Ha, he'd finally got one back on her, aside from the comment he'd made about the running bra, which he knew had hit a homer.

"I better get going. The frat boys will be here soon, and I have to rifle through your cabinets. Where do you keep the Mazola oil, by the way?"

Man, she was quick. "Just stay out of my toy cabinet, Miss Makris," he said, barely above a whisper. There was a pause, and he chuckled. That was two for him. Cain glanced over his shoulder to see whether his client was listening. She'd given him space, but not a lot.

"No way," she spouted.

"Good night, Mika."

"See ya when you get home...here," she corrected quickly. "Bye, Cain."

She hung up, but he kept the phone to his ear. With another shoulder check, he saw Carrie had a pissy look on her face. Ignoring the high maintenance alpha female with a short fuse if all the attention wasn't on her, he raised his voice and said into the dead line, "Listen, maybe I should come home now. If it's that bad, I'll come." He paused for effect, seeing Carrie's expression change to shadowy interest. "Tomorrow. Okay, don't worry." He hung up and joined the cold executive with a personality like a spiny fish.

45

"Sounds like trouble," she said, her arms sliding around his hips.

He brushed a strand of hair from her cheek with a practiced hand. "Something needs my attention."

She applied a pout to her lips. "I need your attention. At least for tonight."

"One more night, but tomorrow I have to leave." Carrie's Botox lips eased into a demure smile.

She urged him back toward the bed. "I don't know if I ever want you to go."

He took control of her seduction and the bedsheet gymnastics, hating every second of it. Women were a commodity. Several years ago, he'd stopped feeling anything but a cold disdain for his clients. His resume could include acting with spontaneous emotion deployed at crucial moments. Attentive to their needs, he offered them what they wanted. His Master's Degree in computer engineering hung in his office, but he'd shunned his analytical mind and taken a one-way highway to hell instead.

Carrie's body twisted, moaning with his touch. Cain was good at what he did. Easing on a condom, he got down to business. He stroked her dry core with a controlled cadence. Carrie's head rolled back in ecstasy enjoying the ride. He'd carved an elite clientele list that grew yearly with his reputation. With discretion, he serviced wealthy women. The more he gave, the emptier, he'd become.

He paused as Mika's smiling face floated into his mind. The sweet feminine tone of her voice followed. A pulse of excitement suddenly ripped through his chest, as Carrie's channel milked his shaft and she scratched his arms with her manicured nails.

How long could he do this before he completely hated himself, or had he reached that point already? If he told Mika, she wouldn't bat an eye, but she'd tease him mercilessly. The chemistry between them had been instantaneous and easy.

Carrie's passion began to spike, her cries and hips climbing higher. Another pulse made his lust swell. He closed his eyes and saw the pretty young woman in his cottage. Her thick, dark hair spread across a pillow, her hands gripping his hips, urging him closer. He groaned, realizing he was going to come fantasizing about his tenant. His breath grew shallow, his body tightening. He plunged his shaft to the hilt into Carrie.

"Oh, God you're good at this, Cain."

He didn't hear the coarse, empty woman beneath him, he heard another voice—gentle, innocent. His darkness wanted him to ignore her, but he heard her clearly, and she was calling him from beyond the wasteland he'd made of his life.

****

A brush with insanity. That's what Cain decided as he drove down the road to his house thirty-four hours later. He scanned the dash. Six o'clock. The evening sun threw its failing rays across his home. There they were, and he exhaled with relief.

47

Mika had bought a ball tosser, and she swung it behind her and threw as hard as she could, sending the ball and Breeze flying across the lawn. She waved and jogged toward him as he parked the car.

Breeze barked and ran full-tilt toward him, her front paws landing on his chest. "Hey, girl." He gave her a big rub while her tongue slobbered his face. "Missed you, too!"

"You're home early, aren't you?" Mika came to a halt a few feet away in her new jogging suit, the curvaceous figure beneath her loose clothes evident but hidden. He'd expected her to pick-up tight-fitting Lycra and a low-cut tank. Not Mika. She dressed like a middle-aged Phys-Ed teacher.

"Finished my business early."

Mika's brows came together. "Do you wrestle with wildcats?" she asked, looking at his upper arms.

He cleared his throat. "No, bear trainer," he shot back, embarrassed that he'd forgotten to hide the scratch marks.

Mika's brows rose. "Really?"

He snorted. "No, not really." Then he laughed. The darkness flew from his chest like someone opened a trap door and released the demons.

"Well, it's good you're home early. I can meet the girls tonight for dinner. I'll bring over Breeze's food and bowls before I leave."

When she quickly turned away from him, his stomach knotted. What did he expect her to do—hug him and welcome

48

him home? He watched her saunter away and shook off the odd feeling of disappointment.

During the long flight back, he'd made a decision. It was time for a resurrection instead of an erection. Two years ago he'd put his degrees to use, starting an internet company that he'd nurtured—slowly. The time had come to give it more effort.

"Hey!" he shouted.

Mika turned halfway between him and her cottage. "What?"

"Did she have her run today?"

"Four kilometers." Mika did a happy dance as if she'd scored the winning touchdown in a football game.

He waved. "How about six more, girl?" he asked Breeze, whose ears perked up.

Thirty minutes later, with a good sweat on, he and Breeze finished their run. The familiar smell of Douglas firs and the sea confirmed he loved living in British Columbia. His leg muscles burned in a good way, vaulting the steps from the beach to his front yard. Breeze dashed ahead for her water bowl, made a mess lapping it up, then shot across the property toward the cottage.

"Breeze!" he shouted. "Breeze!" he shouted again. "Damn dog." He chased after her.

The cottage screen door opened, and Breeze slipped inside. Obviously, dogs had their preference of living accommodations as well. Mika stayed by the door, propping it open with an arm.

49

Natasza Waters

"Breeze, you gotta go home," Mika said, with her head turned when he stopped on the porch. "Come on, Breeze," Mika commanded, stepping back inside.

He followed her to find a salty, wet dog lying on Mika's couch. "That's why I don't let her on the furniture," he said. The smell of wet dog permeated the room.

"It's all right, it's an old couch," Mika said, pointing at the floor for Breeze to get down.

Breeze gave her one yap, as if sassin' her off. "Manners," he scolded. Breeze's ears leaned forward with the reprimand. Shepherds had strong wills. Either you commanded them or they took charge. "Looks like she's picking up some of your attitude."

Mika straightened as if he'd insulted her, and maybe his tone had been a bit too serious.

"I don't lie on your couch sopping wet," she fired back.

Holy shit. His cock hardened just like that. The thoughts he'd had while fucking Carrie but seeing Mika were insatiable, and he had to drown them right now.

"I'd have to agree. Besides your tongue isn't quite that long."

Mika's eyes popped open and then narrowed. Bring it, girlfriend, he thought. He was in control of setting the stage when it came to women. Friend or not, she'd be getting the same treatment. He treated them all the same. That's how he kept his distance.

50

"Take your evil ass and your little dog, too, Dorothy, and go home. My favorite show is on." She plunked down on the couch and grabbed the remote control, punching the button, bringing the TV to life.

He cleared his throat and gave a low whistle. Breeze trotted behind him. He scooped up her bowls and pinned the bag of dog food under his arm.

"Mika?"

She swiveled and kneeled on the couch, leaning her arms on the back. She'd taken his advice about the running bra, and it rounded her breasts into a luscious bunch. He'd had a lifetime worth of breasts in his face. Why did hers have an impact on him?

"Thanks for taking good care of Breeze. I appreciate it."

She cocked her head just a little and blew her bangs from her eyes. "You're welcome."

He nodded, and she turned to watch the ridiculous reality show *The Bachelor*. Was Mika looking for her bachelor? Although she treated him like a landlord and never batted a flirtatious eye at him—not like her friend Jen—he imagined she wanted romance. All women wanted the soft words and the chase. It had made him a rich man.

****

Cain's ears perked the same as Breeze's when he heard Mika's crappy Toyota drive past his house. He checked his

51

watch. Four-thirty, as usual. A week had disappeared into the ether. He'd put hours and hours into the internet company. He'd found two more backers this week. His family ties didn't hurt. The fact that the strings that bound them were few wasn't common knowledge.

He'd give Mika half an hour to unwind from work and change her clothes. Hovering the mouse over the close button on the site, a mail message popped up. A request form from his *other* business. He opened it. A picture of Kaitlin Conners stared at him. Rich, curling brown hair, large green eyes and a perfect smile radiated on the monitor. He read her mail.

Hi Cain,

An acquaintance informed me about your services. I've filled in your questionnaire, and I hope I'll hear back from you soon. I have a place in Miami. It would be wonderful to have you visit this weekend. I know it's short notice, but I'm very busy. I'm sure you are, too, and my friend assured me you are completely trustworthy and discreet.

He checked the form. His finger hovered over the accept button. She'd receive an auto response, then he'd make contact with her for details. With a glide of his index finger, he brushed the return key, but not hard enough to send it.

Even guys like him took a vacation. He pushed away from the table and closed the email.

"Later," he said to the laptop.

He rushed upstairs and changed. Closing the front door, he saw Mika doing her stretches. They ran together every day. He still offered pointers, and she was pushing her limits. He joined her on the lawn. Breeze lay down and waited for them.

"How was work?"

"Same." Her voice held a grumpy tone.

Her stretches were only half-hearted, and he stopped and walked over to her, gripping her ankle to indicate she wasn't doing it right. She huffed and did the stretch again.

"Doesn't sound like it was fine," he said.

"It's my boss. I'm pretty sure she hates me. She hates everybody, but I think today was my day to be picked on."

"Find another job," he said.

"Don't want another job. I like my job," she said, starting her squats.

"Everyone has someone higher than them on the ladder. Talk to them."

Mika stopped and stared at him. "You run your own business, don't you?"

He pinned his lips together, hoping she wouldn't ask more. He didn't want to lie to her. "Yes."

"Thought so," she said, straightening her arms and lunging forward on one leg. "If I complained about Lt. Vickers, I'd be in an even bigger doghouse."

"Then let's run it off." He grabbed her hand. "Take your running jacket off, it's too hot."

"No, I'm good. Let's get down to it," she yelled, heading for the forest trail. Her ponytail swayed, along with her gorgeous ass.

Wow, running was making a difference. He inhaled a deep breath and chased her. His mom had two boys, but he set his mind on pretending he had just adopted a sister.

After kilometer six, she struggled to keep up. He palmed her shoulder. "You're too hot. Take off the damn running jacket."

She stopped and bent over shaking her head. "I'm giving up."

"I'm going to keep going," he said through heavy breaths, and she waved him on. Breeze halted and looked back. "Go with her," he commanded through clenched teeth.

After eleven clicks he hit the shower and stood under the rain of water. Stretching his neck, the force of the drops slapped his face. His palms pressed against the walls, and his body screamed for relief. An unfulfilled sexual tension wracked his lower extremities. *How the fuck could he, of all people, be unfulfilled?*

****

At nine p.m. Cain walked through the darkness toward the light beaming like a beacon from the cottage. She never shut her door. Like her personality, it always remained open. As he drew closer, he saw her standing next to the kitchen counter. His brows tightened. *What was she doing?* She had something in her hand, pressing it against her bared belly. He reached the porch and stopped dead. *What the fuck?* Seeing the needle pierce her skin, his temper soared. No fucking way. He almost tore the screen off the hinges as she withdrew the needle from her stomach and reached for a cotton swab.

"What the fuck is that?" he yelled.

She startled, and her eyes flew open. Yanking her shirt down, she glared at him. With a quick turn, she snatched the needle off the table and ran from the room. He paced the floor.

"Get off the couch," he roared at Breeze, who pinned her ears and slunk off the couch.

Mika came around the corner, her face taut.

"You take drugs? I can't fucking believe this. I ended up with a goddamn dope addict after all!" he yelled.

Her face paled and she shook her head. "I don't take drugs. Not *those* drugs."

"You were injecting yourself." He stormed toward her, angrier than he'd ever been in his life. He didn't bother to ask himself why. She was his tenant, nothing more. "That shit will kill you, Mika. Do your friends know?"

Mika didn't move. She barely breathed. "It's not what you think. And yes, they know I have to do this."

He ground his jaw. The anger failing him. "What? What do you mean, you have to do this?"

55

Natasza Waters

She bowed her head, and seamed her lips. "I just do."

"Are you diabetic?" If she was, he was going to feel like an idiot.

She shook her head, staring at the floor. "It's not illegal, okay?"

His heart raced in his chest, thumping its way to his head. "Mika…you have to understand, I can't have you here if you're taking narcotics. I won't stand for it."

She licked her lips and brought her gaze to his. "It's not."

He swallowed thickly. Staring into her dark brown eyes, he didn't see a lie. He saw hurt. He saw embarrassment, and his chest tightened with a strange sensation very similar to worry.

"How often do you do this?"

She brushed past him and grasped the kettle, filling it with water and putting it on the burner. "Once a week," she said meekly.

He placed his palms on the counter, watching her. "Are you sick?"

She shrugged, failing to look at him. "Not exactly."

Did he even have a right to ask her? Damn right, he did. He could worry about her if he wanted to. They stood in silence watching the kettle come to a boil. Mika dug for a tea bag in a small ceramic container she kept on the counter and filled the cup with water. She didn't ask if he wanted one. *Why didn't she ask? Why do you think? You just finished yelling at her.*

56

"I'm tired." Her voice hitched when she said, "I'm going to bed."

She gave Breeze a pat between her ears and left him standing like the moron he was, in her kitchen. He heard the bedroom door quietly close. Why hadn't he just calmly asked her instead of accusing her of something illicit? Forking his hands behind his neck, he released a deep breath.

Breeze looked up at him, and he swore she had the doggy version of "you're a shithead" in her eyes. He needed to apologize, and right now. Breeze followed him down the hallway and sat on her haunches at the door. He listened. His heart tightened into a hard ball and pitched into his stomach. Mika's soft sobs drifted from her room.

Breeze pawed the door and whined.

"Go home, Breeze." Her voice stuttered back.

He tapped on the door. "It's not Breeze. Well, it is, but…it's me, too."

She didn't answer. With gallons of reservations, he turned the knob. Breeze vaulted inside and jumped on the bed. She pushed her nose into Mika's face nestled against her bent knees. He didn't enter. That would be stepping over the line. Way over the line.

"I overreacted. I should have asked, not yelled." He released a nervous breath. The irony obvious. A bedroom was the last

Natasza Waters

place on the planet he normally felt nervous. "I just...I was just concerned."

Concerned? More like scared to death that the bright smile he'd become accustomed to in such a short time could be a slave to a habit that would kill her. Scared that Mika wasn't who he thought she was. Somehow, her open and honest personality had become a healing balm to him. Could he be any more of a hypocrite? She didn't know anything about him or his profession. Even if she did, he'd bet a million bucks, she still wouldn't condemn him. Before he knew it, Cain sat on the edge of her bed.

"Is it something I need to know about? I mean, is it something I should know about in case you need help?"

She shook her head, and her shoulders jerked with a sob. "Listen, I just had a bad day."

Wasn't he Prince Charming? Her boss had shit on her, now he had. His hand moved to cover hers without thinking. She sniffed and looked up at him. Her beautiful eyes glistened, and he swept away the tear on her cheek.

"I guess I've stepped way over the bounds of landlord, but I see you..." He paused, his heart beating hard with the truth. "I see you as a friend, but I didn't act like one. I deserve a good lashing from that sharp tongue of yours."

Breeze saw a chance to help too and licked her. She added a girly woof as if agreeing.

"Don't need your help sucking up," he said to Breeze.

58

Mika sniffed again and curled her arm around Breeze, who leaned into her. "I'm sorry I ruined your dog," she said.

He chuffed out a small laugh. "You didn't ruin her. You girls have to stick together against assholes like me."

Mika blinked. "You're not an asshole."

He tore his gaze from her. "Yeah, I am." He stood up. "I'm sorry for jumping to the wrong conclusion, Mika. I really am. Please accept my apology."

Her bottom lip disappeared. "Thanks." She rocked a little. Her arms wrapped around her legs as if trying to comfort herself.

"I'll let you get some rest." Breeze hadn't moved from her side.

"Night."

He left his dog with Mika and closed the front door. Once again, reminding himself he needed another key. Back at his house, he settled down in front of his laptop. An email notification popped up. Kaitlin had sent a second message.

Just wanted to make sure you got my request form. I haven't heard from you.

He brought up her original request and selected the *reject* button. Walking upstairs toward his bedroom, the house felt cold and lifeless, unlike the cottage that held a warm heart.

He tossed and turned with frustration. Why did Mika need the injection? There was no way to know until she trusted him

Natasza Waters

enough to share with him, unless he wanted to start digging through her trash.

He let out a frustrated breath into his pillow, his gaze landing on the calming scene outside the window. The full moon lit the low swell washing up the shoreline. The number of people he considered friends with no strings attached were few. Mika had somehow streaked to the top of that short list, and he'd almost alienated her tonight.

Chapter Five

Mika snarled at her phone. "God, I'm throwing you in the garbage," she yelled at the little device in her hand. How could a piece of technology drive her so nuts? But it did. Tech savvy, she was not.

"Updates?" She poked the buttons on her phone. "Well, where's the damn update? I don't see any damn update."

Since she didn't live with Dinky anymore, she didn't have Jeff close at hand anymore either. He always helped her with her computer and her phone.

"Stupid thing," she shouted and dropped it on the table.

"Everything all right in here?" Cain asked from the screen door.

"No! I hate technology," she barked, annoyed as hell with herself.

Her landlord leaned inside, his brows arched beneath his bangs. "Problems?"

Cain had already helped her with her barbeque. Acting as if she were tied to the railroad tracks and squealing for help once a month was enough.

She blew out a frustrated breath. "I'm fine."

The screen opened wider, and he stepped his handsomeness inside. Why wasn't a guy like him all tangled up with a girlfriend or married with forty children? Men like him didn't wander around the planet without some gorgeous woman stalking him.

"You're sure?" he asked.

With elbows on the table and her cheeks smooshed up in her palms, she stared at him. "You're just going to make fun of me again," she said, making a pouty face. "And I don't have a piece of barbeque to chuck at you."

"I'm sure you've got something to throw at me, and considering how I acted the other night, I'd deserve it."

She gave him a squinting smile. "I'm trying to download an app and it keeps telling me I need IOS13, and I can't find it."

Cain nodded once. "Can I take a look?"

She blew her bang out of her eyes. "Sure. I'm throwing up the white flag and this phone in the ocean."

Cain rounded the table and looked over her shoulder. "Well, you're almost there, so I don't think you have to sacrifice it to the sea." He propped his hands on the table on either side of her and took control of the mouse. "You need to back-up your phone first."

"I know. I can't find it." He clicked a couple buttons and voila, a back-up started. She groaned.

A low chuckle by her ear made her skin tingle. Cain's aftershave smelled so good. Being this close to him, she had to stop herself from craning her head and shoving her nose into his throat for a deep breath.

"I hate computers," she drawled.

"You're not alone." The back-up finished. "Okay, let's get the latest version into your phone."

This time, he clicked his way through her phone as if it were second nature, and the prompt for updating the new version came up. "What the heck," she spouted. "How do you do that so easily?" He shrugged, his chest brushing against her back sent a warm shiver through her body.

"This laptop is ancient."

Now it was her turn to shrug. "I'll get a new one after I get a new car."

Cain continued clicking, going into the guts of her computer. Places she didn't even know existed. "I'm surprised it hasn't crashed on you."

"It wants to. It just feels sorry for me and keeps working."

He smiled. "Listen, I have an extra one I don't use anymore. It's a lot newer than this one. I'll get it for you."

She turned her head and his face was right there. His sharp jaw, perfect lips with a strong cusp and flawlessly proportioned nose within heart-thumping millimeters. She swallowed her own tongue when he angled his head and gazed into her eyes. *Talk. Say something! Don't stare, you moron.*

"Umm, no. It's okay. Thanks anyway." He stepped away from her, and she let out a breath. Maybe one that was a little too audible.

"Do you back up everything on your computer onto an external drive?"

She shook her head. "I can barely find my 'C' drive let alone anything else. I can cut, copy, paste and save. Word processing stuff, but that's the extent of my abilities."

"How about you borrow my laptop, until you get one of your own?"

"I could rent it from you, maybe."

A smile broke onto his lips, and he went from mysteriously seductive to jaw-dropping, make-your-pulse-pound, magnificent. "I'll be back in a few minutes."

The least she could do is put a kettle on to boil. "Do you like tea?" she asked as he opened the screen.

"I do." His voice filled with sensual inflection and warmth.

When she turned, she rolled her eyes, mostly at herself. His words weren't filled with anything, but her sex-starved nerve endings were.

An hour later, Cain had the new laptop connected to hers, and had transferred all her files, which were mostly work-related and a gazillion pictures of her and the girls. The last file finished copying. He unhooked her old laptop, walked into the kitchen, and dragged her garbage can from under the sink onto the floor.

"No," she squealed and scrambled to her feet. "Not Christine, you can't."

He laughed and held the computer over his head. He had a good six inches on her. She attacked, pulling on his raised arm.

"Christine?"

"Yes, she's possessed, but she's mine." She yanked on his arm. Trying to manhandle his marble strength didn't get her anywhere. Cain's other arm wrapped around her waist.

"Time to let go, Mika. Bid her farewell." A fully-loaded smile shot across his face.

She had no choice. Her watering pot was on the counter. Without a second thought, she poured it over his head and jumped back, laughing, then clamped her hands over her mouth.

Shock, surprise, and then a wicked glint flickered in his eyes. The laptop dropped square into the garbage, but she was already running out the door with Cain behind her. She zigged and he zagged, tackling her onto the lawn. Breeze ran from the main house barking.

"Help, Breeze!" she screeched, then laughed as Cain rolled her onto her back, shaking his head, spraying her with water. He had her trapped, and she just laughed harder, her face dripping, but not as badly as Cain's hair. She'd gotten him good!

"Get her, Breeze," he said, holding her down.

Breeze showed her empathy by licking Mika's face dry. She squealed when she got a little doggy tongue in her mouth and sputtered. "Oh, you're evil."

Breeze lay in the grass beside them, licking her chops. "Two against one, Miss Makris. You give?"

Cain hovered over her. Mika's breath became a pant for another reason than her fast retreat. "Until I find another pail of water."

He swayed his head. His eyes were so incredible. There had to be an auditorium filled with women pining over this man. The laughter stopped, but her pulse picked up. Cain's grin faded as he looked into her eyes. Slowly, he released her. He pulled on her hands, helping her up. A faint, distant smile crossed his lips.

"You are hereby released from Christine's possessive powers. And a towel would be good, too."

She laughed. "That I can do." They walked back to the cottage. "Thanks for letting me borrow the laptop."

"You're welcome," he said, glancing across his shoulder at her. "But it's not a borrow. It's yours."

His broad shoulders rolled as he walked. He was one of those rare men with an electric magnetism, but he was her landlord and maybe a friend. Mentally, she unplugged the outlet on the electricity coursing high wattage ideas through her head.

She looked into the garbage can. "Poor Christine," she cooed.

"Consider the garbage a final resting place for that piece of crap. I mean, Christine."

She grabbed a towel from the bathroom and flopped it over his head as she passed by the kitchen table. He'd just swallowed the last drop of tea, and she watched the cords of muscles running down his throat flex.

He dragged the towel away. "Thanks."

She gave him a cocky smile. "Welcome."

He settled the cup on the kitchen table. "Is this you?" he asked, expanding the image to its full size.

A picture of her and the girls standing on the shore at Shawnigan Lake displayed on the screen. "That's us eleven years ago." She glanced at him, and he had that questioning look in his eyes again. "What?"

"This is in the middle of summer, right?"

"Yes."

Uh-oh. She hurried to the fridge and started pulling out vegetables. Holding them under the tap, she rinsed and placed them on her cutting board.

"I'm making a stir fry. Guess I should feed you for letting me borrow your computer." He turned in the chair as she chopped up a carrot. *Don't ask. Don't ask.*

"Thank you, I accept. So what's with the parka-like clothes in this shot?"

He had to ask. The crisp celery snapped off the stalk, and she sliced it into long strips. "They are not."

"Long sleeved shirt, collar up to your neck, and jeans. Everyone else is wearing bikinis."

"I remember," she lied. "I was getting over a summer cold."

Cain's deep blue eyes rested on her, but he didn't dig any deeper.

Twenty minutes later, she said, "Dinner's almost ready." Cain had been quietly checking out all her pictures. He took his time as if researching each one.

He slowly closed the laptop when she slid two plates and cutlery across the island for him to place on the table.

"I'll go get a bottle of wine."

"Only if you want some. I'll pass," she said.

He tilted his head. "Then I will too. Water is fine."

She joined him, and they dished out the stir fry. Raising the fork to her mouth, she stopped and stared out the window toward the sea. A soft, orange glow from the falling sun filled the room.

"Mesmerizing," Cain said, pulling her attention to him. He swallowed and gave his head a jerk. "The sunset," he added quickly.

"Yes, it is."

They talked about her friends mostly. How long they'd known each other, and when the girls had met their husbands, and what everyone did for a living. Cain didn't offer a lot about himself, and she got the feeling he didn't want her to ask.

After a leisurely dinner, he collected both their plates and put them in the sink. "I better feed Breeze."

She nodded. "Thank you for all your help."

She followed him to the door. Cain stopped and turned toward her. "You're welcome. Come and get me if you have problems. I don't mind getting a little wet over you." He winked at her and whistled for Breeze.

His Perfect Imperfection

Oh, if only that were true. "See ya, Mr. Landlord."

****

Mika left Old Tess running while she knocked on Cain's door. Her landlord returned last night from a five-day business trip. Just before going to bed, Cain had knocked on her door. Tired from a long day at work, she was a little grumpy. He'd come to collect Breeze. Other than reporting everything was fine, she didn't feel like talking. This morning, she felt guilty for being so abrupt.

The warmth of the day reflected off the opaque glass, heating her face. She'd ventured out with a pair of jeans and a long-sleeved top. Too much clothing for the scorching eighty-five degree June day the meteorologist promised this morning on the news.

Dinky and the girls had told her the scars on her arms and legs weren't that bad, but her embarrassment hadn't paled enough to allow Cain to see her flaws. Baring her ugly to his ripped, exotically handsome landlordism was something that would never happen.

Cain swept the door open. "Morning."

"Hiya, I'm going into town for a veggie run. Do you need anything?" Cain's hair glistened with moisture. He'd showered but not shaved. Scruff suited her new friend better than any man on the planet.

Staring down at her, he replied, "Where'ya going?"

Natasza Waters

"The Hudson Farmer's Market. Thought I'd wander around for a bit."

"I'll come with you. Hang on."

He disappeared into the house, leaving her with a question scrunching her brow. "Err…" She expected, "Yeah sure, pick me up some green peppers," not "I'll come with you."

She hustled back to her car while he locked the front door, turned then stopped dead, staring at Old Tess.

"What?" She poked a finger toward him, seeing the wrinkle of disgust on his face staring at her four-wheeled red wagon. "Youuuuu snob."

He snapped his teeth together, giving the car a brilliant white grimace. "We can take my car," he offered politely, looking like someone told him he had to sit in a pool of toxic green goo.

"No, we'll take my car."

Breeze appeared at the window and used her "I'm angry at you" bark. She hopped up on the glass and barked again.

"Think she wants to come."

"Breeze, no," Cain commanded, but Breeze wasn't listening.

"You better let her come or your fancy dining room table will be nothing but wood chips when you get home." Mika laughed and shrugged at him. She opened Old Tess's back door.

Breeze bounded out and shot straight into her backseat while Cain disappeared for a moment to retrieve her leash.

When he got in, Cain looked around the car as if he might catch a virus. "Would you stop that? Old Tess serves me well. She's been very dependable."

He bit down on verbalizing his thoughts and pinned his gaze to the front window. His jaw sharpened, trying not to laugh.

Mika shifted into drive, and Tess released a healthy burp from her exhaust. "She just lets off a little gas once in a while, like any old timer."

Cain buried his face in his hand and laughed. Mika ignored him and straightened her shoulders. She lowered the rear window. Breeze stuck her head out with a happy doggy look, and they were off.

She found a parking spot close to the main doors of the farmer's market, but there wasn't much shade. We can't leave Breeze in here. It's too hot," she said.

Cain leashed Breeze, and they walked into the main entrance. They'd come early and didn't have to battle the crowds that would soon arrive. She loved the market with stall after stall of fresh breads and vegetables. Artisans displayed their handmade soaps and jewelry. The open, high-ceilinged warehouse offered an industrial backdrop in contrast with the colorful mix of food and flower venders.

"Good morning," a young woman said as she and Cain stopped to look at the girl's handmade crafts, the greeting directed at Cain, as were the girl's eyes.

71

He offered her a shallow smile. "Good morning."

It hadn't taken Mika long to get used to the drawn-out looks Cain received from women. Some shoppers even cranked their heads around to stare when they walked past.

"What a beautiful dog," the girl said, gazing at Cain instead of Breeze.

Cain didn't answer. "Thank you. She is, isn't she," Mika said, holding Breeze's leash and surveying the thick multi-colored candles on one of the tables. She picked up the wax cylinder and sniffed. Cain's hand landed on her shoulder, and she held it up. He took a sniff and panned a look at her, shaking his head with dislike.

"Those are infused with natural scents," the girl explained, walking to the other side of the table. "These over here have a muskier scent. Kind of sexy." She handed the candle to Cain.

Mika refrained from rolling her eyes.

"These are designed for men. That one is Wood Fireplace." She pointed to another. "That's Fresh Cut Lawn, and this," she nudged the deep brown wax with her finger, "is Campfire Mesquite."

Mika surveyed the table. "Designed for men, huh? Got any beer belch or peperoni stick scents?"

Cain broke into a hearty chuckle as he turned a look Mika's way, his hand still gently gripping her shoulder. The girl took note, and the glint in her eyes dulled. He picked up the Campfire

Mesquite and let Breeze have a sniff. The dog snuffled then sneezed.

"That's very inventive," Cain said, putting down the candle. "Think Mika would like something a little less outdoorsy."

Mika chose two thick candles, one with an orange scent the other with a rich, peach scent, both approved by Cain and Breeze's acute sense of smell.

They thanked the gal and left with the clerk burning a hole in Cain's ass. Mika decided to have a little fun.

"Do you know how many women gawk at you?" She pivoted on her toe, realizing he wasn't beside her.

Cain had stopped next to a leather stall. "Does that bother you?" he asked.

"Who me? No, pfft. I'm used to it when I go anywhere with Jen."

Cain un-looped a belt from a display, running the leather across his palm. He peered at her with a questioning gaze. "Are you sure they aren't checking you out instead of Jen?"

She barked with a Julia Roberts-style laugh. "Definitely sure."

Cain clipped the belt back on the display board and plucked a woman's belt with a big chunky buckle from the rod. She stilled when he reached around her, his eyes never leaving hers, and wrapped it around her waist. He cinched it gently then

Natasza Waters

stepped back. She tipped her head and flattened her blouse to see it.

"I wouldn't be so sure of that. When we look at ourselves, we don't see what others see."

Her nerves plucked out a tune on the high end of the scale, the one that shatters glass. Oh, how very true, she thought, with a waterfall of sarcasm wanting to pour off her tongue.

A young girl with a creamy-smooth complexion and likely still in high school, approached them. "We'll take this," he said, his fingers releasing the belt from around Mika's waist.

"You're a clothes horse, aren't you?"

Cain turned his attention to the pile of summer shirts on a maple table. "I like feeling comfortable and presentable."

"I'm presentable," she fired back, taking offense when she probably shouldn't.

The look he dropped on her made her squirm as if she'd said the world's biggest lie, and he'd caught her in the act.

Cain leaned in, his mouth next to her ear. "You hide behind them, and you shouldn't."

Should she be insulted? Indignant? For some stupid reason she felt two inches tall. Ashamed that he'd guessed the truth. "We can't all be fashionistas."

"Hello, Mika."

The voice made her cringe. Tormented by the woman all week, the last person she wanted to see was her boss. "Lieutenant Vickers. Good morning, ma'am."

She'd never seen her boss in civvies before. Vickers won the best nasty manager award every year. Mika didn't mind her being a perfectionist, but the woman thrived on berating and belittling. She was a magician at it, never crossing the line of harassment. Mika usually kept out of her line of fire. Most of the time, she picked on the newest girls in the office. Sally Vickers had to be fifty-five, but she kept herself in top condition. At lunch she went for a run, showered, and was back at her desk to look for her next victim by thirteen hundred hours exactly.

Vickers eyed Cain with interest and waited for an introduction. Mika's fingers tightened into a ball behind her back until she felt Cain's strong hand encase hers.

"I'm Mika's manager, Sally Vickers."

Cain pressed his frim body against her side as if to say, *"Don't worry, Mika, I'm right here."*

"Cain Sallas."

An expression she'd never seen on his face before made her quirk a brow. She couldn't call it a smile. Couldn't call it suggestive, but it was all sexy handsome.

"Mika has told me she enjoys working for DND."

Vickers gaze locked on Cain like Medusa in heat. She realized even if Vickers wasn't panting, she was entranced. *Double yuck!*

"Mika always finishes her assignments early," Vickers said, making her feel like she was in grade one, and Cain was getting her quarterly report card.

Cain's hand palmed Mika's arm. "You're lucky to have her. Any corporation would love to get their hands on her—skills."

Vickers lips twitched. "Yes, I'm sure they would." She nodded. "Your project is due Monday morning, Mika."

"Yes, ma'am. I'm reviewing it on Sunday, but it's complete."

"Have a pleasant weekend."

"Relax," Cain said next to her ear as they watched Vickers disappear into the Saturday morning shoppers flowing through the front doors and filling the wide aisles.

"I am," she lied.

He searched her face, his brow worried. "You're not. Is she the reason you come home frustrated so often?"

Mika stared up at Cain's handsome features his morning shadow a masculine contrast to the empathy in his deep blue eyes. How did he know she was frustrated?

"I guess. The woman loves to belittle people."

"We can pick up one of those dolls we passed a couple stalls ago and burn it in effigy if you want?"

She grinned. "Thanks. I'd hate to be responsible for her demise, although I may have plotted it once or twice."

"Just say the word, I'll have her taken out."

Mika couldn't help but chuckle. "Thanks, Cain. You're a real pal."

Putting the old battle-axe behind them, they wove through the thickening crowd. Breeze behaved very well. She didn't shy with the gaggle of legs she had to navigate. Arriving at the fresh veggies, they filled the basket Cain carried, while she kept Breeze on a short leash. Next was the bakery. Loaves—long, short, square and oval—covered the tables. The browned crusts layered in cheese and infused with herbs, smelled divine.

"Why don't we get something to eat and take it to the parliament building?" Cain suggested.

"Picnic?"

He nodded and looked across the mass of delicious choices. They purchased a French loaf and a couple others for home. Eventually, they reached the cheese display, and both groaned.

"Love cheese," she said, seeing all the different varieties.

"Me, too. Tried this one?" he asked, handing her a block of creamy cheese.

"Nope."

"We'll take this," he said, giving it to the gal who hovered nearby.

"Excuse me," someone said from behind them.

It wasn't Vickers, it was worse.

"Market Security."

Uh-oh, Mika thought. She figured this might happen. Cain turned, but she didn't.

"I'm afraid you have to leave. No dogs are allowed in here."

She slipped her shades onto her face and turned with a jerky motion. Adding a haughty tone to her voice, she said, "I assure you Breeze is an extremely well trained dog."

"Uh." The security guard, who was really a pimply-faced kid, took his job very seriously, but his severe expression slackened with doubt.

Mika raised her hand and swept it through the air. She did it again, as if blindly searching for Cain's arm. "Come on, Cain. Obviously, we're not welcome here."

Cain caught on pretty quickly and wrapped his hand around her upper arm. "We'll leave, but we're stopping by administrations to make a complaint first," he said harshly.

The kid stepped back. "No, I'm sorry. I didn't realize. The dog doesn't have an assistance halter."

"She doesn't need one," Mika quipped. True but misleading.

Breeze sat on her haunches, her Shepherd ears perked with interest.

"Sorry to bother you, folks," the kid murmured and walked away.

She and Cain didn't move. Slowly, they both looked over their shoulders to make sure he was gone. Mika lowered her chin and gazed over her shades at Cain.

They started laughing at the same time and knocked their heads together. "Ouch," she cried.

Cain rubbed her forehead. "If I ever need a wingman to rob a bank, you're it." He grinned. "We better get out of here before they realize you've got twenty-twenty vision."

They snapped up a few more cheeses and quickly purchased them. Cain gripped her hand, holding it against his upper arm, and wouldn't let go as they swept by a few more stalls to grab a basket of fresh strawberries and grapes. With arms loaded, they made their escape.

They cracked the doors on the car, the inside blazing hot already, and waited for it to cool off. A sports car with a couple of yuppies drove into the spot next to them. The girl's eyes zeroed in on Cain as soon as she got out. The guy's did the same then swung to Old Tess.

"Morning," the yuppie said.

Mika knew exactly what the guy was thinking, and she started to bob her head. Poor Cain, a wealthy man riding around in a beat up, red Toyota. He'd probably have nightmares over it.

"Nice car." Cain threw a look over the top of Old Tess that said, *'You are never getting me in this car again.'*

She busted a gut laughing and slapped the hood.

The yuppie looked at Old Tess with disgust. "Yeah. Thanks, man."

The couple linked hands, and Mika said, in her best southern accent, "Honey, you don't wanna bright, shiny car like their'ssss, do ya? I thought you loved momma's little red wagon."

The couple snickered at each other as they walked past. *Pompous assholes.*

Cain's forehead *thunked* on the roof. "Get in the fuckin' car." He could barely get the words out, he was laughing so hard.

Chapter Six

They drove around the stately legislature building five times before they found a spot in the shade. Cain grabbed their picnic lunch from the backseat, and they strolled along the sidewalk. Breeze wanted to sniff the horses decked out and hitched to a carriage. They let her investigate the massive hooves and powerful legs for a few seconds and carried on.

"Have you ever taken a horse-drawn ride?" Cain asked.

A woman in brown riding pants approached and offered Cain a Tally-Ho pamphlet with the prices. He nodded his thanks and tucked it in his pocket.

"Who, me? No." She shrugged. "I've lived here all my life. It's more for tourists and lovers."

They rounded the corner onto Belleville Street and crossed the lawn in front of the BC Legislature Building.

"Your prom date never took you for a romantic ride?" he asked.

"No, afraid not." She neglected to tell him, she had gone solo to her prom while the rest of her gang had dates.

People lay in scattered groups on the lawn and watched the tourists wandering the sidewalks. She and Cain passed the massive fountain burbling in the center of the immaculately kept grass. Rhododendrons bloomed with bouquets of pink and white in the landscaped gardens. Tulips mingled with pansies soaking up the beautiful day. They found a patch of grass and settled down with an uninterrupted view of the masts swaying in the harbor. The boats in the marina, glinted under the sun.

"Aren't you hot?" Cain asked, his eyes running over her clothes.

Everyone wore shorts. Girls wandered around with bare stomachs and sleeveless shirts. Some even had on bathing suit tops. A group of young women strolled by looking for their own patch of grass, and they all smiled at Cain.

"I'm fine." People like her were used to bearing the heat. No way was she going to show her battle scars.

Breeze settled between them and sniffed at their bags of food. She'd found the one with her treats inside. Mika pulled one out, and Breeze took it gently from her fingers, chomping happily.

"Do you like living here?" she asked.

Cain peered at her from under his bangs. "I do," he said, "It's an island, but very different from Greece." He paused as if deliberating. "That's where I grew up."

She nodded. "I've never been there, but my dad was born in Greece."

Cain offered a warm smile. "Have you travelled much?"

"Went to Disneyland once," she said, then popped a piece of cheese in her mouth.

Cain rolled onto his side, his muscular body strung out like a centerfold. "I lived with my brother in Los Angeles before I moved to Canada. Came here for business and I liked it."

She nodded. "Yeah, a lot of people fall in love with the island. Where's the rest of your family? Are they all in Greece?"

"Most of them."

Another couple strolled across the lawn, and a beautiful German Shepherd bounded ahead of them. Breeze noticed and her ears perked. The other dog's did too, and headed straight for them. Breeze jumped to her feet, the fur on her back standing up.

"It's okay, Breeze," she said, flattening the ruff with her hand.

The other couple didn't seem concerned and continued to walk arm-in-arm, talking. Breeze stepped out, meeting the other dog. They sniffed and then turned circles around each other.

"Caper's friendly," the guy said as the couple walked toward them. But Caper had other ideas, and playfully bit at Breeze's neck, then tried to mount her. Breeze was having none of that, and she ran away, Caper giving chase. They tore after each other, then stopped and sniffed again.

Cain gave a sharp, short whistle to call her back.

"Looks like spring," the woman said before kissing her boyfriend.

Mika smiled up at them while the dogs romped around, playing with each other. "Think today is the first day of summer, actually," she said, plucking a blade of grass.

Breeze ran back to them, her tongue lolling out. Mika took one of the empty food cartons and filled it with water, then accepted a big slobbery kiss on her cheek. She didn't bother to wipe it away. If she couldn't have man kisses, she was happy with Breeze kisses.

The couple concentrated on each other's lips. Must be nice, she thought to herself, and felt a tiny twist in her heart. If she ever became a rich woman, maybe she'd hire an escort, someone who was a professional and wouldn't freak out seeing her battered skin. For one night, she could live the fantasy. Then again, maybe she had options closer to home.

She was in remission, and Ben, a guy who worked on the base, had asked her out. She'd refused, but maybe she should reconsider. Sure, he was a man-whore and everyone on the base knew it, but he seemed nice enough. He flirted with her all the time. She'd zing him with a one-liner, he'd laugh, then turn his attention on someone else, on the prowl for a one-night stand.

She glanced at Cain, seeing his gaze held a question. She chose to focus her attention out toward the ocean instead of giving him a chance to verbalize it.

"Why don't we take a walk down on the waterfront?" he suggested.

She nodded and leashed Breeze. They joined the throng of people enjoying the sunshine and walked on the lower seawall, stopping to listen to a musician with a crowd gathered around him. Breeze sat on her haunches between them and cocked her head, which made Mika chuckle.

Sweating under the broiling sun, she brushed her wrist against her forehead. A little shade to hide under for a couple minutes, wouldn't hurt, but the benches were taken under the cherry trees behind them.

Cain's brow scrunched with concern.

"Mika, are you okay?" His palm pressed against her cheek. "Woman, you're boiling to death. Let's get you home and put you in some shorts."

"Good idea. Think I'm melting."

Cain's hand fell to the base of her back and guided her to the stairs. She blinked away the dizzy spell. His fingers slipped between hers, leading her up the steps. As they walked back to the car a text popped up from Kate.

SQUEEE, Tad scored tickets for all of us to Bon Jovi tonight. Front row!!!

Awesome!

Cain's invited. Jen's emphatic he come.

She held her phone out to him. "Like Bon Jovi?"

"Sure, why?" he asked, and took her phone reading the message. He stared at the text a lot longer than it would take to read it. Handing her phone back, he said, "I'm driving."

She grinned. "Sure, you can drive Old Tess. I don't mind."

"Not what I meant," he fired back.

She made a huge display of being offended. "What are you saying, Rhett? Why, this car has been in my family for years!"

Cain opened the back door for Breeze. "When are you buying your new car? This thing is a piece of shit."

She covered Tess's side mirror with both hands. "Don't listen to the pompous rich guy, Tess. He doesn't mean it."

Cain rolled his eyes. "Get in," he growled playfully.

She grinned all the way home. She even honked at a few people just so they'd turn and look at them. Cain's face was buried in his hand again, but he smirked all the way to their driveway.

Once Cain had retrieved his groceries, he said, "What time are we meeting everyone?"

"Eight o'clock."

****

After shoving all his goods into the fridge, he snagged his laptop and settled on his patio with a cold beer. He tried to concentrate on his website, but his damn leg kept jiggling. Maybe he should go for a run. The forest provided enough shade, and he wasn't making much headway on his strategy plan. He kept looking over toward the cottage.

86

Mika appeared and knelt down in front of the garden bed with a flat full of summer annuals. What the hell was she doing? He wandered over and hunched down in front of her.

"Why haven't you changed out of those jeans?" She leaned back on her haunches, a big serving spoon in her hand. "And what the hell is that?"

She said very slowly, "Aaaaa spoooon." Picking a yellow Gerbera Daisy from the flat, she plopped it in the hole, then filled the dirt in around it. Shuffling on her knees, she started to dig another hole.

"You know if you wanted more flowers, you just had to ask. I'll have the gardener plant some."

"And what fun would that be?" she asked, squinting into the sun. With an upward blow, the wispy bang over her eye flew up then straight back down to where it had been before.

Before he even knew what he was doing, he fingered the locks away. The way she looked at him for a single heartbeat stopped his pulse, then she put extra energy into digging the next hole.

"Thanks," she said, furiously scooping dirt with her spoon. "But I can do this."

What the hell was he doing? "I'll get you a proper hand shovel, put the soup spoon away."

"By the time you get back here, I'll be done."

"Wanna bet?" he fired back.

Her eyes narrowed. "Yes, I do."

"Bring it," he said. "What's the bet?"

"We trade cars for a week," she said, continuing to cheat and plant at double-time.

She was losing this bet. "Done, if you win. If I win, I've got something else in mind." He was up and running for the shed. He yanked open the door, grabbed the hand shovel, a small rake and watering can, and bulleted back to the cottage.

The dirt was flying from that old kitchen spoon, and she had two plants left, but only one hole dug. He rammed the shovel in the dirt giving her a lazy smile of victory.

"Time, Miss Makris." She rolled back onto her bum and crossed her legs. "Now, let's talk about what you owe me."

Five hours later he was showered, shaved, and pacing his living room. This, he thought to himself, should be good. He chuckled and looked at the clock. It was six-forty-five. Close enough. He headed to the garage and raised the automatic door with his fob. Tonight they'd drive in the jag, but he couldn't wait to see what walked out of her cottage door.

His price for winning the bet was simple. No baggy jeans. No baggy shirts. He wanted it black and he wanted it tight. He couldn't forget the look in her eyes when she saw the couple kissing on the lawn. Longing flashed for an instant, then it was shuttered, as if she drew herself behind a curtain to hide. Tonight, she'd have everyone staring at her.

He wore a button down, cotton, navy blue shirt and a pair of snug jeans, and his most comfortable boots. The evening was balmy so he left his leather jacket behind the seat. He pulled up in front of the cottage and got out, leaning on the car to wait for her.

The front screen opened and so did his mouth. Mika stepped out in a pair of skinny black jeans and a blouse that made him shove his hands in his pockets. The off-the-shoulder blouse hugged her upper arms, and built in cups pushed up her assets. A silky, almost see-through material fluttered down to her waist. She wore boots too, but with five inch heels. The black choker around her neck dripped with a blood-red heart.

Fuck me, that woman is definitely Greek!

After they'd made the bet, she'd jumped in her car and zoomed down the driveway. She'd gone shopping, quickly. He'd bet a heap of money everything she owned was loose and bulky. Why? The woman's Marilyn Monroe figure had him holding his breath. She'd applied makeup and done her hair, falling in a bed of curls around her bare shoulders. Wanting to show his appreciation, he clapped.

She shot a glance his way. Uncertainty replaced her cockiness. She shook her head and headed for the passenger door, but he intercepted her, pulling the belt he'd bought this morning from beneath his arm and stringing it through the loops of her black jeans. Her cheeks flushed as she laughed. The belt

89

buckle sat low on her hips, making her look all kinds of hot. Tucking her under his arm, he held up his phone, and they put their heads together. Mika grinned up at him. He took the pic, then gave her a slap on the ass to get moving.

"Victory picture."

She chuckled, opening the passenger's door. "Whose victory, mine or yours?"

"Miss Makris, I definitely won't be the one being stared at tonight."

He found parking near the Save-On-Foods Memorial center and slipped the Jag into the spot. He'd been right. As they walked with the hundreds of people heading to the concert, guys actually bumped into each other when their gazes fell on Mika.

"The gang should be up here on the left," Mika said, totally ignorant to all the looks she was getting.

"Mika?" Dinky called out, and then covered her mouth.

Sarah, Kate, Jen and Cyn all gawked. Tad, Jeff, Sam and Mac took a second look then Tad gave a long wolf whistle.

"Whoa, what did you do to our Mika?" Tad asked.

The girls all hugged, and Tad gave him a curious look. "She lost a bet." Cain laughed when Mika stuck her tongue out at him.

Jen sidled up. "Hey, Cain." She gave him a hug and left her body snuggled to his side. "Glad you came."

Another guy he'd never seen before stood between Tad and Jeff. Tad introduced them. "Mika, Cain, this is Wyatt. He works with me in sales."

Mika had explained Tad worked for Save-On-Foods, which was how he'd met Kate, who worked there too.

Wyatt's eyes hadn't wavered from Mika. When she finally put her attention on him, he shot a look Cain's way. He should have backed up and indicated Mika wasn't his. Obviously, Wyatt had been brought as Mika's escort, and Jen, who had a snug grip on Cain's arm, was his. He couldn't move. Didn't want to when he saw the interest in Wyatt's gaze.

"Hey, Wyatt," Mika said, stepping away from him and offered her hand. "Nice to meet you."

Poor ol' Wyatt looked a little confused. *Too bad.*

"You guys ready for this?" Dinky asked, jumping up on her toes and hugging Jeff with both arms.

"I've wanted to see these guys in concert forever," Jen said, wrapping her arm around his like a python.

"How did you get front row seats, Tad?" Mika asked.

"Top salesman this year. The perks don't hurt."

Jeff hammered him on the arm. "Neither does being your bud," he said, grinning.

Cain's smile slipped a little when Wyatt's hand planted itself on the shallow of Mika's back—more like the top of her ass—as he walked beside her.

"Shall we?" Jen said, nudging him.

He didn't really hear her. Cain's thoughts wandered to whether Wyatt, who reminded him of a salesman cut from cream

91

Natasza Waters

cheese with a dentist-enhanced smile and hungry eyes, would know how to kiss Mika. Would he thumb her soft cheek? Gently pull her to him so she could feel his shaft hardening just by looking at her. Appreciate the heat in her beautiful eyes? Then tease her mouth before kissing her.

"Cain?"

"Sorry?"

Jen gave him a wink. "Gang's leaving."

"Yeah. Let's do it."

"Anytime, handsome," Jen said, giving him a sweet smile.

He didn't say it, but the words played out like a marquee in his head. *Not unless you've got a lot of money, babe.*

Chapter Seven

Working their way down the stairs, Wyatt held Mika's hand, and the rest of the guys steadied the girls as their high heels clicked on the cement surface—except for Dinky, who wore ankle runners with a flirty summer dress, which somehow worked on her.

The opening act was a group from Victoria, who warmed up the crowd. When the lights went out, the anticipation and the roar of the crowd went up. The lights flashed on, and Bon Jovi was on stage ten feet away. Words curled into a circle on a screen behind the stage. *Hope. Fear.* The sticks hammered the drums, and their guitars strummed. "Can't Go Home" started and the girls went nuts, jumped to their feet, and gripped the barricade. Six beautiful women, their hips swaying, their arms pumping in the air, reminded Cain of teenagers. He sat with his arms crossed, grinning. He looked across his shoulder at Mac, Cyn's husband.

Mac leaned over and said in his ear, "Cyn and I started dating when we were thirteen. I've seen those asses shaking for seventeen years, and I never get tired of it."

Cain laughed. Mika had a picture in her cottage. The girls couldn't have been more than seventeen. They were all splayed over Old Tess, but she wasn't old, she looked brand new. Still ugly as shit, but whoever took the picture had captured the budding beauty of the women.

As the girls danced with their arms wrapped around each other's waists, his gaze wasn't on Jon Bon Jovi, it glued itself to Mika, her body sleek and getting sleeker from the running. Her dark curls bounced like black coils of silk under the brilliant lights. Desire pulled at him, and it wanted him to smash through the darkness he'd walled himself behind.

The music droned in the background to the beat of his pounding heart. What he wouldn't give to rise up right now, step behind her, brush his palms up her stomach to cup her breasts in his hands, and slide his lips over the beating pulse in her neck. Feel it flutter as he bit his way down to her beautiful shoulder.

"You're just a friend of Mika's, right?" Wyatt yelled in his ear, shattering his thoughts.

With a crank of his head, he paused, the answer stuck between "yes" and "screw you."

"Are you fuckin' her or what?" Wyatt asked.

Mika deserved better than this dickhead. He didn't answer, but his glare did.

Bon Jovi had the entire stadium rocking when "*Living on a Prayer*" powered through the speakers. The girls turned and danced for their men. Mac, Jeff, Sam, and Tad jumped to their feet, and snagged their women. Mika kept her back to them, her entire body a writhing, sexy wave of woman. As he rose like a snake from a basket hypnotized by her, Jon Bon Jovi looked straight at Mika, leaning over, he sang to her. Jen appeared in front of Cain, throwing her arms around his neck. He almost tossed her out of his way, but by the time he'd untied her arms, Wyatt stood next to Mika.

Fuck that shit. He stepped around Jen, clasping his hands on Mika's hips as *"You Give Love a Bad Name"* played. She twisted, pointed at him and sang her heart out.

Oh, how right she was.

All twelve of them stood in a tight group, rockin' to the tunes, the music blaring and Cain's heart shedded its skin from years of living a solitary life.

The concert ended after two encores. Mika smiled up at him. "I'm deaf."

"So am I, but that's from you singing off-key all night." He broke out laughing at the big "O" her mouth formed. He threw his arms around her and pulled her to his chest laughing. "I'm kidding."

He and Wyatt walked on either side of her, herded with the rest of the fans leaving the auditorium. Mika's hand rubbed against his, and he felt a twinge of possessiveness when their fingers linked. A small action, but her touch electrified him.

People were doped up and drunk, their emotions ramped from the concert. A few guys started yelling at each other off to the right. Cain and the other five guys in their group drew the girls closer and pushed for the exit, smelling trouble. Some punk swung at another guy, and a mob fight started. People panicked, shoving through their group and separating them. He let go of Mika to ward off a gangly teenager who'd been pushed into them. When Cain turned, Mika was gone.

He saw Wyatt ahead of him and he had Mika. The anxiety in her expression yanked at his heart when their eyes met.

Wyatt yelled, "I've got her," and drew Mika away. Cain had to block a fist from some fucking kid swinging beside him.

"Cain?"

He turned, hearing Jen's scared call.

"Cain!"

She was behind him, trying to reach him through a crush of bodies. Just like that, she was down. Some guy slammed into him, and he pushed the kid off him with little effort, then swam against the tide of people. Jen was on her knees. He used his body to shield her, pulling her up by the waist. On her feet, Jen pinched his fingers like vise grips. He held her under his arm and used his weight to break a path. He was bigger than most guys and a head taller.

"Where the hell is security?" she asked, an octave higher than normal.

Two guys tumbled into them, and he yanked Jen out of the way. The rush for the doors was like a herd of cattle being prodded down a chute.

Cain heard his phone beep with a text. He read it once they'd made it outside.

96

We're at the meeting place. Jen?

"It's Mika," he said. Jen clutched his waist with an iron grip. Sirens bounced off the buildings, Victoria's finest on their way. Finally, more help was coming. They needed to get out of there. He saw Mika waving.

"Shit, do you believe that?" Tad said, holding onto Kate with both arms. "Fucking idiots."

Mika stood next to Dinky. Wyatt gave him a nod. Cain was grateful he'd gotten her out safely. Jen hadn't let go of him yet, and he didn't like the look in Mika's eyes as she watched her friend pressing her breasts against his arm.

"That kind of ruined the night, didn't it?" Jeff said. "You guys feel like getting something to eat?"

"I feel like downing a couple beers," Tad suggested. "Babysitter is good till midnight, right babe?"

Kate kissed her husband and nodded. "Wanna hit the casino?" she suggested.

"Cain, would you give me a ride?" Jen asked. She pressed her cheek to his shoulder. "I took a cab here."

What started off as a great night ended on a shit note, but he didn't need this situation getting out of control, either. He didn't do girlfriends, and Jen's body plastered to his side delivered a definite intention.

"Sorry, Jen," he said, stepping toward Mika. "We brought the Jag." Putting emphasis on *we*.

Natasza Waters

"No worries, man," Wyatt piped up. "I'll give Mika a ride. What d'ya say, gorgeous?"

Wyatt plastered on a smile he probably used a hundred times to weaken women's knees. Mika glanced at him, and then Jen. She crossed her arms. "Sure."

She was mad at him. Cain could feel it. Was she jealous of Jen or was it something else?

"We'll see you guys there," Jen said, pulling on his arm.

They crawled with the traffic leaving the city, headed for View Royal, Cain's finger tapping the steering wheel in time with the unsettled beat of his pulse.

"I hope Mika finally takes the plunge tonight," Jen said, looking out the front window. "She's a ticking sexual time bomb." She shifted in her seat to look at him. "How did you convince her to wear some decent clothes?"

His brow curled. "Her clothes are fine." Cain ignored the rising burn in his gut. He wanted Mika to feel good about herself when he'd made the bet. He just hadn't expected her to be in another man's car after the concert. "Why is she a ticking bomb?"

Jen inspected her nails and raised a brow. "I certainly can't live without hot, sweaty sex. Wyatt would be perfect for her. He looks like he knows what he's doing, since Mika doesn't." Jen paused. "So do you." Her gaze skated over him. "We don't have to go to the casino, could take a detour."

98

Cain chewed on his inner cheek, ignoring Jen's innuendo. Maybe Mika had been burned in a bad relationship. His phone bleeped, and he checked it when the streetlight turned red.

You let go of me.

Mika's text made his guts cinch the knot in his belly.

No. You let go of me.

Jen reached over and turned up his stereo. The light changed to green, but they weren't going very far with the sea of taillights ahead of them.

Did not.

You were safe.

He looked into his rearview mirror. Was she behind them or ahead of them?

Thanks to Wyatt.

Were they actually having a text fight?

You okay?

He smokes. Yuck.

Jen crossed her long legs, and her dress hiked even higher on her thin thighs. He rolled his eyes.

Asked if you were okay?

No.

He selected her number, and she picked up on the first ring. "What's wrong?" he asked, his concern overriding his anger.

There was a pause. "I'm going home. I'll let Breeze out." Mika huffed. "And I'm keeping her for the night since you won't be home."

"Where do you think I'm going?"

"Talk to you later."

"Hey," he barked at her. "I'm dropping Jen off at the casino. Wait for me at the front entrance." He was sure Wyatt had other plans. He shouldn't stop her from hooking up with him if that's what she wanted. What bothered Cain was *he* didn't want her hooking up with Wyatt. "Unless you want to go with him." He could hear Wyatt prattling on about himself in the background. "Does that guy ever shut up?"

"No," she said, sullenly.

He grinned to himself. She didn't like him. *Good.* "The traffic's breaking up. Wait for me."

After thirty minutes, they rolled up to the casino entrance. Without hesitation, Jen slid her hand to his shoulder. "Come in for a drink." She leaned over as if to kiss him when the door yanked open.

"Hey, guys," Mika said, stopping Jen's advance.

Jen's expression pinched. "Sorry," she whispered.

He wasn't. "See ya, Jen."

Jen pressed closer. "Oh, come on. One drink isn't going to kill you."

Mika leaned over. "Sorry for interrupting." She closed the door and headed into the casino at a run.

He gripped Jen by the shoulder and pressed her back. "I'll park the car. Find the girls."

"I'm buying my hero his first drink." She winked at him.

His heart raced in his chest. As soon as Jen was out of the car, he was on his phone, but Mika wouldn't pick up. He disconnected and tried again. Then three more times.

She finally answered as he got out of the car about to go find her. "Get your ass outside," he commanded and hung up.

She took her sweet time, but when she appeared, he didn't waste any. "Don't you ever run away from me again."

She stared down at the ground, her fingers pinned in her pockets. "I didn't mean to interrupt you and Jen."

"You didn't interrupt anything. Listen, what happened back there freaked everyone out, including me." People milled around the casino entrance, most lighting up a smoke. "The fight wasn't your fault, or was it? Couple guys start fighting over you?" he teased.

"Don't do that," she fired back unexpectedly, not an ounce of humor in her voice.

She leaned against his car.

"Do what?"

She pinned him with a hard look, her brow tight. "Don't lie to me to try and make me feel better about my image. I hate when people feed me bullshit, especially one who I thought was my friend."

101

He dropped his fists on the roof of the Jag, pinning her between them, anxious energy straining to be released. The draw to follow her bare collarbone to the graceful arch of her neck dug grappling hooks into his restraint. Wyatt had done exactly what he expected any guy to do when they looked at Mika. Desire her. Except when it happened, he didn't like it.

"I am your damn friend, and I don't lie."

She crossed her arms tightly. Oh, no, she wasn't going to push him away. He knew how to read a woman's body language better than most men. He gripped her wrists and yanked them to her sides. A brilliant light atop of the entrance shone down on them. Standing so close, he saw Mika's bottom lip had a natural little pout, its fullness a temptation to any man. But he wasn't any man. His jaw clenched, resisting the strongest draw he'd ever felt in his life.

The angry mob had scared her, but two things had scared him—the crowd taking her from him, and Wyatt wanting to do the same thing.

His hand curled gently around her neck. "Mika, I shouldn't have let go of you. It happened so fast. I'm sorry."

Her eyes darted to his, and she threw her arms around his neck and hugged him. "Me, too."

He buried his face in her hair and folded her tightly in his arms, knowing she'd quickly back away if he didn't. It was a let's-be-friends hug, not a signal she wanted more of him.

He cocked his head back. "You want to go home?"

102

"I'm hungry, and they serve a steak and mushroom hoagie that's making me drool just thinking about it."

"What? You're going to eat something other than water and celery?"

"Are you mocking my food?" she tossed back, her eyes narrowing.

"Hell, no. I want one of those hoagies, too. I'll save your conscience and we'll share it."

They parked the car and walked into the casino together, his arm around her shoulders and Mika's arm wrapped around his waist. It felt good, really goddamn good. Before they found the gang, he said, "I don't like that guy, Wyatt."

She shrugged. "He's okay."

"I'm just warning you," he said as they took the two steps down to the casino floor.

"About what?" She looked up at him, her big brown eyes accentuated with dusty rose eye shadow.

Her eyes were extraordinary, and he had to admit to himself, whether he wanted to or not, he loved looking into them any chance he could.

"Wyatt is prowling for one thing, and I don't want you lured into his bullshit."

She gave him a hip bump. "Jealous?" She laughed.

Yes almost came roaring from his mouth. "Just protecting your reputation."

"Aw, thanks, buddy."

The gang stood in a huddle at the bar. The drinks had been ordered and everyone seemed to have forgotten the incident at the concert. Jen pinned a curious look on him. He wasn't letting go of Mika, and when his gaze strayed to Wyatt, the message he deposited at his front door was simple. Stay the fuck away from my friend.

He and Mika shared a hoagie, and when the gang filtered onto the casino floor, he noticed Wyatt talking Jen up. Disaster averted.

"Hey, Cain. Sorry man."

He turned and Tad gave him an apologetic expression as he set his empty beer on the bar.

"For what?"

"I didn't realize you and Mika...."

The girls hadn't gone far, all of them huddled around Kate, who played a slot machine. Cain slid off his stool. "Nothing to realize. I know Wyatt's an associate of yours. He's just not good for Mika."

"Know someone who is?" Tad asked, giving him a sidelong look. Kate and the girls squealed, and they wandered down to see what she'd won. Cain grinned seeing the twenty dollar win counting up, and Kate clapping like she'd won a million.

He wasn't an idiot and could read the expression on Tad's face. They headed for the tables. "Why doesn't she have someone?"

Instantly, Tad became wary. "She's got her reasons. They're not good enough for the sisterhood over there, but Mika has always run solo."

"Does this have something to do with the injections she takes?"

His brows arched. "You know about that, eh?"

"To a point. Why does she need them?"

"Sorry, man. Not for me to share the details."

Mika's friends were loyal to the core. "Obviously, you know. I assume you all do."

Tad reached in his pocket and pulled out a few twenties. "You want to join me for Pai Gow?"

"Okay, I get it. You're not gonna divulge. Just tell me this, is it serious?"

Tad deliberated for a couple seconds. "Yes."

His heart squeezed with worry. "Enough to kill her?" He'd keep asking, if Tad kept talking.

Tad jerked his head to follow and wound his way through the other visitors, looking for an aura hanging over some slot with a jackpot ready to burst. "If it got bad enough, yes," he said.

"Then I want to know what it is."

Tad sighed. "Mika is embarrassed by it. It's not one of those diseases people greet with instant pity. People like her are ridiculed. Because of that, she lives like a nun." He paused. "We're all used to it, but Mika has a tendency to disappear when it's really bad." Tad slid onto a chair at the Pai Gow table and pushed his money across to the dealer. "When she's ready, she'll share." The dealer counted out his chips, and Tad piled them on the felt. "I can tell ya one thing for sure. She'll never let you be more than a friend, so if I were you, I'd store that look in your eyes."

"I don't have a look."

Tad nodded and tossed his bet on the table. "You can bullshit strangers, but not friends," Tad said, landing a knowing gaze on him.

Is that how they saw him? They were accepting him into their group?

"Giants are playing the Cowboys tomorrow. Guys are coming over," Tad said. "Five o'clock."

"How big's your television?"

"Seventy-two incher, man."

Cain looked over his shoulder and saw Mika searching the crowd until she found him. "How about hundred and ten. My place."

Tad blinked. "You got high def hundred and ten?" He was almost drooling.

He nodded. "You can see the laces on their shoes. See ya at five."

He wandered back toward the women and placed a hand on Mika's shoulder. "How come you're not playing?"

106

"Editing procedure manuals doesn't really pay." She grinned up at him.

"Find me a machine."

She raised a brow at him and then gripped his hand, dragging him behind her. He chuckled. She knew exactly where she was going. Laying her hand on a slot near the entrance, she said, "This one."

"Sit."

"You sit. You're probably luckier than me."

He prodded her into the chair, then slipped a bill into the machine.

"A hundred dollars," she squeaked. "Are you crazy?"

He bent over and snuggled his cheek to hers, wrapping his arms around her seemed so damn natural. When she didn't move, he picked up her hand and placed it on the buttons. When she tried to slide her hand to the forty cent bet, he moved it to three bucks.

"Bet big, win big, sweetheart."

She chuckled. "Okay, your loss."

Every time she won a little, she did a sexy little seat dance, and he laughed.

By the time he parked the car in the garage it was two a.m. He sat in the dark and watched her sleep, memorizing the gentle curve of her lips. She didn't wear lipstick, just a little gloss, and he liked that. Her cheeks had a gentle swell, tempting him to

107

trace them with his finger. She didn't have money or prestige. She was an everyday girl with a pretty face and an easy smile. His heart beat faster. The draw too strong to resist, he brushed her cheek. So soft. He withdrew his hand.

Cain gently squeezed her shoulder. "We're home," he said quietly.

Her long lashes fluttered open. "Sorry, I fell asleep." She pushed herself up and blinked a couple times.

Regret handed him a reality check as she reached for the door handle.

"Night, Cain."

He had one thing to be happy about. Mika had come home with him and wasn't lying under that prick, Wyatt. "See ya tomorrow for a run."

She waved and wandered up the gravel path toward the cottage. He watched her until she was safely inside, then let Breeze out.

When he checked his laptop, he had three more requests for his services. Each woman was wealthy with average good looks. Sitting at his dining room table, his attention was drawn to the cottage. He watched as the lights flicked off.

"Night, Mika."

He released a deep sigh, rejecting each request, then closed the lid.

Chapter Eight

One day a week she allowed herself to indulge in caffeine. Granted, the cup was big enough to fit a puppy inside, but she refrained from refills. Mika settled in front of her laptop. The summer sun shone in her windows, laying a warm track across the wooden floorboards of the cottage. Crisp air curled through her screen door. Vickers had her tongue guns trained on her this week, but living here made it all worthwhile.

The laptop booted up. She needed to replace Cain's and give his back. Maybe he'd go shopping with her and help buy a new one? A text from Dinky popped up on her phone.

Coming over. Squee. Only one week away.

Mika chuckled. Cyn, Kate, and Sarah had all been crazy as loons a week before their weddings, but Dinky was a psycho bride. She'd decided on a themed wedding, surprising everyone who thought it would be a mix of punk and Goth, but typical Dinky, she dropped every jaw when she announced it would be Victorian. She wanted all the men in tuxes and the ladies in lace.

A hunky torso appeared on Mika's desktop. From the neck down to his sexy hips and torqued abs, the mystery man she'd sniped from Google images gave her something to dream about.

Cain craned his head in the door. "Morning. You wouldn't happen to have coffee?"

"You smelled it from your house, didn't you?"

He broke into a smile. "You always have coffee Saturday morning."

"In fact I do, and you can save me the temptation of drinking the rest by finishing the pot."

He strolled by, leaving a trail of sizzling magnetism wavering behind him. The man always smelled good. "Is that your aftershave or what?" she finally asked.

"Hmm," he murmured tipping back the coffee cup, a stupid but puzzling grin on his lips.

"You stink good."

He chuckled. "Thanks." He leaned over her shoulder "What the hell is that on my computer?" he asked.

She crooked her brow and craned her head back. "What? You gave it to me."

Cain's brow creased looking at the hot dude on her laptop. "He ain't that great."

"You take your crazy pill already? He's hot."

Cain rubbed his jaw and gave her a cocky grin. "I should have left a selfie on that."

She snorted. "Yeah, right."

He settled in the chair across from her and slipped the newspaper from under his arm onto the table. "I wear Clive Christian No.1."

"Never heard of it." She Googled it and her mouth gaped open. "It's twenty-three hundred dollars a bottle!" she screeched.

Cain's brow barely creased. "You said you liked it."

"Well, you're not getting that from me for Christmas."

"What do you wear?" he asked.

She signed on to Facebook to see if anyone from her group was online or had left messages.

"Eau de goat's milk soap."

He spit out a laugh and opened the first section of the Victoria Times. "Sexy," he drawled.

"We're not all rich snobs."

With only a handful of groups dedicated to her disorder on Facebook, she'd chosen the smallest, with four thousand people.

"Scent is not what I'm talking about, and every woman has a bottle of perfume," he said, flipping up the paper.

"Nope. Not everyone."

Like many online groups, most folks just lurked. She'd joined the group during its early days and she'd come to know the men and women who were most active on the site.

She'd lived with her enemy since she was three, and had run the gauntlet of home remedies, creams, and pills for what she and twelve million other people struggled with. To the group, she had become a reliable resource. She'd literally *done it all* to keep the monster inside her quiet. She had ten personal messages and a string of posts where she'd been tagged.

"Would you wear something, if I bought it for you?" Cain asked, lifting his mug with a raised brow.

"Miss an old girlfriend or something? Buy a teddy bear and spray it."

A deep rumble of a laugh erupted from his chest. "Still not what I'm talking about."

She ignored him. Taking a sip of her coffee, she began to read and make comments. This group was closed because people bared their souls, including pictures. When it had first started, the two administrators had kept it open, but that didn't last long because the heartless idiots of the world came storming in to make rude comments and nasty remarks.

"You don't wear anything?" he asked.

She stopped typing and looked across the table, but he was hidden behind the paper. "I wear clothes. Haven't you noticed?"

He dropped the paper and gazed at her. His lids shuttered then he stuck his tongue in his cheek as if stifling a laugh. "Yes, I notice everything."

"I bet you do."

He flipped the paper up. "Uh-huh."

Cradling her coffee, she read the second PM from her friend Karen, who lived in New York, instead of being concerned with her landlord-clothes horse.

I'm really struggling these days, Mika. Not only am I fighting a flare, but Gavin can't deal with it. He won't come near me. He makes horrible comments like, "You're not trying hard enough. Why can't you make this go away?" The worst one was

112

last night. "We're not having sex until you get that under control. It sickens me."

Mika put her cup down with a deep sigh of regret. Karen wasn't the only woman who had an unsupportive husband. When they'd married, her enemy had been under control, but she'd gone back to work after having two children, and the stresses of her corporate position had pushed her autoimmune system into chaos. Her dermatologist had put her on Methotrexate which helped, but didn't render a complete remission. Nothing could cure what they had.

Mika typed a response to Karen and moved on to the other messages. She heard a car and saw Dinky driving up the road.

"By the way," Cain said and slowly dropped the paper, grinning at her.

"What?" she drawled, waiting for another lesson on how to smell. He looked as if he'd found out some dirty little secret he was going to hang over her head.

He leaned over the table with a sublime smile. "If you wore that incredibly sexy see-through negligee you have on all the time, you'd have guys lining up outside your front door."

Her guts rolled over in terror. She dropped her gaze. She'd totally forgotten she had on her nightie. Her *see everything nightie.* She screeched and ran from the table.

"Holy fuck," she blurted, diving into her bedroom and slamming the door. How in God's name could she have ever look Cain in the eyes again?

"Morning, Cain." Dinky chirped her greeting.

Cain was still laughing.

"What's so funny?"

Mika threw on a pair of jeans and overly big sweater, and stomped back down the hall.

"You could have said something earlier," she stormed at him.

Cain sat back in the chair, looking all friggin' relaxed and sex-on-a-stick handsome. He raised his hands. "Hey, I'm not complaining."

Dinky's head swung back and forth. "Should I leave?"

"No," she sputtered. "But Cain is!"

"Before you go, here." Dinky gave him an envelope.

"What's this?" He opened it and grinned. "I'll be there. Thanks, Dinky."

Dinky dropped the big book she carried on the table.

"You've changed your mind about something—again, haven't you?"

Mika's bestie brushed past her into the kitchen. "Yes." She poured herself a cup of brew and said to Cain, "You need a tux, Victorian style. Most of the guys are using Tuxes Galore."

"Think I can manage something."

Dinky got that look on her face and Mika knew there was more coming. "Mika, you've always gone solo to all the weddings and we just kind of thought…."

Mika slammed her eyes shut. "You didn't, Dinky."

"What," she said, accompanied with a perky smile.

"You asked Cain to be my date?" She groaned. "Seriously?"

"Mika, it's not that bad. I mean, why not?"

Cain leaned forward, one perfect eyebrow arched. "Yeah, why not?"

She sputtered. "Oh, I don't know. How about people will think we're a couple, and the poor guy will be stuck with me all night."

"I don't think he sees it that way." Dinky cranked a look at Cain. "You don't see it that way, do you?"

Cain rose with a shit-eating grin on his face. "Not at all. And don't forget clothes aren't optional, Mika."

She grabbed the first thing she could find, which happened to be a magazine. Cain put it into high gear and shot out the front door just as the mag slammed against the doorjamb.

Dinky cocked her head like an ostrich. "Um, ya sure I shouldn't come back later?"

"Not unless you bring back lye, duct tape and garbage bags, so I can bury my landlord," she yelled at the door.

"Lovers spat?" she asked.

"He's not my lover," Mika growled. "I'm going to end up solo again anyway. Every single woman there is going to be lusting over him, especially Jen."

"Jen has a date."

Mika rubbed her neck and let out a frustrated grumble. "Cain looks like a Greek god when he wears a pair of torn jeans. Imagine what he'll look like in a tux? I hate you sometimes."

Dinky offered her pearly smile. "No, you don't. You love me." She tapped her chin. "I'm guessing he could make 007 look like a swamp beast."

Mika shook her head. "Don't play matchmaker. Cain is most definitely out of my league."

Dinky rolled her eyes, and they settled at the kitchen table over the book of flower arrangements. "Your flowers are gorgeous. Why are you changing them?"

She waved her hand in the air. "There's too much pink. I'm thinking yellow for summer."

"You're driving my mom crazy, so make up your mind."

They hovered over the thirty options and pared them down to five before they took a break. Dinky sucked back her water, which she never went anywhere without. A month ago she decided she could lose ten pounds. This from a natural born string bean. Mika had teased her, asking if they had negative sizes in dresses. Which her best friend responded, "No, I'm gonna be a perfect zero."

Dinky patted her hand. "Let's go out for lunch and then drop by the dress shop."

"You've been there so often, they know what you're going to name your first child."

"It's for your fitting. Now come on, let's get going."

****

Wednesday afternoon the limousine picked up all the girls for Dinky's bachelorette party. Mika had rented the limo for the night, and they'd crawled through the clubs. Yes, literally crawled after club number four.

Thursday morning at five a.m. she'd staggered to bed, and stayed there. Breeze kept her company in her miserable state, and she'd begged off running with Cain.

She found nothing funny about standing at her front door in her bunny PJ's at two in the afternoon and her hair standing up on end, but Cain did.

He took one look at her and said, "Wow, you're in agony, aren't you?"

She squinted even with three Advils and a miracle shake meant to eradicate the screaming harpies from her head.

"Guess you're not running today," he said smirking.

"Guess not." And she slammed the door shut in his face. A tap made her open it again. "What? Can't you leave a woman to die in peace?"

With one hand propped against the jam, he grinned at her. "Just wondering what time we're leaving on Saturday."

She dragged her fingers down her face and tried to make her brain function. "Butchart Gardens, the wedding starts at two. Dinky rented rooms at the Empress. We've got hair appointments at eleven then back to the hotel to get dressed, blah, blah, blah."

Cain chuckled and her stomach tightened. It did that every time the man smiled, never mind making her toes curl and her legs quiver. He was just too darn handsome for his own good.

"I'll drive you to the Empress in the morning. How's that?"

She shrugged nonchalantly. "Sure."

He nodded once and backed away, giving her that look he had with his head a little tilted and a sexy, inquisitive stare from beneath the slashes of his dark brows.

"'Kay." He huffed out a laugh. "You really need some TLC."

"Oh, shut up." She didn't have a good one-liner to fire back at him.

Cain had been out of town on business for most of the week. She thought it was kinda cute that he'd called each night to check on her. They didn't talk long. Just a quick convo to connect. Mika considered herself lucky to have a good friend like him.

"I'll be back later with some dinner. Go to bed."

"Intend to." After shutting the door in his face, she walked straight to her bedroom and stuffed her head under the pillow.

Good to his word, Cain came back at five with dinner and some awful-looking yellow concoction.

"Seriously, it'll help," he said and nudged her hand to drink.

She downed it and gagged. "Oh my God, what is that?"

"Buffalo piss, but it works wonders."

Her eyes flashed wide open. "Whaaat?"

He doubled over laughing, putting his hand in the air. He tried to talk, but couldn't stop laughing. "You should see your face."

"Yours is gonna be in a coffin if I just drank buffalo urine," she barked.

He grabbed his stomach and fell onto the couch laughing. Shaking his head, he couldn't control himself. She stood over him with her hands on her hips, ready to make her threat a reality.

"What the hell was that?"

He yanked her down on the couch beside him, stretched his long legs and set his heels on the coffee table then grabbed the remote.

"Feeling better?" He broke out laughing again.

She actually was…but. "Tell me." She slugged him in the shoulder.

He wrapped an arm around her shoulders. "We going to watch your stupid show?"

"Which one?"

"Exactly." He clicked the TV on. "You should read more."

"I do read." She tucked her feet under her butt, and leaned against his sturdy shoulder, pulling the blanket up to her chin.

They watched *The Bachelor* and Cain groaned halfway through. "Why do you watch this crap? None of it's real."

She sighed. "It's kind of romantic."

He looked down at her, and she looked up. They were almost nose to nose. "Why do women search for a fantasy instead of looking for the real thing? I mean, why sit here and watch this instead of going out and finding a real guy?"

"Because there's no good ones left," she said, turning to stare at the television.

"Jeff, Tad, Sam and Mac are decent guys."

"They are," she agreed.

He paused then said, "How come you haven't brought anyone home? You never go out."

"I like my little cottage. I've got my friends." She turned up the sound, and he got the hint. It wasn't long before she'd nodded off.

Mika woke up cradled in Cain's arms, the room dark, and the TV off. Instead of interrupting his sleep, she eased herself from the couch, pulled the blanket over him, and went to bed.

****

Saturday morning, Mika stepped outside to drink her herbal tea on the patio. The breeze off the ocean had a nip, but the sky was clear. A beautiful day for Dinky's wedding.

Four hours later, Mika rearranged her bestie's train and gave her a kiss. They'd gotten all their crying done before the cosmetician had applied the makeup. Dinky didn't want the traditional wedding song. She'd found a beautiful Gaelic tune to honor her Irish roots.

The rest of the girls had already walked down the aisle.

She'd been in Cyn, Kate, Sarah, and now Dinky's wedding party. Her dress was very different from the other girls. They all had dresses that came to just above their knees and halter tops covered in lace and beads. They were dazzling. Mika had to cover more of her skin, so she wore a floor-length mermaid dress in shimmering gold. The dress fit snuggly with full-length sleeves and a very revealing off-the-shoulder bodice. The dress clung like a layer of Saran wrap around her hips.

As the maid of honor, she was up next. Dinky had chosen yellow and white flowers, which had been wrapped around the lamp posts.

She rounded a sculpted hedge with the perfect, practiced walk of a bridesmaid but never a bride. A red carpet covered the gravel path. She caught the smiles of family and friends as she walked past the early summer flowers of Butchart Gardens.

Mika kept her shoulders straight and her chin up. She smiled at her mom, who sat with their friend's parents. Mom blew her a kiss and she winked back. By chance, standing on the aisle across from Mom, was Cain.

Her breath rushed from her lungs, and she almost tripped. She'd been wrong. 007 didn't hold a candle to her landlord. Cain was outstandingly handsome wearing his period tux. With his gaze focused on her, she felt incredibly self-conscious.

His mouth curved into a fetching smile, causing her pulse to thump madly. She joined the wedding party, then watched her best friend walk up the aisle. Instead of following the bride, Cain turned and stared up at Mika. Her mom saw him doing it, and the little hat she wore tipped as she panned a look at her and back at Cain.

When the ceremony was over, guests wandered through the gardens as the photographers snapped pictures. Jeff's brother, Jordon, was his best man. As soon as Dinky and Jeff disappeared to sign the paperwork, Jordon's wife appeared. Once again, Mika was solo and stared across the sea of smiling faces.

"Mesmerizing." She heard a voice behind her.

She turned and grinned at Cain. He hadn't seen her in the dress because the wedding party accompanied Dinky in the limo before the ceremony.

"More beautiful than a sunset," he said.

His gaze made her stomach flip. "Thank you. Better than jogging pants." Something in his stare unnerved her, or maybe it was just the fact that he was staring. Intently. "We have a half hour before group photos."

"Mika?"

"Mom." They hugged each other, but her mother's attention was set on Cain. "This is my landlord, Cain Sallas."

Mothers and daughters often had a slight resemblance, but some, like she and her mom, were mirror images of each other.

"Nice to meet you, Cain."

"Mrs. Makris, it's my honor." He accepted her hand as if she were royalty.

Her mother smiled with approval. "Is that a Greek accent I hear?"

"Yes, ma'am. I was born there."

"My husband, Mika's father, was Greek. He was born on the Island of Rhodes."

"We have a business there, and several of my relatives live there as well."

"We traveled to Greece when Mika was a baby."

"I just remember Disneyland," Mika said.

"You were only six months old. We wanted to show you off to your grandparents. They were overjoyed to have a granddaughter." Her mom paused. "Sallas." She nodded. "Did you know there is a Sallas Winery? Old vine is very popular."

He nodded. "That's right. It's one of my family's most popular lines. It's quite well known."

She smiled brightly at Mika. "Your father loved that wine."

Mika didn't know that and shrugged.

"My daughter doesn't drink very much because of her condition."

"Mom," she warned, and gave her a covert look to be quiet.

Her mom rubbed her temple. "Not sure how long I'm going to stay, sweetheart."

"Haven't you gone to the doctor's yet?" Her mom was a busy woman, but they talked almost every day.

"This time of year is extremely busy. I haven't had a chance. Not to mention Dinky changing her mind a hundred times," she joked.

"Mom owns a flower shop in Victoria. The Creative Stem," Mika explained.

Cain watched her mother with concern. "You're not feeling well?"

"I just have headaches sometimes. More than I probably should. Don't worry, Mika. I promise, I'll see the doctor soon."

"As in next week, Mom."

She nodded. "It was nice to meet you, Cain."

He took her hand and held it, giving her one of his warm smiles. The one that made a lady's pantyhose melt. "I hope we see each other again."

"I hope so, too. Excuse me, I have to say hello to some friends."

Cain watched her mother wander down the path toward a group of their friends' parents. "You look just like your mom."

She nodded. "Yeah, that's what everyone says. People think she's my older sister, not my mom. My parents had me quite young. She's forty-eight."

"And your dad? He isn't here?"

She glanced away. "No, he passed away five years ago. It was a heart attack."

"So young."

She sighed and clenched her hands together. "Mom's never been interested in another man. We tried to set her up on blind dates a couple times." She chuckled. "She finally told us all to lay off. She still loves Dad, even if he isn't around. She says she feels his presence looking out for her."

"May I?" A man said, stepping up to them. A leather bag was hooked over his shoulder and he held an expensive looking camera. Dinky had hired a team of photographers. "Would you and your escort mind standing over here," he asked, pointing toward an enormous azalea bush with bright red blooms.

Cain's brow creased. "I'm not her escort," he said harshly.

"Uh." Her heart sank and she flushed with embarrassment. "He's a friend of Dinky, I mean, Dina and Jeff."

Cain's deep blue eyes darkened even more. "I'm her date, not her escort."

Mika stilled, not understanding what the difference was or why Cain seemed angry.

"You're a beautiful couple," the photographer said. "Would you mind if I followed you and took some pictures?"

She put her back to the photographer. "You don't have to do this, Cain."

He cleared his throat and glared at the ground. "Sorry. I'm not fond of that term." Cain's masculine features creased as if perplexed for a moment, then he leaned in, putting his mouth next to her ear, causing goose bumps to coat her flesh. The photographer was already snapping photos. "Would you accompany me through the gardens, Miss Makris?"

She smiled, their cheeks touching. Years from now, she could stare at the pictures, filling her head with silly dreams.

"My pleasure, Mr. Sallas."

"You really are stunning, Mika."

He offered his arm and they walked through the gardens, stopping when the photographer asked them to pose. Thirty minutes later, they found their way back to the Sunken Garden. Cain waited while the photographers ordered the wedding party into their groups for the photos.

When they'd finished, Cain joined her again and placed his fingers on her cheeks and massaged them. She chuckled. "I think they're permanently frozen there."

"Shall we?" he asked, offering her an arm once again.

For some strange reason, Cain had the ability to make her feel like someone truly special. They walked toward the exit with the rest of the entourage.

"Now, we get to relax," she said. "And eat. I'm starving."

Cain opened the passenger's door of the Jag. Once she'd buckled in, he squatted beside her.

"I've been to a lot of weddings, but I don't think I've ever seen a more beautiful maid of honor. You outshine the bride."

She raised a brow at him. "Did I miss an open bar?"

Cain held his phone up. His wallpaper held a picture of her, standing in front of a blooming magnolia tree. Her head slightly turned and her expression distant.

"In Greek legend, Helen was the most beautiful woman ever known, and the indirect cause of the Trojan War. I've seen many paintings of her, but none surpass this image on my phone."

Her mouth gaped a little, and Cain gently lifted her chin with a finger.

"See you guys at the Empress," Jen called out, clinging to her date.

She waved. "Right behind you." Cain stared at her, and it made her incredibly uncomfortable. "If I'm Helen of Troy, then you're most definitely Adonis. All the single women have been drooling all over themselves since you arrived. Your dance card is already full, and we haven't even gotten there yet."

Cain's gaze swept across her face. "There's only one name on that card this evening. I'm ready to dance with you all night."

"Hope you wore steel-toed shoes."

127

He whisked a stray curl from her cheek. "Your feet will never touch the floor when you're in my arms."

Her mouth gaped again, but this time Cain backed away and closed the door, a sizzling, mischievous grin on his lips.

****

The Empress Hotel served an exquisite dinner. Laughter and tears were shared as the speeches followed. Mika made it through hers without crying, but Dinky and Jeff swept their cheeks when they played the video she'd made for them. It had taken her a couple months to decide on what pictures to use. She'd hired someone to put it all together with their favorite song.

Love swept through the luxurious banquet hall and joined every guest in celebration of their marriage. Luckily, Dinky wasn't big on too much pomp and ceremony.

After the bride and groom had their dance, the guests all joined in. Cain had been seated with her friends' husbands during the meal. When the guests began to mingle, he rounded the head table and escorted her onto the dance floor.

He carried a masculine strength and elegance that no other man in the room possessed. His eyes never veered from hers, making her feel anxious. Cain's large palm pressed against the arch of her back and drew her closer for the slow dance. Mika truly didn't want to embarrass herself and step on his toes. But he led her with ease, all she had to do was follow.

She couldn't put her finger on it, but it felt like he was professionally trained to be the perfect gentlemen. He came from a wealthy family, maybe he'd been taught the finer nuances of society.

The conversation of the crowd, the eyes watching them, everything disappeared as Cain created a bubble around her. He held her snugly as they danced to a romantic melody. When the song ended, she glanced at her friends who were close by, and they were all staring at her. She hated being the focal point in any group and blushed.

Cain's reserved smile creased his firm lips. "I feel honored to be here tonight, but especially in your company."

Oh, my God. Her cheeks heated. Because of the occasion, her alcohol abstinence was on hold for the evening. After that comment, she needed a couple ounces to calm her nerves. Cain didn't step back, instead he held her close, as if they still danced. The warmth of his palm on her back seeped through her dress, causing her blood to tingle.

As usual, when she felt uncomfortable, she quickly resorted to a joke. "Think I should be paying you this evening."

A storm cloud shifted across his expression, wiping out the smile and he immediately released her. "I'm going to the bar," he stated coldly. "Want anything?"

The magic instantly broken, unease slithered up her spine. She chased him and gripped his arm halfway to the bar. "Cain. I'm sorry. It was a joke."

He rounded on his heel, his attractive jaw clenched. "I know that."

"Then why are you angry?"

He exhaled and closed his eyes for a second. "I'm not."

Although it was probably totally wrong, she forked her fingers with his. "All I meant was that you look so handsome tonight." She snorted. "Who am I kidding?" She shrugged. "You always look handsome."

He gazed at her as if trying to work something out, then his brow creased with chagrin. "I…" Cain scratched his forehead. "Let's get a drink."

They walked toward the bar, joining their friends who had the same idea. She expected Cain to release her hand, but he didn't, and that made her smile.

****

They arrived home around one a.m. Mika clutched the bouquet she'd caught in her hands, along with all the little wedding gifts Dinky had plied on her. Her feet were sore, and she thought she might just slip into a bath before bed.

Cain had been very quiet on the drive. "Thank you for being my escort," she said. They stood in front of the garage as the door lowered. Alcohol always made her a little braver, and she winked at him.

His tie was undone and his jacket draped over his arm. Her smile evaporated when he looked at her so seriously. "I really don't like that term, Mika."

"Why? I mean aside from accompanying someone, I don't see anything wrong with the profession." Slipping off her spike heels, because she couldn't stand them pinching her feet, she wiggled her toes to bring the feeling back. "I've even thought about hiring one someday for myself."

He took an angry step toward her, and her pulse quickened. "Don't do that. Don't *ever* do that."

Shocked at his vehement response. "Why? Twenty-first century, ya know. From what I've read, they're very popular with executive types and women who are too busy to hang out and wait for some man to take notice. They're educated and always polite." She shifted the load in her arms. "I saw an article that said they'll accompany someone to an event or a party, and that it's not all about sex. In fact, that part is a separate contract, agreed on by both parties in a very mature way. I don't see anything wrong with that."

Cain's chest expanded with a deep breath. "Why would you do that? Jen said you haven't gone on a date in years. You get asked, but you don't accept."

She shrugged. "I've got my reasons."

"What are they?" he shot back.

Her friend was getting too nosy. Cain's jaw ground into a tight line. Instead of answering, she decided to head toward the safety of her cottage to avoid more questions.

"Mika," he said sharply.

"I'm tired, Cain. Good night."

"I want you to talk to me first before you ever consider doing something like that."

She laughed and tossed over her shoulder, "Why, you gonna give me a cut rate?"

"What?"

Within a second, he was beside her and dug his fingers into her arm then swung her around.

"I'm kidding. What is the matter with you?"

Cain blinked and swallowed deeply. "Nothing—good night." He turned and strode toward his house of glass.

Strange. She walked down the gravel path, the cool sea air refreshing on her skin.

"Hey!" he called out. "I hope you save me a dance at your wedding." His deep timbre cut through the darkness.

She thought of twenty self-deprecating comments. Everything from "if miracles happen, sure" to "no one marries monsters," but instead she smiled to herself. "Night, Cain."

Chapter Nine

Mika's heart raced with fear. She came to a screeching stop near the main house. Leaving the car running, she bolted to the front door, hammering on it.

"I can't run today," she said, when Cain appeared. She didn't wait for a reply and ran back to her car.

"What's happened?" Cain shouted, stepping out in his bare feet.

"My mom," she yelled back. "Her neighbor called. She thinks she's had a stroke."

She threw the car into drive and stomped on the gas, headed for the Royal Jubilee, where they'd taken her.

Running into the emergency department, she checked with the reception desk. Her mom was still being assessed. The clerk said she'd notify the doctor that Mika had arrived.

Over the years, she, like most people, had visited the hospital for a cut or a sprain. The last time was the worst, when her dad had a heart attack. Dinky, Jen, Kate, Cyn, and Sarah had waited with her and Mom. Her younger sister, Stephanie, was back east attending school.

Five years had gone by since that day. She and her mom had cried in each other's arms, her friends clutching them, when the doctor came to tell them he was gone. It was like they'd all lost a father, since they'd known each other all their lives.

She sat in the hard, plastic chair and watched the people come and go. The hands of the clock on the wall seemed to take forever to move. After an hour, she checked with the reception desk again.

The young woman said she'd notify the doctor.

Her cell rang.

"Are you okay? How's your mom?" Cain asked.

"I don't know. Nobody has come out to talk to me."

"Are the girls coming?"

She didn't answer for a moment. "No, I haven't called them."

"Where are you?" he asked.

"Royal Jubilee. ER."

"Mika, I'm sure everything is going to be okay."

She nearly burst into tears when Cain rounded the corner ten minutes later. His strong features coated with concern as he caught sight of her. He sat down and hugged her. "Anything?"

She shook her head. "They keep saying they've told the doctor I'm here, but I haven't seen him, and they won't let me see her."

Cain gave her a reassuring squeeze. "Give me a second."

She watched, her heart still beating in high gear as Cain spoke to the clerk at the desk. She saw the woman lift the phone and dart looks at Cain's broad physique while she spoke. He nodded at the woman and returned to sit with her.

Before long, a doctor came through the emergency room doors. "Ms. Makris." They began to rise, but the doctor shook his head and pulled a waiting room chair in front of them to sit down. "Ms. Makris, I'm Dr. Sinclair. We're moving your mother into surgical pre-op." He gave her a compassionate look. "Unfortunately, she's had a severe stroke. The MRI revealed a rupture. That means there's blood leaking into her brain. We're going to operate within the hour, but I have to tell you, I believe there is already permanent damage due to the size of the tear."

Mika gulped down air. "But she's only forty-eight." Cain's arm wrapped around her shoulders tightly.

"What kind of damage?" he asked.

"She's paralyzed on her left side and she's lost the ability to speak. Thirty minutes ago, she slipped into a coma." The doctor cleared his throat. "We may be able to save her life. With long-term therapy, she may even improve. It depends on many factors. I have to be honest with you, from the scans I would say there is little hope for a full recovery."

"O-okay," her voiced stuttered, and tears rained down her cheeks. Cain wrapped both arms around her and pressed his mouth to her ear.

"Don't give up hope, Mika. Don't give up."

"Are you Mrs. Makris' son-in-law?"

135

"No, a friend."

"I assure you, we'll have the best surgeons on this. They're on their way now."

"Thank you," Cain said. "Should we wait?"

The doctor shook his head. "It would be better if you went home. The surgery is going to take several hours. I'll call and let you know how it went and what the prognosis is."

"Can I see her?" Mika asked.

She saw Cain nod and after a long pause, the doctor said, "Yes, please follow me."

Cain helped her stand and held on to her as they walked into the emergency room, past beds filled with patients, young and old. Completely numb, this all felt like a horrible dream.

The doctor stopped in front of a curtained bay. "She's in a coma, but talk to her." He slid the curtain aside.

A mask covered her mother's face, feeding her air. An IV dripped into her arm, and several cables connected her to machines beside the bed. Cain gripped her hand, or maybe she gripped his to leash herself to something real. She slid between the curtain and the bed to stand beside her mother.

Her mom's dark hair surrounded her heart-shaped face, her chest rising and falling in time with the sound of the machine. "Mom?" she said in a weak voice. Pain like she'd never known struck her, and she let out a small cry. "Mom?" Cain led her hand to rest on her mother's, which was cool to the touch.

"Mom, I want you to get better, okay? I'm not ready for you to go."

Tears fell on her mother's blue hospital gown. "The doctors are going to operate. Try not to worry." She leaned her forehead against her mom's and clutched her hand. Her mother had been healthy as a horse. Why was this happening? Through her rampaging heart, she heard Cain speaking with the doctor behind the curtain.

Cain's concerned voice asked, "The chance of any kind of recovery is not very good, is it?"

"I'm afraid not, but we're flying in Dr. Sun from Vancouver General. He's an excellent neurosurgeon. The best in hemorrhagic strokes."

"Why did this happen to her? She's too young."

"I understand your concern. In this case, I'd say it's hereditary. Sometimes we're born with thinner veins, and they burst with unattended high blood pressure. She probably didn't even know she had it. I'll be assisting Dr. Sun, and I can tell you more once the surgery is complete. Take Mika home. We'll call as soon as we can."

"I will. You said hereditary. Does that mean Mika could have the same condition?"

"It's quite possible."

"I want her to have an MRI, too."

137

"Her GP can make arrangements for that." The doctor walked into the stall and stood across from her. "We have to take your mother up to surgery, Mika. Make sure reception has your number so I can call you."

She nodded, kissed her mom's forehead, and backed away. Cain's large hands gripped the top of her shoulders. "Come on. Let's go home."

In the parking lot, Cain guided her to his car. "I want you to eat, then I'm taking you home to bed."

"I should wait here," she said, turning around to head back inside.

Cain gently gripped her arm. "Sweetheart, you—you can't do anything here. Let's go home."

"My car…."

"Is fine. We're coming back. Now, please get in."

The next twelve hours crawled until the phone rang. She answered before the first ring ended.

"Miss Makris?"

"Yes, what happened?" she asked, recognizing Dr. Sinclair's voice.

"Your mother survived the surgery. We've put a coil around the bleed. I don't want to dash your hopes, but she will not be the same woman you remember. She may not even wake from the surgery. As the inflammation recedes, we could see some improvement, but I have a number for you to call. This is an agency that can help you find a placement for your mom. They have an advocate here at the hospital."

"I can't bring her home?"

"I'm afraid not. She'll need medical attention round the clock that only healthcare facilities and professional nurses can provide."

She wrote the number down. "When can I see her?"

"Come tomorrow morning, visiting hours begin at eight. Check in at the nursing station, and you can stay as long as you like."

"Thank you."

"You're welcome. I wish I had better news."

She hung up and Cain, who'd been watching her, crossed the room and sat next to her on the couch. He hadn't left her side for a second. He'd made her a light dinner, which she'd barely touched. He'd made her tea and forced her to drink it. He turned on the television, which she didn't hear or see.

She folded her hands and brought them to her forehead, closing her eyes. "I have to find a home for her. They saved her life, but her life is over." She looked up at him, tears welling. "She'll be bedridden until she passes away."

Cain exhaled heavily and wrapped his arms around her. "Do you want me to call Dinky?"

She shook her head. "I'll do it tomorrow after I visit Mom. They said I could stay as long as I want."

"I'll take you back in the morning." He rose and urged her to lie on the couch, draping a quilt over her, then knelt on his haunches beside her. His hand brushed a calming sweep across her hair. Breeze jumped onto the couch and settled behind her legs, resting her chin on Mika's hip.

"Close your eyes." He gently caressed her temples. "You've got friends who love you, and you'll find a safe place for your mom to live out her life in peace. But you can worry about all that tomorrow. For now, I want you to sleep."

"I have to call my sister. She's in Alberta."

"Tomorrow will be soon enough."

Cain continued to gently caress her head with soothing sweeps. She gave up trying to fight the need to be brave. *Why did this happen? Why her family?* No matter how much she wanted to, she couldn't change a thing, and that brought a wave of heartbreak.

Cain's warm lips kissed her forehead.

"I'm right here." He squeezed in beside her and coiled her in his arms. "I've got you, sweetheart." He cocooned her in his strength, and she cried all over him. As his large hand rubbed comforting circles on her back, eventually her mind drifted toward the darkness.

****

The next morning she called her sister, Stephanie. They had a tear-filled conversation and her sister was going to fly out the day after tomorrow, once her husband, Kevin, booked off work.

Two days later, the reunion at the airport was a somber one, and she clutched her younger sister and held on tight. Kevin held Cash, their six month old son, and she pulled them both to her for a hug and a kiss.

"Maybe knowing Cash is here will help, Mom," she said.

Stevie brushed the tears from her cheeks. Her name was Stephanie, but when they were kids, she was more tomboy than girl.

"I don't know if I can face this, sis," Stevie said.

She rubbed her shoulder. "It's going to be a shock. I won't lie about that. I don't know if she knows we're there, but I pretend she does."

Cain had lent her his SUV, and Kevin secured the baby carrier in the back seat.

"You finally get a new car?" he asked.

"No," she said, helping him. "This belongs to my landlord."

"I was wondering," Kevin said, strapping Cash into the seat. The little one shook his toy and grinned. "Thought maybe you got a huge pay increase to afford a Mercedes."

They drove straight to the hospital. She held Cash, while Stevie and Kevin visited their mom in ICU. While waiting, her cell rang.

"Everything okay?" Cain asked. "Did you get your sister and brother-in-law?"

Cash cooed and tried to grab the phone from her. "No, no, Cash." She leaned her head back.

"You don't have cash?"

"My nephew." Cash decided to show off his powerful lungs and shouted his dislike for not being able to play with the phone.

"How old is he?"

"Six months. Stevie and Kevin are with Mom. We'll be home later. While I'm here, I'm going to talk with the advisor about assisted living options."

"Are you okay?"

"No, but thank you for lending me the SUV."

"Come home soon."

"I will."

She told the ICU nurse where she was going in case Stevie was looking for her.

The advocate for assisted living loaded her up with paperwork and told her to visit the facilities, but the truth was, it would be hard to find a place on the island. She might be forced to put her mother in a home on the mainland. Mika's questions fell on sympathetic ears.

Forty-five minutes later, she returned to ICU to see Stevie's face buried in Kevin's shoulder as she sobbed. Mika understood. It was a shock to see their mother like this, and the worst part was, there would likely be no improvement. Her mom's eyes had opened, but she didn't acknowledge them. The doctor said to keep talking to her. Mom could breathe on her own, but she would have to be fed by tube.

"Think we need a little time to digest this," Kevin said and took Cash from her.

When they got home, she showed them to the guest room, and they sequestered themselves there for a couple hours, coming to terms with the future. At least Stevie had Kevin and Cash.

Her phone rang. "Hey," Dinky said.

"Hi."

"Did you get Stevie?"

"Yeah, they're here."

"Listen, we're all coming over. I don't care if you want us there or not. We're coming. We're bringing dinner, so you're just gonna have to deal with it."

She gulped down her tears. "'Kay."

Emotionally bereft, but anxious at the same time, she piled dishes and cutlery on the kitchen counter.

A knock on her screen door made her turn.

"Hi," Cain said, entering, but stopped just inside the room.

"Hi," she said, watching him.

"I didn't want to intrude, just wanted to know what the advisors told you."

She sighed and shook her head. "Not good. They don't think there's a bed for her here on the island. They gave me a list of facilities to check. I'll take Stevie with me tomorrow, but they said I might have to put Mom on the mainland."

Cain rounded the counter to stand before her. He grasped her hands. "You'll find a place here. I'm sure of it."

She toyed with his strong fingers, brushing his thumb, dazed and existing on autopilot. "Maybe, but I've heard about some of these places. Some are better than others, and the good ones are difficult, if not impossible, to get into."

She heard the sound of cars outside on the driveway. Dinky must have called when they were already on their way.

"Company's coming," he said, seeing the headlights.

"It's the gang. They're bringing dinner."

He nodded. "Good, call me if you need anything."

"You're leaving?" It shot out of her mouth as if he were abandoning her. "Sorry, I'm muddle-headed. Thanks for coming." She sounded like an idiot, her thoughts scattered.

He turned his broad shoulders and gave her a look she couldn't read. "I don't want to intrude." He cut off his sentence as her brother-in law walked in the room.

"Sorry, didn't mean to interrupt," Kevin said.

Cain shook his head. "Cain Sallas. I'm sorry for your misfortune."

"Thanks. I'm Kevin, Mika's brother-in-law."

Stevie rounded the corner with Cash in her arms. She'd showered, but her face was still a little puffy from her tears. It looked like she'd gotten a good cry out, and now she was ready to face the world again.

The screen door opened, and the chatter of voices filled the cottage. They all called out and greeted Cain, but his eyes never left hers until Jennifer cut him off from her view.

The girls all hugged Stevie. The guys gave Kevin a high five and pats on the back. They'd been part of the gang before Kevin was forced to move to Edmonton to keep his job.

Jen slipped her arm through Cain's and gave him a little pull. "Hey, good to see you. You're staying for dinner, right?" she asked with an enormous smile.

Mika watched Jen paw at Cain.

Something clicked in her brain.

She was tired of the few things she deemed special in her life being snatched away. Tired of dealing with her disease and the knowledge she'd never have a husband like all her friends. Tired of a God that took her father early, and now left her mother in a state where she would never recognize her own grandson.

Mika pushed her way through the group, clasped Cain's hand and shot a look at Jen that should have left her dead on the ground.

Cain's eyes ate her up, and his fingers swept into her hair, gently clasping her neck. Her heart pounded, scared of losing him. A ridiculous thought. Cain was her friend. So was Jen. But for now, she needed his support. For a heart-stopping moment they stared at one another.

"As if he could read her mind, he said, "I'm not going anywhere." He smiled sadly.

A little embarrassed that he recognized her selfish actions, she said, "I want you to meet my sister."

He kept a hand on her shoulder. "Stevie, this is Cain Sallas. He's my…" Cain gently squeezed her shoulder. "My friend and landlord."

Stevie looked up at him with her big brown eyes and gave him a sweet smile. "Hi, Cain."

"And this," she said, hauling her nephew into her arms, "is Cash."

"Hey, buddy," Cain said, gently gripping his little hand. The baby's drooling lips and big blue eyes darted up to Cain, then he smiled and shot his other hand in the air, gripping his favorite toy.

The ladies started uncovering the dishes they'd brought, and the guys piled food on their plates.

Cash was back in his mother's arms. His hands flexed on her boob. "Somebody is hungry," she said, looking down at her son. "Kevin, make me a plate. I'm just going to feed your son in the other room. Cain, thanks for being there for my sister the last couple days."

Cain returned her smile.

Kate's son had just turned three, keeping Tad and her fit, chasing him down whenever he made a fast getaway. Because the girls often came over with their kids, Mika had baby-proofed her house. Sarah held her two year old daughter on her hip, and Sam held her twin. Mac and Cyn's four year old son was wedged on his dad's hip.

The little cottage was overloaded, but she was ever grateful.

"I want you to eat. I'll get you a plate," Cain offered.

Those who couldn't fit at the table sat on the couch or the floor around the coffee table.

****

Cain considered inviting everyone to his place. He had more room, but there was something healing about all of Mika's friends and her family talking over top of each other. She needed the distraction.

Kevin and Stevie seemed like good people. Mika's sister looked a little like her, their eyes sharing a resemblance. The rest of Stevie's features must have been from their father. Cain had been shocked when he'd seen her mother. Mika looked just like her and his heart stilled, seeing her mirror image struck down and barely hanging on to life. He never wanted to see Mika like that. The thought sent his pulse pounding and his thoughts racing back to why she took the injections.

Jennifer sized up the spot to his left on the sofa, teasing. "Oh, is that for me?" She pointed at the plate he'd set down.

Natasza Waters

"No, it's Mika's." He moved to the left so she couldn't sit down.

Mika rounded the bodies cloistered around the coffee table and slipped in from the other side.

"Thank you, Cain," she said, when he offered her the plate, once she'd seated herself on the couch beside him.

Mika looked over at Jennifer. "Spot just opened up at the table, Jen. Help yourself." She filled her fork. "Oh, wow, this is good. Kate, this is your homemade mac-n-cheese, isn't it?"

Kate tried to keep her son's fingers from grabbing a handful. She rolled her eyes and gave up while her son smooshed macaroni all over his face. "Yep. Junior here loves it as much as his father."

Tad chuckled. "My son's a growin' boy," he said proudly.

Jen, who appeared gobsmacked Cain hadn't tripped over himself to have her sit beside him, headed to the counter to get her own plate. Mika pressed her lips together to stop from smiling.

He leaned over and very quietly said in her ear, "That was catty, and I'm very proud of you." He was determined to see her smile again.

She leaned into him and whispered, "Only gay guys use the word catty."

He choked on the mouthful of food he'd just deposited on his tongue.

"Hey, I've got nothing against them," she said.

148

He turned his head, and they were nose to nose. She leaned back when he offered up a soul sucking, sizzle-a-girl's-panties glint in his eyes.

"You'll pay dearly for that one," he said under his breath.

"You're not?" she asked, lifting her brow.

"You're kidding!" Everyone else at the table was loud enough to drown out their quiet words to one another. "Why the hell would you think that?"

Her brows popped, and she gave him a cheesy smile. "Umm, mmm, errr, because no straight guy ever turns Jen down."

He'd come to the realization that Mika had never been kissed by a guy in the heat of passion. She'd probably been to a few parties during university. Maybe she'd even lost her virginity, but had she known the touch of true desire? He doubted it.

From what he knew of Mika, he could probably write her life story. Her knowledge of lust and the intricacies of sex had probably come from her girlfriends, books, and a couple pornos they'd watched when one of the girls found their father's stash. Real passion wasn't anything like a young woman's failed sexcapades with some college guy.

He gazed at her, riveting his eyes on her soft features. With a slow slide, he surveyed her entire face and ended on her mouth. She blushed all the way down to her neckline.

Oh, yes, she was woefully inexperienced, and he knew he'd just laid her in a bed of soft down and sought out every sensual spot on her body with just a look.

She'd teased *him* enough times. He leaned toward her. "I'm not gay, and I enjoy every irresistible curve of a woman's body," he breathed on the shell of her ear, making her shiver.

"Well, if you have crazy monkey sex with Jen, do me a favor and don't share any details."

"That will never happen," he said. "Now eat, you look a little...flushed."

Chapter Ten

Mika walked into her manager's office with a sense of dread. "Ma'am, could I have a word?"

Although Mika wasn't military, the battle-axe who ran their department was. Every day she came to work, hoping with thirty-five years of service, Vickers would announce her retirement. Although Mika didn't drink, she knew she'd be tossing a few back the day she heard those words.

Lieutenant Vickers sat back in her chair with a churlish expression. "What is it, Mika? And why are you late?"

Mika didn't bother to sit in the guest chair. "Ma'am, I'd like the week off. I'm ahead on my current project for Commsec."

"Sorry, Mika. If you're finished, then I have another job for you."

"Ma'am, my mother had a severe stroke. I have to find her a care facility."

Vickers sat forward. "Sorry to hear that," she said without an inch of empathy, "but you can do that on your time off. I can't approve the leave."

"I don't have a choice. She's incapacitated. I have to find her something where she'll be comfortable and cared for." Vickers scared the crap out of her, but she wasn't going to back down. "You have a duty to accommodate in family-related matters. You can't deny me the leave." She said it firmly and knew when she returned to work Vickers would ride her for at least a couple months.

Vickers mouth tightened into a thin line. "Fine," she growled. "One week."

"Thank you, ma'am."

She backed out of her office and bolted for the door. She jogged to the car, where Stevie waited. Kevin was working remotely from Mika's place. She and her sister had one more day to find a facility for their mother, or the hospital would deposit her in the next available place.

Cain shook his head when she'd tried to return the keys of the SUV to him after picking Stevie up at the airport. "Keep it," he'd said. He'd been too good to her and her family.

"What's wrong, Stevie?" she asked, sliding in behind the wheel.

"Just got off the phone with Golden Years Extended Healthcare. It's at the top of that list I made last night. They don't have room for her and said they've got a year and a half waiting list." She shrugged and looked sadly out the window.

"Okay, well let's go see the second best."

Stevie shook her head. "Called them, too." She bunched the paper in her hand. "I called them all and stopped when I got to the ones that had bad reports from family members concerning the care of their loved ones."

"Where on the list is the one they told us they would put Mom in temporarily?"

Stevie sucked in a deep breath. "The bottom."

Mika gripped the steering wheel. "I don't want Mom on the mainland. It's too far." Her phone rang. "Hello."

"No luck?" Cain asked.

"Worse than no luck. It's just as the advisor told me. The good ones all have waiting lists, and the one they're sending her to have bad reviews. I don't know what to do."

"Which one did you want?"

"Stevie made a list. The best one is called Golden Years, but we've talked to them. There's no room."

"It'll work out, Mika. Don't worry."

She sighed. "Can't seem to stop worrying. What are you doing?"

"Kevin is working out in my gym, and I'm babysitting. Well, Breeze is actually babysitting. Cash has pulled at least two fistfuls of fur out of her, and she hasn't flinched."

Mika smiled. "She's such a good dog."

"She keeps licking his face, and he keeps laughing. I'm just sitting here watching them instead of getting my work done."

"Sorry, we'll be home soon."

"Take your time. Breeze has it under control. In fact, when I tried to take Cash away from her, she growled at me."

"Ho." Mika laughed. "Seriously?"

"Yup. Don't think she trusts me with the kid."

"I'm sure you'll make a great dad."

The line went quiet, and she thought maybe they'd lost the connection. "Hello?"

"How come you're not married with two point five kids?" he asked.

Now, it was her turn to go silent. "I'm good being an aunt," she answered. "Talk to you later." She disconnected. "You wanna go see Mom?" she asked her sister.

Stevie swiped a tear away. "I hate living so far away from you."

She gripped her sister's shoulder. "So do I, but it won't be forever. You okay? I can drop you off at home, instead."

Stevie nodded. "Is that awful? I hate seeing her like that."

"I know." Mika pulled into the traffic, and drove home to drop Stevie off.

An hour later, she walked into the ICU, said hello to the nurses she recognized from yesterday, and headed down the hall to her mother's cubicle.

"Hi, Mom." She spoke loudly like the nurses suggested, then kissed her mother's cheek and gripped her hand as she sat down. Her mom blinked, but her eyes didn't focus. "You feel like sitting up a little today?" she asked. She pushed the button on the bed, raising her mother's upper body. Mika pulled a small brush from her purse and ran it through her mom's thick hair. "There, that's better." She sat down again, wishing her mom would

154

squeeze her hand. "The hospital is going to move you to a place where you can be more comfortable. You'll have a semi-private room and won't have to listen to the noises in this place anymore."

A nurse came by to check her mother's blood pressure. She rolled back the pronged stand with an empty bag. Remnants of a yellow substance visible through the plastic. Her food. This was no way to live a life.

Mika worried that her mom could exist like this for a long time. The doctor had confirmed her fears. Her heart was strong and as long as they kept feeding her, she could survive for many years. The doctor explained if her breathing failed, she'd have a choice to make. At that time, she could opt to not continue feeding her mother and sign the paperwork to remove any life-sustaining equipment. She wasn't certain she'd be brave enough to do that, and it would have to be a decision she and Stevie would make together.

"How are you doing, Mika?"

She looked up to see the advocate for home care she'd spoken to the other day.

"Not so good. You were right about the assisted living situation on the island. Is there anything I can do to change that? I don't want her in the home they have her slated for."

Natasza Waters

The woman smiled at her. "That's why I'm here. I got a call from Golden Years. They informed the hospital they have room for your mother."

"What?" She shot from her chair. "Are you kidding?" Violet, her name was Violet. "Are you serious, Violet?"

"Absolutely," she said, with a nod of her head. "I notified the patient transfer office. Your mother will be moved to the facility tomorrow."

"Oh, my God!" A wave of tears filled her eyes. "Thank you."

"I have to say, it's a miracle. They rarely have openings. Not sure how this happened, but I'm glad it did, especially at your mom's age. She'll need good care for many years."

Mika rounded the bed and hugged Violet, then turned to her mother. "It's gonna be okay, Mom. It's the best facility on the island." She leaned over and planted a kiss on her soft cheek. "I've got to tell Stevie. I'll see you later."

She walked at a fast clip out of the ICU. When the automatic doors opened, she skidded to a stop. Cain leaned against the wall, his arms crossed and his gaze pinned to her.

"Guess what?"

He unfurled his arms. "Tell me."

"A spot opened up for Mom at Golden Years."

He walked up to her and palmed her cheeks. "I told you not to worry."

156

She threw her arms around him, hugging him fiercely. A warm, rumbling sound came from his throat, and he held her snuggled in his strong embrace.

"We need to tell Stevie and Kevin."

"They know. The hospital called the house and talked to her."

She placed her hands over her face. Now she was crying with relief. She had to stop this sloppy, wet stuff.

He gently pulled her hands away and leaned over. "No more tears. The worst is over, at least for a while. I was thinkin' I'd take you all out for dinner tonight. Would that be all right?"

"Thank you." She burst out crying again. "Thank you for being such a good friend." She hugged him and soaked his shirt.

"Don't go spreading it around. Wouldn't want to ruin my reputation as an asshole."

She chuckled through her tears. A Kleenex appeared, and she plucked it from his fingers. "It's not used, right?"

He laughed and swatted her butt. "Get moving. I'll follow you home."

****

That night, they enjoyed a dinner in downtown Victoria. Cain had chosen a restaurant with large dollar signs attached to the entrées. They toasted the small blessing they'd received. They spoke their sympathies and acknowledged that whoever had left to make room for their mother had more than likely passed on. Tomorrow afternoon Stevie and Kevin would be returning home after their mom was settled.

After dinner, Mika excused herself to go to the washroom, and Stevie followed. Done washing her hands, Stevie leaned up against the counter waiting for her to finish.

"What's the real deal between you and Mr. Hotness?"

She blinked. "Who?"

Stevie's brow knit together. "Umm, ya know, the rock star sitting beside you in the restaurant."

"Cain? Nothing. He's my landlord."

Stevie shook her head. "Are you lying to your sister?"

Mika pulled a soft terry towel from the pile on the counter to dry her hands. "Of course not. Why would I lie to you?"

Stevie stared at her strangely. "So, you're trying to tell me he stares at you with that intense need, and you've never seen him naked?"

"Stevie, you know me better than that."

"But you're in remission. Now's the time to catch up. What are you waiting for? He wants to devour you whole."

She laughed at her. "I think you better stop reading those bodice rippers for a while. He's my landlord, that's it."

Stevie snorted. "Nobody looks at a tenant like that. Are you just refusing to see it because of the P?" she asked.

"No. He's become a good friend."

"Does he know?"

"Heck no. He caught me taking an injection once." She laughed nervously and crossed her arms. "I didn't tell him what it was for." She headed for the exit before her sister went all "Dear Abby" on her. Stevie put her hand against the door before she could open it. "Look, you get the white picket fence, I get to be an aunt and spoil Cash rotten."

"I want you to have a happily-ever-after, too."

Mika sighed. "No guy is going to love me with my condition. At least until there's a cure. That's the reality."

Stevie shook her head. "You're wrong. I'm not saying it won't take a special guy, but one is looking at you all the time, and he's sitting outside."

"You're dreaming, Stevie."

"I'm not. Don't pretend you don't see it. Why don't you tell him the truth?"

She yarded on the door. "There's nothing to see. He's a friend. A really kind, thoughtful friend. Why would I want to ruin that?"

"A hot, obviously wealthy, amazing friend, who stares at you when you're not looking," she corrected, following her out. "I bet he's been sending you signals and you've been ignoring them."

Mika laughed. "No signals. Sorry, sis."

"What does he do for a living, anyway?"

"His family are vintners." They edged to one side to pass a couple of women headed to the bathroom. She shrugged. "He works out of town sometimes. Usually no more than five days." She furled her brow. "I'm not quite sure what he does."

They seated themselves at the table and Cash started to fuss. Kevin handed the baby to Stevie.

"I recognize that face," Stevie said. "Think our quiet dinner is about to be ruined, but you've been Mom's good boy, haven't you?" she said, raising her son over her head. Cash went from a frown to a gurgling smile. "Thank you for dinner, Cain, and allowing us to stay at your place during all of this."

Cain nodded and threw his credit card down on the bill. "My pleasure." Kevin reached for his wallet, and Cain shook his head. "Put it away, it's covered."

"Thanks, man. Appreciate it."

Great. Stevie had tossed a bunch of loose ideas into Mika's black pit of a mind, and she was worried all over again.

"Cain, what do you do for a living?" Stevie asked.

He handed the maître d' the card and the bill. Without a pause he said, "My family are wine makers."

"Oh, an international company?"

He nodded.

"Mom met Cain at Dinky's wedding. She said Dad's favorite wine was from the Sallas wineries." Mika shot Stevie a glare to stop. She had no business prying.

160

"Mika, are you going to move into Mom's house?" Kevin asked.

"I guess I could," she said. She hadn't even thought about disposing of their mother's possessions. Their mother's flower shop remained open, but Mika would have to deal with that as well.

Stevie nodded. "Whatever you want to do is fine with me. If you want to sell it, then go ahead, but if you lived in it, we could hang onto our family home. Mom owned it outright. There's no mortgage."

Cain signed the receipt the server put on the table. "Mika?"

Suddenly, she felt overwhelmed again and looked at the one person who balanced her racing thoughts.

"Don't make any decisions right now. Give it a few days." His brow creased.

Cash's face contorted and everyone knew what was coming next.

"Okay, we better go," Stevie said, rising with help from Kevin.

****

The next day, Cain joined Mika and her family at the long-term care facility. The staff showed them around, answered all their questions, and then they were greeted by the man in charge, who introduced himself as Mr. Baxter.

He shook all their hands, ending with Cain. "Mr. Sallas, I hope you've found this facility to be above standards."

Everyone's eyes fell on him. *Oh, shit.* He didn't blink. "It is. Mika and Stevie can rest easy. Their mother will be well cared for."

"I had to personally come and thank you. You were more than generous," Mr. Baxter said. "If you have any concerns, please bring them to my attention personally. Your mother should be arriving shortly." He nodded and left them.

Cain cleared his throat. Killing the little, fat, bald guy crossed his mind. His wishes were explicit when he'd made the arrangements for Mika and Stevie's mother. The proverbial pin dropped on the carpeted floor where he currently looked.

"Cain?" Mika's voice sounded wispy. "What did you do?"

He rubbed his jaw, and his gaze jerked up to hers. He shrugged. "Nothing." They all continued to stare at him. "Shouldn't we go wait at the entrance for your mom?"

"We'll go ahead," Stevie said, and pulled Kevin by the hand.

Mika's face paled. She stepped closer, and he drilled his hands into his pockets. "We should go."

"Cain," she said again, this time hushed. "What did you do?"

"Nothing."

"Tell me," she said, gripping his arm.

Fuck! Mika deserved nothing but the truth, but this is one he didn't want to share. "I just made a charitable donation, that's all."

"How?" Her voice stuttered. "How much of a donation did it take to get my mother in here?"

"That's not what happened."

"That's exactly what happened," she said quickly. "Why would you do that for us?"

"I help several non-profit causes every year. It's not a big deal." He met her gaze, and his pulse leaped. With a tug on his jacket and the straightening of his tie, he said, "Come on, don't you want to be there when your mom arrives?"

"How much, Cain? Tell me."

He sighed. "Mika," he said sternly, "are you coming or not?"

Chapter Eleven

They waited in the shade of the overhang while the transport ambulance unloaded her mother's stretcher. The family followed as if they were behind a funeral procession. Mika had to remind herself that her mother would be treated with dignity in this facility. She was close, and could visit every day on her way home from work. She prayed her mom wasn't trapped in her body, her mind screaming with no one able to hear her.

They passed the administration office where Mr. Baxter spoke with one of his employees. With a quick right turn, she darted inside.

"Mr. Baxter?"

He turned, his portly belly protruding over his belt. "Yes, Miss Makris? Is everything all right?"

"Yes, I was just wondering." She paused. "If the donation was acceptable or if more is required?"

"Oh, my." He approached and gripped her hand. "Never say that to a facility such as ours. We can always use Good Samaritans such as you and Mr. Sallas. Two million dollars will go a long way, and I graciously thank you."

Her heart thundered. *Two million frickin' dollars.*

"Mika." Cain's harsh call made her jump, and when she turned, his brows were seamed together. "Are you coming?"

She bid Mr. Baxter thank you and closed the door behind her.

Her hands covered her mouth in complete shock. "Oh, my God." She shook her head. "Are you kidding me? Even if I rented your cottage for the next hundred years, and sold Mom's house I couldn't pay that back."

"Mika, this is not a loan."

"I don't understand? You hardly know me—us."

He drew his teeth over his top lip as he removed her hand from her mouth. "You needed help. I was in a position to help, so I did. It's as simple as that. Now, can we go?"

"I don't know what to say."

"I can hear your wheels turning," he said, pulling her to his side. "Please, just accept it, and stop thinking about it."

Later that afternoon Mika gave Stevie, Kevin and Cash a big hug goodbye. "I love you guys."

"We love you, too." Stevie hugged her once more.

Cain joined them and shook their hands. Stevie whispered something to Cain, and his deep blue eyes filled with an indiscernible shadow. "Have a good flight home," he said and stepped back.

Mika sat quietly in the SUV as they drove home. Halfway down the Pat Bay Highway she couldn't stand it anymore. "What did my sister whisper to you at the airport?"

"She just thanked me."

"You're fibbing. I'm sure I know what she told you, and you can ignore her. She's a meddler."

Mika looked over at him. A dark afternoon shadow covered his cut jaw. Although his handsome features and toned body sat relaxed behind the wheel, his expression was anything but comfortable. It was drawn tight.

He totally ignored her statement. "Want to go for a run when we get home?"

Okay, so he didn't want to talk about it, and neither did she. "Sounds good. Hey, can you stop at the mailbox? I haven't checked it in a few days."

"Me either."

He pulled over to the community box.

Mika slipped the key he'd given to her out of her purse. Yuck. Bills and about a dozen envelopes were inside. She turned them over and saw they were all from Greece. Some had funny squiggles and little hearts on them, others had balloons. The stiffness had to mean there were cards inside. She got back into the SUV and separated her two pieces of mail. "The rest are yours," she said.

"Thanks." He took them, his eyes skirting them quickly, then he tucked them beside his seat.

"It's your birthday, isn't it?"

He turned down the road leading into his property. "Yes."

"When?"

"Saturday."

"July thirtieth, and..."

He pulled up to the five-car garage and pressed the button on the remote attached to his visor. "And what?"

She leaned over. "And, how old are you going to be?"

With his eyes shaded, he said, "Thirty-five, and I don't celebrate birthdays."

He practically growled it at her. Pulling in, he parked the SUV between his silver sports car and the Jag. Before she opened her mouth, he jumped out and slammed the driver's door. She hurried out but Cain was already halfway to his house.

"Cain!" His steps slowed. She didn't chase after him. "I don't know why you did it, but I'll never be able to thank you enough." Her mysterious landlord turned to look at her, the handsome image of a noble man, but his expression bothered her. Was he angry at her?

"Are you going to move into your mother's place?"

She strolled up to him. The closer she got, the easier she could see his rigid stance. "I need to sell it and pay you back. At least some of it. Or I could move home and pay you back on a monthly basis."

Cain shook his head. "I won't accept it."

The way he said *'it'* made her pause. She wasn't certain if he was speaking about the money or her leaving. "If I move home, you can rent out the cottage and I could pay you back as well."

Natasza Waters

Cain swallowed and his expression grew dark. "Do what you think is right, Mika."

****

On Saturday evening, she stood in her kitchen and called Cain. "Hi. Got a problem," she said when he answered.

"What's going on?"

"Need my landlord."

"Okay, you going to tell me why?"

Cain had literally hidden from her all week. Aside from taking a run, he'd made himself scarce. "I have to show you. I can't explain it."

Cain grunted. "All right, I'll be over in a second."

Mika grabbed the candle, stuck it in the middle of the pie and lit the wick. Cain came through the door and stopped, staring at her.

"I lied," she said. Leaning over the kitchen island with one cheek in her palm, she pushed the pie with her finger. "Happy being born day."

He tilted his head, peering at her with a sideways smile. "Guess I'm making a wish this year."

"Guess you are," she said, watching the man who constantly took her breath away walk toward her. "Do you have a good one? You only have one candle, so you have to make it count."

"I only have one." His full lips formed a sexy bow when he extinguished the flame, but his gaze remained locked on her.

168

She slid a couple of plates toward him and a knife. "It's apple and pineapple."

"Sounds good."

He looked anything but good. He looked sad to her. They sat down at the table, and she poured them both a coffee. He drank his with a little cream, like she did. Spooning in a mouthful of pie, he nodded, making an approving noise.

"Do you have a date tonight?" she asked, noticing he was in jeans and a fashionable button-up shirt.

He shrugged. "Not really, was just going to head into town."

Breeze started to bark from the main house, and she darted a worried look out the door. "She's pissed you didn't bring her. Trying to keep us girls separated?"

He raised a brow. "No." His concentration on the plate.

She'd been right, and her sister had been totally wrong. Whatever Stevie had said to him at the airport created an uncomfortable gap between her and Cain. The other option was unlikely. Even if she moved out, they'd still be friends. He had to know that.

Cain seemed distant as he stared at the kitchen tabletop, leisurely drinking his coffee. When he was done, he put the dishes in the sink.

"I better let Breeze out. Thank you."

"No problem," she said and watched him leave. Either this was going to bomb big time or it would repair their friendship.

169

She waited till he rounded the back of the house, then she ran full speed toward the front. Mika threw open the front door at the same time Cain opened the patio door, and the gang pounced.

"Surprise!"

He looked totally shocked, then his face lit up. His eyes met hers, and he shook his head. "I knew you were up to something."

She shrugged, and let her friends fawn all over him. Jen deployed her sexy sway meant to drop any man on the spot. With a coy move, she slid her hand around his neck and gave him a kiss. A long kiss. Mika swallowed deeply.

Cain stepped out of Jen's grasp and glanced at her. Mika winked at him, just like a good friend would. The fact that her heart twisted with jealousy didn't eradicate the smile on her face.

Sarah's husband, Sam, found the stereo and docked his iPhone, cranking the volume. The guys pushed some furniture aside. Kate and Tad hit the makeshift dance floor. Jen grabbed Cain, pulling him into the center of the room, doing her best to wag her ass at him and throw meaningful glances his way.

The gals had made too much food as usual. She manned the bar set up on the marble kitchen counter and did a dance for one with the sink, while her friends cut a rug. Digging for her inner *Tom Cruise a la Cocktail*, she made everyone drinks from the list she'd copied from the internet.

An hour later Cain thrust the patio doors open, the summer evening bringing onshore winds and cooling the sweat off their brows.

A crystal glass appeared in front of her, and she gently pushed it away before she realized it was attached to Cain's hand. His fingers came to rest on her hip. "Here, try this," he said, next to her ear.

She shook her head. She was downing her water and ice by the bucketful. "I'm good with water."

"It's my birthday, and I want you to join me for a drink." He placed it in her hand.

"What is it?" She tried to live a purely organic, almost vegetarian lifestyle. Once in a while she cheated, but her condition could flare without warning, and food was a big part of that.

"A family recipe. It's refreshing. Try it."

She sniffed the glass. It smelled like raspberries. She tasted a little, and then a little more. "Seriously, if this is goat piss, you're in big trouble."

He grinned. "A sparkling wine," he said, staring down at her. "Just like your eyes."

Not too heavy, the drink thirst-quenching and bubbly. "I like it." Then his words struck home. "My eyes? What?"

"Cain, get back here, I've got more calories to burn," Jen yelled over the music, waving her arm then took a little staggering step.

Cain ignored Jen, instead his gaze traced a path to her mouth. "Thank you, Mika. For the party, and for sharing your friends and family with me."

She gave him a thumbs-up. "We've always got room for one more friend." His face inched closer. Mesmerized at the strong cusp of his lip and the dark scruff on his jaw, she allowed a dream bubble to float from her secret wish list, and the thought made her over-indulged fantasy of kissing him, come to life.

"Mika, you trying to steal my workout coach?" Jen asked, slipping up beside them. The blue dress she wore fit like a glove around her slender curves. Her breasts popped out the top of her dress, but not in a sluttish way, just enough to make a man hungry.

"Need another drink, Jen?" she asked.

"You bet, girlfriend." She blew her a kiss and threw an arm around Cain's waist. "Make me thirsty, big guy."

Jen drew him away, but Cain's gaze stayed with her. He gave her a slow nod before Jen demanded his attention.

"Hey, Cain, that hot tub open for business?" Tad yelled out, dancing with both Sarah and Cyn.

He grinned. Within thirty seconds, the guys were down to their skivvies and the girls were ripping off their dresses to their undies. Mika's eyes fell on the bottle Cain left on the counter, and she refilled her glass and chugged it back, then filled it again, and downed that one, too.

Fuck it.

With the room vacated, and the sound of water splashing accompanied by the hoots of her friends from the patio, she grabbed cold beers from the fridge. The first thing she saw outside was Jen with her back to Cain, and him slowly unzipping her to reveal her baby blue bra and thong.

Cain unbuttoned his shirt, and the girls started catcalling. When he took off his pants, the guys started booing and chucking shit at him. Shoulder to shoulder, they filled the hot tub. The oohs and ahs falling from their mouths.

"Here you go," Mika said circling the tub, depositing a beer in each of the guy's hands. When she got to Cain, he turned and swept back his bangs, making a piece stand on end. She laughed and patted it down.

"Get in here," he said and gripped her hand.

"No, thanks. No more room." She met Jen's gaze, and right then her jealous little heart hated her friend. Jen had staked her claim. "Okay, ladies, who needs what?"

Cain had downed a few drinks and smiled more because of it. "Mika, are you, okay?"

"Course she is," Jen said, sliding a hand up his abs to put his attention back on her.

Mika wanted to hurl.

Jeff whistled and held Dinky's sopping bra high in the air. Dinky screeched and jumped to get it back which started everyone howling. It's not like they hadn't seen each other naked dozens of times before. They'd been friends for so long it was like seeing a brother or sister. They'd streaked together and spent many summers at the lake skinny dipping.

Jen's fingers wandered south, following the sexy indent where sinew ran beneath Cain's briefs. Mika had seen enough.

"Refill for the girls?" she shouted.

"Yeah, Mika!" they called out.

Cain's hand shot to Jen's and stopped it at the waistband of his very revealing, tight underwear. Mika couldn't watch this.

Not with Cain.

She didn't give a damn what Jen did with all the other guys she tumbled into the sheets with, but not Cain.

"I'll be right back. Nobody drown in the meantime."

The blender crunched the ice, mixing the Margaritas into a slushy concoction. Her landlord stepped into the house, the machine drowning out his words. "Need another beer?" she yelled.

He rounded the island to stand in front of her, soaking wet and sizzling hot. With the press of his finger, he turned off the blender.

"Why aren't you coming in?"

Definitely a little drunk, and a lot more talkative, his mood had brightened. Her evil plan had worked.

"I'm the official bartender, haven't you noticed? Now, go enjoy. I'll be out there in a few." Putting her attention on finishing the drinks, she lifted the lid. Cain pressed himself against her back. "You're soaking wet."

His arms slid around her waist. "Now you are, too," he whispered in her ear. "So there's no reason for you not to come join me. You have a beautiful body, and they're all your friends. I can't imagine you're shy."

"I'm not. They've seen me naked tons of times." Cain's grip tightened.

"Then it's only fair I catch up. Why are you hiding?"

"Can't. Now let me get these drinks out there or the girls are gonna be meowing like cats in heat."

Jen stepped into the house. "Need some help?"

Mika rolled her eyes. Once Jen had her sights on a man, she became territorial. They all knew it and had made a rule when they were thirteen. If one of them had a bead on a guy, all the other girls agreed to back away.

"We'll be out in a second," he said.

Jen's wet bra and thong hid very little of sexy body.

"Here, Jen, take these, and I'll bring the other two." She slid the Margaritas across the island.

"Sure," Jen said, giving Cain an inviting smile. "Coming?"

"Excuse us." The command was clear. *Get out.*

When she left the room, Cain trapped her against the island. "Can't or don't want to? There's a difference."

175

Natasza Waters

"Can't," she said. "Now shoo, enjoy your birthday gropes from Jen." She pressed against his arm, and it was like trying to break through a steel girder.

"You're jealous, aren't you?"

She coughed out a laugh. "Of course not."

He gripped her chin. "Yes, you are."

She wrinkled her brow. "Am not. Why should I be?"

His lips dipped closer to hers. "Maybe for the same reason I didn't want Wyatt near you."

Mika's heart thundered through her alcoholic haze. With her gaze zeroing in on the floor, she couldn't miss the impressive bulge in Cain's shorts. She bit her lip, knowing if she was just a little drunker, she would have been brave enough to admit she'd passed jealous an hour ago.

Mika hated her sister for seeing through her façade.

She gripped the counter behind her, the only piece of stable real estate to keep her steady. Sparking blood cells and a racing heart made her dizzy. Although she wouldn't know what to do with him, she wanted to climb those abs of his like a monkey up a tree.

"It's my birthday. Every one of your friends has kissed me."

"They're kissy people." She swallowed thickly and kept her eyes on the slate floor.

"And you're not?" he asked.

She took a deep breath, palmed his jaw and popped one on his cheek.

Her heart fluttered madly. In truth, she wanted to die.

Cain's warm hand cupped her cheek, his blue eyes sucking her into an abyss. With little effort, he held her in place. "Not good enough."

His perfect mouth brushed against her lips, then possessed her. It was like being swallowed by fire. The flames licked her toes, pulsed through her veins, and streaked straight to her brain, roaring like a storm. Her knees shook. Her body shook. Cain's warm mouth drained her willpower, her strength, and replaced it with an ache she'd never felt before. Her eyes remained closed when he withdrew. Slowly, she opened them and saw the intensity in his gaze.

She blushed and with a stuttered breath said, "There, happy b-day."

Suddenly, Cain's brow creased as if confused. He cleared his throat and backed away from her, his cut jaw, rigid. His gaze jumped around as if he didn't know where to look.

She swiftly went back to pouring drinks. "Now you're gonna have to wait a whole year for another one."

Her landlord rounded the island. God, the man was ripped and blow-a-girl's-mind sexy.

He stretched his arms wide and gripped the counter. "Will you be here next year?" His throat flexed with a deep swallow. "Or are you leaving me?"

177

Natasza Waters

She shook her head and grinned. "Doubt that. I forgot to tell you, I'm never moving out of that cottage. It'll take an excavator and a forklift to pull my ass out."

"Is that a promise?"

She and her friends had a steadfast rule. Whatever was said while drunk, didn't count.

"Here, take these out, and I'll get another round of beers." Cain picked up the Margaritas and headed toward the patio.

Her hand drifted to her lips, and her mind replayed the kiss, then rewound and played it again. Guys had kissed her before, but they were all frogs compared to Cain.

"Don't ever let me do that again, Mika," Cain's low timbre cracked her fairytale thoughts, not realizing he was still in the room by the door watching her, his expression caught between anger and confusion.

A sour bite of rejection pierced her heart.

When she was a little girl, her mother used to tell her tales about dragons, and the warriors who hunted them. Those who failed to slay the dragon would commit Hara-Kiri, an old Japanese custom that ran in her mother's blood. Mika had scales too, and she'd pretend they were different colors, brilliant hues of blue and green. They protected her against the mean words of the kids who'd teased her. Over time, her skin had become thicker, not only because of her disease, but to shelter herself. Cain's warning sliced a little higher and to the left.

178

She inhaled a slow stuttering breath, her head bowed, she bobbed it with understanding.

"Shit." The sound of glass landing on the marble counter made her flinch. "No, you don't understand," he said.

Cain rounded the island, coiling his arms around her. She withdrew the sharp splinters of his words from her heart, and looked into his face. She smiled. Her shields back in place. "I do."

Cain's brows creased into a tight line. "No, you don't. Whatever thoughts are rolling around in that beautiful head of yours are wrong."

"Friends say things sometimes, but if you're a true friend, you know it isn't meant to hurt."

"I don't want to hurt you." Cain's arms bundled her to his chest. In the reflection of the refrigerator she saw him slam his eyes closed, and felt him bury his face in her hair. "You confuse me," he murmured. "I don't deserve you. Not any of you."

She palmed his cheek and kissed it, giving him a big smile while her stomach clenched into a tight ball. "You don't deserve to see me naked, that's for sure." Her words carried a double meaning, but he didn't know that.

A slow smile crept across his lips. "But it's my birthday," he said, finally opening his beautiful eyes. "And it's dark outside." He curled his hand around hers and tugged, his muscles moved like a sleek predator in the prime of its life.

179

"Stooop." She laughed.

"I'll turn the patio lights off." He gently drew her out of the kitchen.

"Noooo."

"Yessss," he said, his voice a low rumble. "We're all friends, right!"

She laughed again and shook her head. "Yes, but…."

He stopped, one brow rising. "You're not?" He turned a broad shoulder and flicked the front patio lights off. The flames burned bright in the exterior fireplace. The guys whistled when he doused the lights.

"What are you two doing over there?" Mac shouted.

Cain had her arms stretched as far forward as they would reach. They'd reached the doorway and he gently pulled.

"Be there in a second, just taming a shrew," he yelled over his shoulder.

She gasped. "Shrew!"

The fire caught the teasing glint in his eyes. He yanked her into his arms. "Gonna prove me wrong?"

"Get your ass in here, Mika," Dinky yelled out. Then she started chanting and the rest joined in. "Mika. Mika. Mika."

Cain kept walking backwards, and although she dug her heels in a little, she wasn't getting much traction. "I hate you guys!" she yelled out.

"No, ya don't!" they all yelled back.

She let out an exaggerated sigh. "Fine." The second he released his hold, she darted around Cain, hopped up the two steps and jumped in, clothes and all.

"Booo." The guys called out and splashed her.

She splashed back, and within short order the tub lost a quarter of its water with all of them in a close quarters fight. Cain had a remedy, and everyone screeched when he turned the water hose on them, full blast.

"Where's my beer?" Jeff shouted.

"Get your own," Mika yelled back, giving him a wave of water in his face.

Cain jumped in and pulled her onto his lap. "You cheated," he whispered in her ear.

She laughed. "Your business skills must be slipping. I abided by the terms of the agreement."

He chuckled. "Next time, I'll be more specific."

Chapter Twelve

By midnight the gang had vacated, and she and Cain weren't feeling much pain. They didn't have to drive, and all she had to do was stagger across the lawn.

"Well, I've done my duty. I'm outta here. Happy being born day, Cain," she said, grabbing the door for support, struck by a dizzy spell of tornado proportions.

He'd loaned her one of his shirts. When she'd demanded a pair of running pants, he'd given her an odd look but brought her down a pair while her clothes were in the washing machine.

"I'll walk you home," he said, swiping a bottle from his bar and picking up two glasses.

"I'm going to bed," she said, pointing at him.

"Nope, you're gonna sit under the full moon with me and have a drink."

"Psst, I think I've had enough. Your raspberry hooch is deadly."

He nudged her with his arm. "Only if you drink the whole bottle." He scanned the counter, reached for the wicked raspberry liquor and shook it. "Which you did. Get going."

Breeze followed them out, and they wandered down the gravel path. Cain set the glasses on the patio table she'd bought from a second-hand store. With a big sigh, he settled in one of her new Adirondack chairs.

"Sit, we're going to share."

"Share?" she repeated, taking a staggering step, and realized it was better to sit than to fall. She sat with a plop.

"Ask away," he said, pouring an ounce from the bottle and pushed the glass toward her, then filled one for himself. He held it up to toast. "And then it's my turn."

"Are you hammered?" she asked, then giggled.

"Not nearly as bad as you, but yes."

She picked up the glass and sniffed it. "It smells like licorice. I love this stuff." They clinked their glasses, and she downed the shot. "So, I get to ask questions and you're going to answer. Straight out. No bullshit. Is this like spin the bottle?"

He snorted and nodded with a long, drawn-out tumble of his head.

She bundled up her hair in her hands, staring up at the heavens. "Okay, what do you do for your family's winery?"

"Nothing."

"Nothing? You mean you get to live here and own all this, and you do nothing?"

He sat forward and released a huge sigh. "I make my money another way."

She squinted at the moon's brightness and then at him. "CIA agent? Spy? I know, Russian czar, the accent is bullshit." She laughed at her own joke.

"Escort."

A choir of night critters singing broke the silence. Insects, a couple frogs, and some crickets created a symphony for the moon hanging low in the sky. Her head bobbed toward him.

"Escort what? Armored truck? Money? Politicians?"

"No, to all the above." He poured them another round. When she took it from his offered hand, he said, "I fuck women for a living."

The glass slipped from her fingers and bounced on the wooden slats of the table, covering it with the thick, syrupy Ouzo. She blew her breath out with a deep exhale. Didn't matter if she was ten times drunker, she still would have been thunderstruck.

"I'm—" She burst out laughing. "Okay, you got me. What do you really do?"

He tossed back the shot and slowly turned the empty glass in his fingers. "I just told you. Women hire me to fulfill their sexual fantasies. Now, it's my turn."

"Wait a minute." She threw her hand up. "First off, I didn't say I was gonna share and secondly, I have more questions. You can't just drop that bomb on me and walk away."

"You'll get your turn." He righted her glass and filled it up. "Why aren't you married like your friends?"

"Easy," she spit out. "No one ever fell in love with me." She reached for the glass almost knocking it over. "Guess I won't bother asking you that."

"Hmm." He growled deep in his throat.

"What's your brother's name?" she asked. She'd get back to the escort part when her brain stopped spinning.

"Abel."

She choked on her liquid licorice. "Your parents named you Cain and Abel? Are you kidding me?" Her mouth gaped open, and a twist of anger stirred in her stomach as her thoughts stumbled, trying to figure out why his mother and father would do that. Some biblical tales couldn't be wiped away, but rubbing their sons' noses into the doomed tale seemed cruel.

"Long story," he said somberly.

She watched his mood darken. "Got all night."

He shrugged, but his eyes betrayed the aloof move. "Short story."

"You can start there."

"It's going to end there."

"Don't go all stuffy on me now." She grabbed the neck of the bottle and poured him another shot. "Drink this first, Hooker Boy, then spill."

He chuckled and shook his head. "I never should have told you."

185

"You were dying to tell me. Get it off your chest. I'm a nobody. Who am I going to tell?" She fluttered her fingers prompting Mr. Broody Hotstuff to give up the secrets buried behind his castle-thick wall of don't-get-too-close.

With panther-like smoothness he sat up. "My mother screwed around on my dad once. When they reconciled..." His hands flipped up. "Here I am."

"Because....you're your dad's son, or?"

"Yeah, there's the problem. Dad, thought I wasn't, and to this day, he's of the same opinion."

"Who's older, you or your brother?" She downed the half ounce she'd poured herself. Geez that was good stuff.

"My turn. Are you mad at me for making the donation so your mom could stay at Golden Years?"

"No," she blurted. "No, not at all. I was just dumbfounded. I still don't understand."

"Abel is three years younger than me," he said, answering her prior question. "I did it because." He paused. "Just because."

"That's not a reason. So, your dad and mom were taking a timeout and she got pregnant." She poked his glass toward him with her finger, and he swept it up and shot it back. "Better?"

"Than what?" he asked, plopping the empty glass down on the table, a grim line forming on his pinched lips.

"Doesn't have to be a *what*. You shared." The world tilted a little, and she slumped back, overcompensating.

"And that's going to make me come to terms with the fact the man who raised me always looked at me with disdain, seeing another man's eyes in his son? I was marked by my own father. Cast out. Coined a bastard."

"That's fucked up."

A laugh spit from him. "Woman, you get a colorful mouth when you're drunk."

"That's cuz I never drink." She held up a finger. "In fact, the last time I was this drunk I lost my virginity."

He tsked. "And you probably don't even remember." He swung his glass in the air. "Better that way, I'm sure. I'm guessing he didn't have a clue what he was doing, and tore into your sweet body without a second thought."

"I don't actually. I learned my lesson about mixing booze with sex." She sighed. "Now, I don't indulge in either." She blinked and wavered in her chair. "Well...except tonight."

His chin dropped. "I kissed you. We didn't have sex. Believe me, we'd still be in bed if it were the other way around."

"If you earned all this screwing women, you must be good." She bobbed her head and heaved in a deep breath. "But there's lots of women who don't have sex."

"Everyone has sex, Mika. It's the one true pleasure God gave us. At least, it should be a pleasure."

She squinted at him or both of him. Nope, there was only one of him. "I was eighteen and that was the one and only time."

He coughed. "Wait a minute, wait a minute." He held his hand up. "You seriously can't expect me to believe it's been eleven years."

She shrugged. "I don't drink either. I mean sure, I've prayed to the porcelain bowl a few times when I let the girls override my good sense, but I don't come home, put on fluffy bunny slippers, a red negligee, and suck back a bottle of wine every day."

He rolled his head back and laughed. "That, I would love to see." His brows pinned together. "Wait, I have seen you in a negligee. All of you."

"Hooker Boy, you barely saw a thing."

"Au contraire, Miss Makris. I saw everything above the waist, and I can't seem to forget it." He stared out toward the ocean. "Tried." He ran his hand through his bangs. "Really tried, but man." He shook his head.

"Believe me, I'm forgettable."

"You'll be getting close and personal with that bathroom deity if you don't stop that," he said, watching her pour another ounce.

"Shmeh." She waved her hand. "You need a cheap therapist who really knows what she's talkin' about."

"And that's you?"

"Yup." Then the most unladylike burp galloped from her mouth. On four hooves, it hit the airways full out. "Oops." Her hand flew to her mouth.

At first he was shocked, and then one fine slash of dark brow bounced with humor. "You're fucking hilarious, do you know that?"

She did her best imitation of Tim Conway pie-eyed on hooch. "If you say so. Now, back to your fucked-up family."

"Aw, shit." He fell back in his chair and covered his face with parted fingers. "You know far more about me than any woman."

"Yeah, I call bullshit on that one. I think there's plenty of women who know every square inch of you."

He plucked his refilled shot glass from the table and saluted her. "True." He chuckled.

"So, do I have to knit a story here for you to see the wrongs of your ways, or—" That didn't come out right. She tried again. "The ways of your woes." Nope, that wasn't right either. "Umm, why are you a hooker?"

"I—am—not—a—hooker."

"Oldest profession, and as always, equality is missing between the sexes. Some poor woman is selling herself on the streets and living in low-income housing. You own a multi-million dollar property and a flippin' awesome but ugly house. That's inequality, bub. She spreads her legs and barely gets by. You use your handsome hotness with the same results, but get paid a fortune." She stopped and blinked. "Wait a minute. I got off track."

189

"Yes, you did," he said, grinning at her. "Must have been my hotness."

"You don't affect me."

That sleek brow of his rose and this time his cut jaw sharpened. "Really?"

"What? You think every woman is attracted to you? Your ego is burning on all four cylinders, isn't it?"

His eyes were like molten rocks. "I could seduce you right out of your bunny slippers if I wanted to."

She barked with laughter. "First off, stop changing the subject. Second off." And she lifted three fingers. Nope, wrong, and dropped a finger. "I'm grass roots. You're—not." Did that make any sense at all? Probably not. Who cared? "Just out of curiosity—"

"You've got no end to that."

"Shut it. Listen. What was I saying?" Haze collected in her brain.

"Seduction," he said with a sextastic timbre, still staring at her, which she ignored, but only because she was drunk.

"Yes, I remember," she spouted. "Do you screw all of your clients?"

"No," he said, and a small smile lifted his kissable lips.

"'Kay, then what makes the difference?"

"Attraction. Women—rich women—come in all shapes and sizes. It's my choice, not theirs."

"Doesn't that get a little weird if they start panting and pawing at you?"

His smile broke free, and he tilted his head as if he'd caught her reading porn. "Why so interested? I seem to remember you telling me all about the ins and outs of escorts after the wedding."

"Hey, it's not every day your landlord turns out to be a high-priced hooker."

He scrubbed his jaw with his hand and nodded. "Fair enough. My clients know the boundaries of our transaction before it begins. Chemistry plays a part."

"Chemistry!" A high-pitched giggle escaped her. "Lust, you mean. If she's a beauty queen you'll do her."

"I only accept contracts from older women."

Her jaw dropped with surprise. Before another roller coaster feeling hit her, she jumped to her feet. "How old?"

"I stay away from daddy's rich girls. Learned my lesson early. Late-thirties and up, but I do research them before I agree. They have to fill out an extensive information sheet."

She propped her hands on the armrests of his chair. "Ooooh, can I see it?"

"No."

"Aw, come on!"

"No." He laughed so hard his shoulders shook. "Listen, I think you've had enough. Time for you to turn in."

"No way. I'm going to find you on the web and fill out the form."

"Oh, God." He sighed, leaning his head back and covering his face. When he dropped his hands, he said, "You wouldn't like that Cain. He's dark, unfeeling. He's not the Cain you know."

Her heart fluttered again as she gazed at him. "I love my Cain."

The cricket's song intensified. Had she freaked him out?

He released a deep breath and blinked at her. "You do?"

She gave him her, are you stupid look. "Of course, I do. I love all my friends."

He stared at her perplexed.

Leaning, she picked up the bottle and wiggled it. "We need to drink more. We haven't talked about good old Mom and Pop. I just need water or something."

"You need an oxygen mask and a pot of coffee."

"Nope, I need music." She ran into the house, snapped up the laptop and her speaker, then staggered back outside and plunked it on the dry part of the table, clicking her favorite playlist.

A satisfied growl rolled from his throat. "Going to dance for me?"

She did, but only because if she didn't keep moving she'd hurl. "You must be Greek or something, but I don't belly dance."

"Why not? I dare you to take your clothes off and dance under the moonlight for me. It would be the best present I've ever received."

His gaze glued itself to her while she made a fool out of herself, but being four sheets to the wind and silly, made it easy.

"I'll call Jen to do that for you. In the meantime, I have another question. Is it my turn?" she asked, spinning on the spot.

He shook his head. "Mine."

She waited. "Well?" she asked, when he didn't say anything.

"Are you going to tell me what those injections are for?"

She shook her head.

The next song was John Legend's "*All of Me.*"

Cain rose, his handsome aura wavering around him. She stared as his hand forked between her fingers, reminiscent of another type of joining. For a moment, she considered how many women he must have pleasured.

"I wouldn't make the cut on your client's list, would I?"

His warm strength pressed against her. "Dance with me."

Guess that was a silent but polite 'no'.

He had a nice voice, and sang the words to her as he led her around the patio.

The wind gently swept the heat from their bodies. Locked within his gaze, she let him command her every step.

Natasza Waters

"I've been honest with you." His arm drew her tight to his chest. "I've been so honest, you'll probably never talk to me again."

"Don't be crazy. I'm the last person to judge someone."

He stopped their slow waltz. "You judge yourself all the time and find yourself lacking. Does it have to do with your secret? Your mom called it a condition. All your friends know. Why not me?"

She gave him a big toothy grin, and he swayed his head with frustration. "Because you're a gorgeous hunk of handsomeness and you wouldn't understand."

Cain leaned his forehead to hers. "Mika, if it can harm you, I want to know what it is."

John Legend sang the lyrics that sounded more like poetry, and she closed her eyes, savoring the moment. Would he still be around when the enemy inside her pounced with another attack? She swallowed, the truth tightening her heart. Of course, he wouldn't. Especially, now that she knew what he did for a living. Stevie's suggestion floated through her mind. *Tell him the truth.*

The moonlight draped them in its brilliance. His soothing voice caused her to forget she was on earth and instead, float above the ground.

"Why don't you play that beautiful piano? I've never heard one note drift across the lawn." she asked, urging their dance to resume.

194

Cain's step faltered, but he kept her close. "I learned when I was young. My mother hoped I would become a professional one day. I played classical music. As I grew up, and realized my father didn't treat me the same as Abel, I rebelled and stopped playing." He cleared his throat and searched her eyes. "When I play, I feel the music and the emotion comes out of my hands. I only have the urge to play now to release an emotion I can't destroy."

She nibbled on her lip for a moment. "Will you play me a song one day?"

Cain's Adam's apple bounced with a heavy swallow. "Maybe...if you tell me your secret."

In the arms of her striking friend and her mind muddled with alcohol, she found a reserve of bravery. Her gaze lingered on his.

"I am the perfect imperfection."

Earth came crashing back to the souls of her feet. She pulled from his hold and wandered toward the cliff's edge. No more than a couple seconds passed before Cain's strong arms circled her.

"Not too close. It'd break my heart to see you on the rocks below."

The problem with being drunk was the loss of control. Emotions swung in an instant, and they were almost swaying as much as she was. She sighed, looking out, the navigation lights of the ships twinkling. "It's so beautiful here."

Natasza Waters

"*I'm Yours*" swooped through the air, curling around them.

"Let's talk about you," he suggested.

"Boring. Why did you kiss me?" she asked in a dreamy voice.

He took a deep breath, his powerful chest brushing against her back. "Because."

"Still not an answer." She wrapped her fingers around his wrists crossed below her breasts, feeling safe and content.

"Because you're the first woman in my adult life who didn't pay me to do it."

"And…it's your birthday."

He chuckled. "That too."

He rocked her gently as they looked out over the ocean. "Yes, I was jealous," she admitted. "I know Jen is a very sexual creature, but she really is a sweetheart, too. You're my friend and she's my friend. Truth is, I'd be happy for you both, if something happened between you."

He squeezed her tighter. "You're a pretty good liar."

Her mouth formed an "O," and she turned to face him. "It's true."

Cain shook his head at her. "Like hell it is."

"Speaking of not telling the truth. Why don't you have a DNA test done and prove to your dad you're his son?"

"Too many years have gone by. He's a hard man. His mind is set."

"Where's your brother?"

196

"In Los Angeles. He runs my father's business for US distributions."

"Is it legit or are there more shady dealings going on in your family?" Cain hadn't let go of her, his bulging biceps cradling her.

"No, it's legit. My father owns several wineries all over Greece. He's one of the biggest exporters in the country."

"Do you ever go home?"

He shook his head. "Not often. Once a year to see my mother."

"And you and your brother?"

"We're close, actually. We talk at least once a week, if not more."

"He wants you to stop being a hooker and come work for the family business, right?"

A low chuckle next to her ear made her shiver.

"Yes."

She looked up into his handsome features. "Then why don't you?"

Cain pulled away and shoved his hands into his jeans pockets, then shrugged. He reminded her of the man in a sexy car commercial. The top two buttons of his shirt undone, revealing a powerful, smooth chest.

"I have another venture I've been working on for two years off and on." He cocked his head at her. "Can't be a hooker all my life."

She broke into a laugh and he gave her a slow, tantalizing smile.

"Good to hear." She swayed and took a step to stabilize herself. "I think I've had enough licorice. That stuff is pretty powerful."

"It is if you drink it like water." He leaned forward. "And you did."

"Does that stuff belong to your family?"

He nodded. "Family stock." He stopped her from tipping over. "Think I'll put you to bed," he said and gripped her hand. "Tomorrow's Sunday, you can sleep in." She followed like a little puppy, scooping her laptop up on her way inside.

Breeze ran ahead of them. When they reached the porch of her cottage, he stopped underneath the trellis. The clematis vine curled around the posts. Big purple blooms grew between the green leaves.

"I promise I won't call you Hooker Boy in public." She chuckled, then pulled herself together.

He opened her front door, but when she tried to walk inside—more like stumble—he stopped her.

"What are you doing tomorrow?"

"After having a bottle of Advil for breakfast, I'm going to visit Mom and then go downtown for the BC day sales." She put a hand on the wall and cleared her throat. "Apparently, Jen—you remember her? She wants your body." She paused with a thought. "Would you accept her as a client?"

"No," he said sharply.

Mika cleared her throat. "Anyways, she's a speed dater and thinks my outfits suck, and that jeans just don't cut it. It's her opinion, I look like a schlub."

He grinned. "Schlub is too harsh, but those loose sweatshirts and baggy jeans hide your attributes."

"Pshaw, I don't have attributes."

He gave her a gentle nudge into the cottage. "I know differently. Let's go see your mom tomorrow and then rectify that."

She yawned. "You're going to help me dress all pretty?" she asked, using a bad imitation of a British accent.

He nodded.

She waved a finger at him. "I get it, kind of like 'My Fair Lady.'"

Cain drew her down the dark hallway to her bedroom door. "You are my fair lady. You came out of the blue and now I can't imagine not seeing your face every day."

"Did that just come from your mouth?" Although her brain was fuzzy, she could well imagine the beautiful women he'd been with. "If you like looking at geeky, I'll be here," she kidded.

"Good night, Miss Makris."

She sighed. "Hey, wait a minute. I get one more question," she said, leaning against the wall for support. "What did my sister say to you at the airport?"

Cain grinned at her. "Was wondering when you'd get to that one."

"That's not an answer, buddy."

"She said…"

Mika leaned closer, and Cain did as well, his lips brushing her ear. "What's your secret and I'll tell you mine."

"Cain, come on. I want to know. You've been all 'nowhere to be found' this week, and I think it's because of what Stevie said." She sniffed. "If you don't want to tell me, just forget whatever she said."

"What can be so bad that you won't tell me why you take the injections?"

She nibbled on her lip considering it. Nope, she couldn't. "Hey, do you know any other escorts? I mean someone in the bargain basement?"

Palming the wall on either side of her shoulders, he said, "That's not funny."

She blew her hair out of her eye. "I'm not kidding."

He pressed his nose to hers. "You better be," he whispered. "Or you'll force me to accept your request form."

Even as drunk as she was, her heart slammed to a halt as his words brushed against her lips. Time slowed to a crawl, and then stopped right along with her pulse.

"Are you expensive?"

Cain's gaze heated her to the core. What was she doing? She didn't have a clue about sex, and her words were getting dangerously close to temptation. At the same time, she wondered how much room was on her Visa.

He hesitated, his thumb tracing her cheek. "Very."

"More than a new laptop?"

He huffed out a laugh. "I should have known you were leading me down the path." He kissed her nose. "When you trust me, I want to know what your secret is, but I have one I can share."

"I love secrets," she whispered, and chuckled like the drunken idiot she was.

"You're not just a friend. You're my best friend, did you know that?"

Tears sprang to her eyes as he became lost in the darkness of the hallway.

Mika smiled. "You're mine, too."

When he reached the other end, he stopped and cleared his throat. "Your sister said, 'Cain, I know you're in love with Mika.'"

She covered her eyes. "Ooooh, God, she is such an ass. Sorry about that. Stevie reads too many romance novels." Mika turned and then said over her shoulder. "By the way, Jen is waiting for you."

"What?"

"When we left, her car was still parked in front of the house. My guess…" She wavered and gripped the doorknob for support. "My guess is she's naked in your bed, waiting to give you a happy birthday."

"Seriously?"

She sighed. "Yeah." Her heart twisted into a tiny knot, but she ignored it. "Have fun."

"Mika, I would never do that to you."

He was only a shadow, but even that pulsed with masculinity.

Her policy of always being truthful didn't include hurting her friends or sharing how much it would hurt her. "I'd be the first one up and dancing at your wedding. Jen's looking for perfect. Think you'd fit."

"You forget what I do?"

"You may be a paid fantasy for hundreds of women, but it's because you're the man every girl dreams about. Someone will change your mind one day, Cain. I'm one hundred percent sure."

"What about your dreams?" he asked quietly.

A swift memory of Cain kissing her earlier tonight caused Mika to touch her lips. "That whoever steals your heart, makes you happy. See ya tomorrow." She escaped into her room. Breeze had already made herself comfortable on the bed. "Move over, bed hog."

Chapter Thirteen

Cain waited until the door closed. "You make me extremely happy," he said to the empty hallway. "Happier than I deserve."

A puff of laughter erupted from him when he heard her hit the mattress probably in a starfish-style landing. He inhaled, and a hint of her scent remained with him. A little spicy. A little sweet.

He glanced around her living room. Her eclectic style of unmatched furniture, old with new, colorful with drab gave the little cottage a life of its own. She'd put her laptop back on the table she used to drink her Saturday morning coffee, work, and eat. The one he'd seen her bent over so many times through the screen door in the evenings when the lights illuminated her.

She'd sit there with her hair pulled into a messy bundle on her head. Often she'd blow her bangs out of her eyes just to have them drop back in the same spot. His fingertips twitched, remembering how soft the strands felt. Following her mother's stroke, he'd held Mika until she'd fallen asleep. Two emotions warred inside of him that night—bliss to finally be so close, and anguish for her loss.

Walking past the table, a beep from an incoming email drew his attention. His fingers reached for the mouse, his conscience bellowing at him, but damn it anyway. He clicked on the message.

Thanks for the kind words, Mika. I know you've been there. It's such a struggle right now. Gavin has been horrible lately. It's not his fault. How can I blame him? I can barely live with myself right now. It means so much to me to have you and the others in the group. Especially when we have to deal with this monster. I hope one day we can meet. Thank you again for the shoulder.

Hugs

Karen

Cain read it again. "Group," he said quietly. A support group maybe. *I know you've been there.* Whatever Karen was going through, Mika had already been challenged with the same thing.

He swung a look around the room. Nothing pointed toward a clue. Did this have something to do with the injections she took? Had to be, he thought, and sat down on her sofa.

He leaned his head back and closed his eyes. Toe to heel, he flicked off both shoes and stretched out. No way was he going back to his place. Jen could sleep in his bed if she wanted to. Cain rearranged the pillow and sighed as he stretched out, more comfortable here.

Karen's email rolled through his mind. His phone beeped and he considered ignoring it, then palmed his cell. A text from his brother.

You awake?

He dialed his number. "Hey, brother," he said when Abel picked up.

"Hey, happy birthday. What's happening in the Great White North?"

"My house is a wreck from my surprise birthday party," he said. "Now, I'm lying here in the cottage talking to you."

"Getting to know your tenant better in the carnal way?"

He laughed. "No. As in the friend way. There's nothing carnal about our relationship."

A pause. "Do you even have a woman who's a friend?"

"I do now. We got drunk together. She had me laughing the entire night."

"Well, don't go screwing it up by fucking her then."

"Sage advice, bro."

"Good. I'm thinking about going home in September. Why don't you come, too? Mom wants to see you."

"She might, but Dad won't be happy, will he?"

"Who gives a shit? The old man is never gonna change, but Mom misses the black sheep. Why don't we spend a couple weeks there? We'll hang out, and you can tell me about this internet thing you've decided to resurrect. Which I think is a fuck of a lot better than screwin' rich women out of their husband's dividends."

Cain lay back, tucking his hand behind his head. "It is a good idea, and I've already put the word out. I'm thinking of selling. Hopefully, the news will land on the right people."

"It's one hell of a good idea. I wish I'd thought of it."

"That's because I've got all the brains in the family, but you get all the money."

Abel laughed. "Hey, I told you I'd share, and you've got a place waiting here in L.A. anytime you want."

"Don't want it. I like it here." He laughed, thinking about what Mika had called him. He should probably be pissed at the woman, but it came out of her mouth sounding so cute.

"What?" his brother asked.

"Just thinkin' about Mika. She calls me Hooker Boy."

His brother cracked up. "You told her what you do? That's fucked up. I guess you don't want her for anything else. She calls a spade a spade, sounds like."

"She does. She's the sweetest woman I've ever known."

"Ah, do I hear something else in those words?"

"Hey? God, no," he sputtered. "No, she's just fun. Cute, and has the most incredible eyes. Her mom is Japanese, and it makes a beautiful mix with her father's Greek heritage."

"She's Greek too? You're kidding?"

"Nope, but she's not exotic. She's…she's, ah…." Amazing. Lovely. Innocent. She was all those things, but none of them captured it all.

Abel paused before saying, "And you're looking for exotic?"

"Not looking for anything."

"Why don't you bring her to Greece? I'd like to meet her."

He sat up with a jerk. "Why?"

"I don't know, she sounds interesting. If she's just a friend then bring her. Who knows, maybe I'll fall in love with her."

"She works," he said abruptly. "And I doubt she can get the time off." His mind jumped to her on the private beach of his parents' island, wearing a big, floppy hat and a huge smile. "She's not your type. She's got a brain."

"Ha, I like smart." He paused. "You sure she's just a friend?"

He and his brother talked openly...most of the time. "I'll think about bringing her," he answered, instead of trying to voice the emotions tumbling around inside him, especially since their kiss.

The second their mouths touched, the life he'd turned into a wasteland erupted with sunlight. His heart had thumped with a cadence he'd never known. Cain closed his eyes, the desire to kiss her again rolling like thunder through his veins.

He tuned back into Abel when his brother said, "Even though Dad can be a shit, I know he's glad when you come home. Somewhere deep inside that old man, I think he knows you're his son. I still think you should get a DNA test and shove it in his face."

208

"That's what Mika said too, but it's too late for that. Too much firewater under the bridge."

"You told Mika about Dad too? Man! You sure you're not in love with this chick?"

He'd shared everything with her tonight. Everything, except one important truth. "She's not a *chick*."

"Okay, bro. Well—can't wait to meet her. I'll talk to ya later."

"Later."

He dropped the cell on the teak side table. When he closed his eyes, he saw Mika laughing at him and her eyes sparkling. He gave his head a shake, but she was still there, so he let her stay, and drifted off to sleep with her sweet smile.

****

The sun shining in his eyes made him squint, and he stretched with a groan. Maybe sleeping on her couch wasn't the best idea. Cain had several other bedrooms he could have slept in. He shoved his feet in his shoes and combed his hands through his hair. No sound came from down the hall. He could bring her coffee in bed, and probably some aspirin, but what message would that be sending?

He closed the front door and picked up the nearly empty bottle and glasses from the patio, the remnants of their drunken night of sharing, and headed back to his place. Opening his front door, he blinked. Someone had cleaned up, and he smelled coffee.

Jen rounded the corner wearing the dress she'd had on last night. "Morning," she said, the brilliant smile she always greeted him with, not so brilliant. "I made coffee."

"Thanks, I could use a few gallons." He stepped inside. "And thanks for cleaning up."

Jen stared at him. "I kind of crashed here last night." She rolled her eyes. "Obviously, I thought you were coming back." She paused. "I didn't know you and Mika were...well she didn't tell us."

Silence was his preferred option at this point.

"I'm curious," Jen said, pulling two cups from the rack. "I mean, I love Mika. We've known each other all our lives, but she doesn't seem your type."

He planted the empty glasses on the marble counter. Out of all Mika's friends, he could do without this one if she was about to say something nasty behind her back. He accepted the coffee Jen poured for him. "Thank you."

Her eyes surveyed him. "Or maybe I'm reading this wrong," she said, adding milk to her cup. "Maybe my friend knows me so well, she told you I'd be waiting here for you to come back, and you chose not to."

He pondered his choices. "If Mika's your friend, you wouldn't want to hurt her, would you?"

She took a slow sip of her morning brew, her elbows perched on the island. "Mika doesn't have boyfriends, not in the physical way. I don't think she'd mind if we spent time together."

Interesting. "And why's that?"

"Couple reasons. She keeps men at a distance."

"And the other?"

Jen shrugged. "Our pact. If one of us likes a guy, everyone else steers clear."

He waited, hoping Jen would offer more but instead, she switched gears. "I haven't had a shower yet this morning. Yours looks big enough for two."

He glared at her, taking a drink of caffeine. "Thanks for the offer Jen, but my interests lay elsewhere."

"You're gay?" she spluttered.

Why the hell did women always assume he was gay if he turned them down? "No, I'm not gay. Far from it."

Jen cocked her head, her perfect blonde locks falling across her shoulders. "If you're into kinky, I'm up for it."

Man, this one was relentless in a passive-aggressive way. Jen had to know Mika felt something for him. The blonde was too similar to his clients. Rich. Entitled. Jen wasn't wealthy, but her looks accomplished the same as money. He didn't know her all that well, but he sensed she had a competitive streak. A chick that wanted all the attention and pushed if she didn't get it. Her insensitivity toward Mika was pissing him off.

"Listen. My cock is never going to fuck your pussy. We clear?"

As expected, she wasn't offended, she just raised one of her eyebrows.

"The way you say that makes me hotter."

For fuck's sake. "Thanks for coming to the party." He headed for the stairs.

Jen called out. "A man like you would never be able to deal with Mika's condition. Don't start anything with her. You'll only break her heart." She headed for the front door.

"Wait." He gripped the railing, not wanting the truth but knowing he needed to hear it. "Why would you say that about me?"

Jen lifted her shoulders. "Even though you say you don't want to fuck me, I know you do. People like you and me thrive on the rush. I'm not asking for long-term, Cain. I just like sex with handsome men. You're hot, and Mika's a monster."

Anger rumbled from deep inside him. "Why the fuck would you say that about your friend?"

She laughed. "You misunderstand. Those are her words, not ours, Cain. That's how she sees herself. The truth is, we're all incredibly proud of her. She's braver than all of us." Jen adjusted the purse strap on her right shoulder. "I don't know what I would do if I were in her shoes."

"Why does she call herself that?"

Jen's expression curtained in an instant. "She hasn't told you."

Shit. "I could never see her as a monster, but she's afraid to tell me."

Jen glared at him. "Haven't you noticed she never bares her skin?"

"What does that have to do with anything?"

"A guy that looks like you..." Her brow creased. "You screw models and movie stars. Yeah, you'd run, and you will. Right now, she's in remission, but it'll come back. It always comes back. We all think you're a pretty cool guy, Cain. If you care about Mika like we do, treat her as a friend and keep it that way."

Remission! Did she have cancer? It would make sense. Don't let anyone too close in case... No, no way. Not his Mika.

Jen closed the door, leaving him more frustrated than before. Although for the wrong reasons, Jen's words hit the spot. Mika's heart was more than he deserved, *he* was the monster.

Last night he'd wanted to kiss Mika a dozen times. Alcohol stole his good sense. He couldn't stand it anymore and taunted her into kissing him. He'd never forget the warmth, the need that rushed to every corner of his body. He scrubbed his jaw. This could not be happening.

213

Instead of going upstairs for a shower, he flipped open his laptop. Five requests sat waiting for his response. He looked at each one, his heart hammering in his chest.

Pick one. Anyone. Doesn't matter.

Bethany Coltier. Originally from France. Blonde, blue-eyed, her breasts had been paid for by someone. Thirty-eight years old. One night inclusive package to escort her to a corporate function.

Reject.

Melody Pattison. One week in Hawaii.

Reject.

Karen Worthington. Weekend in L.A.

Reject.

Sarah Pentani. Four days in Florida.

Reject.

Kelly Anderson. My daughter is turning nineteen, and I read your policy on age, but I want someone who will be gentle and professional to take her virginity.

"For fuck's sake!"

He hammered the button. *Reject.*

"Fuck!" he yelled and slammed the lid of the laptop, burying his face in his hands.

Cain yanked on his running gear and left the house. He ran and ran, and kept running. No matter how far or how fast, he would never outrun the past or what he'd become. His chest heaved when he finally stopped in the forest, and listened.

He tilted his head back and stared into the blue sky overhead. Shunned by his own father, his anger drove him to prove he was worth something, but he'd turned to a profession that left him dark and empty, wandering aimlessly without an end like the original Cain.

His confession last night had been premeditated. He wanted Mika to know. No woman in her right mind would trust him, and then she'd floored him. *"I love my Cain."* She'd said it with the words, *"I love all my friends"* trailing behind, but all he heard was the first four words.

He bit back the truth. The ocean breeze brushed the summer leaves with a whisper, and he gave voice to his heart because no one could hear him.

"I love you, Mika. Not as a sister. Not like a friend."

Jen's warning stood on the edge of his thoughts, holding a bucket of cold reality over his head.

Closing his eyes, he resisted the hunger to possess the woman who rented his cottage. He'd never allow his desire for Mika to inhale one breath of free air.

Why?

Because he didn't trust himself. Jen was right. His friendship with Mika meant everything. Changing what they had into something deeper or physical wasn't possible for a man like him. He'd screwed so many women, in some twisted way he'd exterminated his right to truly love someone. He had to protect what he and Mika had now.

One day, some guy would come out of nowhere and take her from him. Offer his heart and a forever.

It would be the worst day of his life.

Chapter Fourteen

"How about this?" she asked with a twirling step." Cain sat back in the leather couch and grinned up at her.

"You rock the red, Mika."

She planted her hands on her hips. The style bared a slit from her thigh down to her knee. It didn't reveal all of her leg, which would have been better in his opinion. Nice, he thought to himself, but as his eyes strayed up her Marilyn Monroe shape to her face, something happened. A squeeze of need, but much deeper, more intense, way more intense than desire, struck him.

"It's so not me," she said, looking at herself in the mirror.

"You're wrong." His voice drifted lower. The heels gave her a little extra height, and the peek-a-boo view of her leg was, was…he blew out a silent breath. Okay, maybe his coming with her to shop wasn't a good idea.

"I'm going to buy it and wear it next weekend."

"What's next weekend?" he asked.

Mika fidgeted. Her fingers locked together, then she looked over her shoulder at him. "I've got a date."

He bolted upright. "With who?"

She shrugged. "A man-whore. He's dated every unattached woman in my office. He works on the base."

"Why would you do that?"

Mika glanced around to make sure they were alone. "I don't know," she said, keeping her gaze on the door that led to the showroom.

"You're doing this with some guy who swims in the shallow end of the pool?"

She gnawed on her lower lip for a minute. "Yup."

"Why?" he asked again. She could have any guy she wanted. Going out with some asshole that wouldn't care about her feelings or how wonderful she was, floored him.

"Man-whore or not, he's springing for dinner, and then drinks at the Blink and Boinker."

Even through his mounting angst, he chuckled. "Are you talking about the Bard and Banker?"

"That's the place. The girls call it the Boinker for obvious reasons."

He nodded slowly, but wasn't sure what his next words should be. This morning he vowed he'd be her friend, and nothing else. "Is this about hooking up, because that's not you?" He thought she'd been kidding when she said she hadn't had sex for eleven years. It just wasn't possible.

She gnawed on her lip. "I saw Jen leave your place this morning. Why should she be the only one to have fun?"

He vaulted to his feet. "Mika, I slept on your couch all night. I saw her when she was leaving. We didn't..." What the hell was he doing? Making damn sure she knew he hadn't...

"Sure ya did."

"Mika," he said sharply, gripping her shoulders and turning her to face him. "I—did—not—sleep—with—Jen."

"Whatever."

The hurt in her eyes betrayed her flippant tone. "I've still got a kink in my back from your damn couch."

"You could have slept in my bed."

"What!" His pulse kicked into high gear.

"The spare bedroom. I've got a bed in there."

He swallowed thickly, keeping every emotion hidden from his expression. "I'll remember that the next time one of your friends climbs in my bed."

"At least with your business you're satisfied. I'm getting bored with my battery operated boyfriends."

As usual, she deferred to funny, but this time it wasn't. As he was about to give her a reality check on the dangers of meaningless sex, the sales woman entered the viewing room.

"Oh my, that is lovely on you."

"Thanks," Mika said quietly.

"Are you sure you don't want to try the one with the halter neckline?"

"It's perfect," he snapped out. Now that he knew what the dress was for, less skin showing was a better idea. Bad enough the drop shoulder revealed her sculpted beauty and regal neckline.

"I bet you would look beautiful in a topaz blue with your coloring. We've got a new line called Greek Goddess. Let me find you some things."

Mika flexed her brows and grinned at him. "Did ya hear that? Greek Goddess."

He wasn't laughing anymore. When the clerk disappeared, he stepped behind Mika. She kept her gaze riveted on the mirror.

"You want to get laid, is that what you're saying?" He caressed the soft skin of her shoulder with his thumb. "You want a man to touch you."

She shook her head, paused then nodded, and finally looked at him. "Don't judge me."

"I'm not." He lifted her long brunette hair and swept it over one shoulder. "Believe me, I'm not. I just don't think you can do that without becoming emotionally involved. That's not who you are." He kept the raving jealousy from tingeing his words. The fact that he wanted to brush gentle kisses along her perfect neck was driving him fucking crazy. "It's not who anyone really is." He palmed her sleeved arms.

"Sure I can." Her forehead furrowed. "You do it. He's a handsome guy, and the word is he'll do just about anybody given the chance. He asked me out a couple times, and I finally said yes."

"Why now?" he said abruptly. *Didn't she believe him about Jen?*

"I'm going to change out of this." She glanced at him. "It works, right?"

"Yeah," he said, giving her a half-hearted smile. "Yeah, it works."

The saleswoman brought three more outfits, and they all were perfect for her. Too fucking perfect, especially the black Goddess dress.

"Find a bathing suit, too," he said coldly.

Mika's head snapped up. "Bathing suit? No, I don't do bathing suits."

He nodded to the sales woman, and she scurried away.

"Cain, I'm not trying on a bathing suit. I don't need one."

"Just do it," he said roughly and left the viewing room.

He paced the store like a caged animal, getting more riled up with every second. When Mika appeared, he took a deep breath and joined her at the register, seeing a bright blue one-piece bathing suit on the pile. When she reached in her purse, he pulled out his wallet and handed the cashier his credit card.

"What are you doing?"

"Late Christmas present."

"No way." She switched the cards and insisted the girl take hers. Without looking at him, she slid his card toward him, then signed the slip. "And I'm buying lunch for your consulting services."

She gave him a big cheesy, satisfied smile.

221

****

The week went by far too quickly. Saturday night came, and when he heard the crunch of stone under the wheels of a car, he swore he wasn't going to look, but he did, and he saw the black Dodge come to a stop outside Mika's cottage. A tall guy, physically fit with a slender build got out. Mika appeared on the porch, stopping the guy in his tracks.

"Fuck," Cain growled under his breath. He gripped his neck and watched the scene like a train wreck. The guy leaned in and gave her a quick kiss on her cheek, then guided her to the passenger side of his car, opening the door for her. Before she got in, her head rose and looked toward his house.

"Don't go. Make an excuse, and don't go," he said, but she only paused for a second and got in.

"Fuck."

He stepped away from the window, his fists clenched, as Mika and her date rolled by. Pacing his kitchen with its cold chrome fixtures, matched his mood. Round the island he went, like a rabid animal. She was the type of woman who made a man look at the future with new eyes. What if this guy saw it and wanted Mika?

He snatched his cell from the counter.

"Hey," he said when the woman answered. "What are you doing tonight?"

After the call, he ran for his bedroom, taking the stairs three at a time. Shoving the hem of his dress shirt into his slacks, he stalled in front of the mirror and stared at himself. Mika had forced him to consider the choices he'd made the night they talked, and maybe every time they'd spent time together.

They both needed release, and although she didn't know it, his sexual frustration was at a peak.

If any man was going to give her that release, it would be him.

****

Ben slid in beside Mika when they were seated at the Bard. Instead of dinner first, they'd decided to grab a drink. Nervous as all heck, she'd put a filter on her mouth and tried to be a little bit reserved. Even a man-whore had to have standards.

"Wow, this place is busy tonight," she said, slipping over and putting some room between them.

The edge of Ben's eyes creased with a smile. "Always is. You've been here before?"

"A few hundred times. I grew up in Victoria. Everyone wants to drink at the Boinker when they're legal," she said.

The two-story pub was famous for its scotch. Polished wood, gold rails and elegant architecture in the tourist portion of downtown Victoria, meant standing room only on the weekends. The band brought in for the Saturday night crowd rocked the place with the first song. With a female lead singer and four guys as her backup, the dance floor was jammed.

223

Ben's arm rested behind her on the leather bench seat. "So, how come you decided to finally go out with me? I'm honored, by the way."

She shrugged. The morning after Cain's birthday, she'd staggered with her thumping, medicine ball-sized head from the bedroom. She'd filled up the coffee pot and found the Advil. Standing on her porch to get a breath of fresh air, she'd seen Jen slip from Cain's house.

The hurt had nearly toppled her. Then she'd rationalized every distraught thought. Both of them were beautiful people. Maybe Jen would be enough to make Cain stop bedding other women for a living.

The tiny bubble of hope she'd nurtured for herself, floated away. The one her heart fired with sweet dreams, and her mind doused with, "get real." She'd gone inside and called Ben.

"You know, I have to throw a tidbit out once in a while," she kidded.

His face lit up, then he leaned in with his mouth near her ear. "You mean, save me from just fantasizing about you?"

He certainly knew the lines, and she was sure there'd be more. Bring 'em, she thought. She'd embrace every one. It had been a long time since she'd been brave enough to accept a date. During university, she'd been on a few, but never saw the guy again when she didn't put out.

Cain had asked her why she was doing this. She wanted to tell him the truth. Tell him that finally she wasn't a monster and her disease was under control. For once, she could look at herself in the mirror and her eyes not mist with shame and hate quarreling in her conscience.

"What do you want to drink?" Ben asked, and she looked up to see the waitress.

"Uh, do you have Tsipouro?"

"Any particular kind?" the girl asked.

"No, just lots of ice."

Ben winked at her. "Never been on a date with someone who ordered that." He ordered a beer from the server, and Mika ignored the long glance he strayed up the girl's slender frame.

After three shots, she was feeling no pain, and the nervous rumblings in her empty belly were gone.

The music boomed through the bar, and Ben pulled on her hand. "Let's go."

"Dinner?"

"Dance floor."

They squeezed onto the small dance floor and dodged the swaying hips and swinging arms. The room was warm and getting warmer because Ben slammed the breaker on his hundred-watt smile.

The next song slowed down, way down, and his hands slid to her hips. "This is what I've been waiting for," Ben said.

She glanced around and saw Cain weaving through the crowd.

"Hey, Cain!"

She waved, and Ben looked over at her landlord's confident, sexy gait, which stopped at the foot of the platform. A couple gals sitting at a table close by nudged each other, ogling his impressive form—tall, broad shoulders and a body that narrowed at his waist.

"Hi, Cain, what are you doing here?"

"Business meeting. I saw you and thought I'd say hello."

"Oh," she said, and her brows shot up. She didn't consider he might do his business locally. For some reason she imagined him jumping on a jet and seducing his clients at a romantic getaway in the mountains or under a palm tree.

"Ben, this is my landlord, Cain Sallas."

"Hey," they both said and shook hands.

Cain glanced at his watch. "Mind if I take her for a turn around the dance floor?"

Ben's amiable smile dissolved a little. "Guess not."

Cain swept in and drew her into the throng of couples dancing to the modern, sexy ballad the singer belted out.

"Isn't your client going to get pissed off?" she asked as Cain drew her close and wrapped his arm snugly around her waist.

"Not that kind of client, Mika. For the new business."

"Oh, sorry. I just assumed...."

"How's the date going? He treating you okay?"

226

"Fine, I suppose. Not like I have a lot of experience." They stared into each other's eyes. Cain was one of the few men she could do that to without feeling self-conscious.

"He made his play yet?"

She laughed. "No, he's been a gentleman."

Cain forked his fingers through hers and warmed her insides. She finally relaxed. Before they were friends, she was nervous and anxious around him, but he'd held her so often it felt familiar and comfortable.

"Not so sure about that," he said, and his gaze shot over her head.

She turned a look across her shoulder and saw a woman standing beside Ben. An amazingly, gorgeous, tall, blonde woman. She spoke to him, leaning in, and Mika saw her breast brush against his hand, which curled over the edge of the high table.

Ben's expression dripped with heat as his eyes caressed the beautiful girl. The gal touched his shoulder, and Ben responded instantly with his hand coming to rest on her waist. The body movement between them sent a clear signal.

Mika's feet stopped and she stared, not sure how to feel. She instantly pushed back against the fear of not being good enough. Every woman felt that from time to time in her life, but women who lived with what she had inside her fell victim to it too often. Ben was a hound dog. She knew this.

The beautiful woman coming onto Ben wouldn't have the scars Mika had on her skin. Her skin would be perfect, never having battled her own body as it rebelled against her. Cain stilled, his embrace pulling her a little closer. They both watched as the blonde laughed at whatever Ben said to her.

Mika used logic, as she always did when the acerbic humor she relied on to push back the deflating image of being less, failed her. Would she actually have the guts to go to bed with Ben? Her skin was clear now, but the war wounds were still present. The song ended, but Ben hadn't looked up, totally entranced by the vivacious blonde.

Cain's low voice rumbled next to her ear as both his arms engulfed her and pressed her to his chest.

"Are you okay?"

A twist of pain tightened her heart, and she gave it a few seconds, hoping Ben would look for her. He didn't. She pulled away from Cain. Tipping her head, her gaze rolled down her dress to the red spike heels on her feet.

Sometimes, the inner battle between confidence and reality ended in an all-out brawl, and her self-confidence walked away with a black eye.

"Mika?"

She looked up and Cain's brows were crushed together in sympathy. That's really what did her in. She hated sympathy. She hated that she'd been born with a defect that couldn't be hidden from the world. A world so damn spellbound by beauty.

Men like Cain, women like the blonde, had it easier. She straightened her shoulders and adjusted the thin purse strap across her chest.

She nodded.

"I think I should take you home," Cain offered.

She nodded again, not trusting herself to speak. Cain broke a path through the dance floor alive with swinging bodies to the fast beat of the next song. She stalled at the exit and looked back one more time. Ben offered his perfect white-toothed smile at the blonde, and they tipped their glasses together, then he finally looked up and searched the dance floor, but didn't seem all that concerned when he couldn't see her.

Cain's warm hand gripped hers. "Come on," he said, and she let him lead her away.

****

Mika sat quietly beside him as they drove through the heart of Victoria. She faced the side window, her hands clasped primly and settled in her lap.

"Are you hungry?" Cain asked.

She shook her head. The silence bothered him. He darted a look her way as they passed beneath a street light. In the reflection of the window, he saw the tears and immediately placed his hand over hers. "Hey, don't shed any tears for him."

She didn't speak.

"Mika." He squeezed her hand. "Talk to me."

229

She finally turned her head forward, and he could see her lip quiver.

"Can't even rely on a man-whore nowadays," she said in a hushed whisper.

Shit. This was not what he'd expected. She was so feisty all the time. He'd expected anger and brimstone. How had he read her so wrong?

"We can't waste that beautiful dress." At the next light, he cranked a U-turn.

"Where are you going?"

"Taking you someplace that deserves your presence."

She sniffed and pressed the heel of her palms to her cheeks. When they hit the next red light, he caressed her arm, but she wouldn't look in his eyes.

"You're beautiful. Don't ever doubt that, sweetheart."

She bowed her head and a stuttered gasp flew from her mouth. Her eyes slammed shut, attempting to stop the tears from gushing out. When the light turned green, he headed for the shoulder of the road and threw it into park. The sports car didn't give him much room, but he shunted onto his hip.

"Hey, come on. What's going on?" She couldn't talk she was crying so hard.

"Need…a…second," she sputtered, opened the door, and jumped out.

Mika appeared in front of the headlights of the car. Her beautiful, dark locks bounced against her shoulders. The silky fabric of her dress clung to her waist and followed her hips with a graceful flow. She was beautiful. Really beautiful, and he bit down on his thoughts. Cain owned her tears. This was his fault.

That fucking guy, Ben, didn't care how lovely she was. He'd only been impatiently waiting to see how loose she was, and if he could open her legs and get inside her.

Cain ground his teeth together. Maybe she would have felt bad if Ben had gotten his way, then never called her again, but right now she was crying because she thought Sofia was a better pick in Ben's eyes than her.

He gazed at the clock on his dash. Sofia had seen them leave, and not long after, she would have dumped lover boy. A text beeped on his phone, and he scanned it.

She's better off without him. He's a dick. Hugs, Sofia.

Thanks

He shoved the phone in his pocket. He left the car running and cracked the door. Mika's shoulders jerked with her sobs. There was something else going on here.

"Mika?"

She swept away her tears. "I'm good," she said sharply.

He stepped toward her. "No, I don't think you are." He didn't pause, he just reacted to what his heart told him to do, and drew her against his chest. "Why are you so upset about this?"

"Says the curl-your-toes handsome guy who women buy to make love to them."

231

She tried to pull away, but he snuggled her in his arms, ignoring her harsh jab. "You're frustrated because he's an asshole? You knew that already. I thought you didn't care?"

Her body shook with leftover emotion. From inside her purse, her phone announced a text. She pulled it out and looked at it. Then typed out a response.

"It's him, isn't it?"

She nodded as she finished typing.

"What did you say?"

"I told him I had a nice time, and I wished him well with the blonde."

Her phone beeped again, and this time a disgusted laugh erupted from her mouth. "You too," she said, reading his response. "Since your landlord wants you for himself." She shook her head. "Typical, hey? He's pawing the blonde, and he makes up lies so it's not his fault." Mika flicked her hand through her curls. A resigned expression coated her features. "Would you mind stopping at a drive thru. I feel like—"

He shook his head. "That stuff is not good for you, and you're not swallowing ten thousand calories because of him. Let's go."

"Where?" she asked, hedging.

"Dinner."

Settled in a quaint restaurant along the Victoria waterfront with candlelight flickering against the walls and a pendent strung above each table, she picked up the menu. When the waiter came, Cain ordered a bottle of red wine. Greek, of course.

"Why don't I have any prices on my menu?" she asked.

"Must be a misprint or something." He eyed her with a grin.

"Yeah, right." She reached for his, but he pulled away.

"Now, now, that's not polite."

"Heck with polite, I'm not ordering something that has the same digits as my lousy paycheck."

He folded the menu closed and leaned on the table. Mika was slowly healing from whatever had ripped a hole in her. "I'll order for you."

Perching her elbow on the table, she rested her chin on her clenched fist. "What if I don't like it?"

"If you'll eat a hamburger, you're not fussy." He cocked his head, digesting her beauty and his deception. "If you want to eat crap, I know you're upset."

She actually stuck her tongue out at him and he laughed.

"Sorry," she said sobering. "About my boo-hoo fest."

He covered her left hand. "I'm glad I was there to sweep you away from the clutches of a man-whore."

"Yeah, but you're a man-whore. Don't you guys stick together?"

"True, but I'm a professional, and when it concerns you, I have good intentions."

"What about your business meeting? Did I ruin that?"

233

He easily shrugged away the guilt. "Concluded." The waiter stood in polite silence and didn't interrupt. "We'll start with the Florina peppers, the Kolokythoanthoi and the Kleftiko for the main dish."

"Very good, sir."

"My mom used to make the best Kolokythoanthoi." Her gaze fluttered away from his and filled with sadness.

They'd visited her mom every weekend together, and Mika always dropped in on her way home from work. "Mine, too. In fact, I bet she'd love to make you some."

Mika grinned. "Does she deliver from Greece?"

"No." He swallowed. "Truth is her chef makes most of the meals, but if you come with me, you can try it firsthand." He hadn't taken his brother's suggestion to heart, not until tonight. Mainly because Abel had scared the shit out of him when he'd said he might fall in love with her. Teasing or not, when it came to Mika, even his brother was a threat.

"Aww," she said sweetly, but with a hint of sarcasm. "I'll just jump on a plane to Greece. No problem." She slid her full glass aside after the waiter poured the wine.

He traded his water with her glass. "Actually, it isn't. How about early September? Can you get time off work?"

Her mouth gaped. "Are you serious?"

"I am," he said, nodding. "We could do some island hopping. I can show you the sights. You'd love it, and my brother's going to be there."

234

Mika stared at him as if he'd suddenly grown a horn out of his forehead, and he almost checked to make sure he hadn't. He waved his hand to break the look of utter shock.

"Hello?"

She sat back and gave him an awkward smile. "Thanks for the invite, but I doubt I'd get time off. Besides, you missed the part about the lousy paycheck."

"Ask," he ordered, maybe with a little too much vehemence. Suddenly, it made a big difference whether he would go at all unless she agreed to come.

"Can't."

"I'm dropping your rent."

"It's supposed to be a ten percent increase each year. I thought you were smart."

"I am. The rent's too high."

"The rent isn't high enough. I know I stretched it to afford having the place, but I love it. I can deal with a little tuna fish to afford the cottage."

"I didn't want some hippy, pot smokin' asshole to come to the door."

"That I can understand."

He pulled both her hands into his. "Now, I want you to tell me the honest truth. What happened tonight?"

She flushed and shook her head.

"Mika." He cleared his throat. "It doesn't make sense to me."

She rolled her top lip and sucked on it, staring at him intently. "It's embarrassing, and I don't think I want you to know."

"What?"

Their appetizers arrived, and he forced the waiter to place them on the edge of the table. He wasn't going to let the food distract them or let go of her hands.

"I have a small window," she said in a quiet voice.

He shook his head not understanding. She tried to pull her hands free, but he held on. "For what?"

Chapter Fifteen

Mika blew out a deep breath. "Why do you need to know?"

"Because Jen said you're in remission, which to me means cancer."

She shook her head. "Not cancer."

His eyes snapped closed with what looked like relief, then with frustration. "Everyone knows. Except me."

"Can we talk about something else and stop making a big deal over this. Believe me, I do that enough myself."

His gaze strayed to the next table with an older couple enjoying their meal. "It is a big deal. I told you something about myself that only a handful of people know outside of my clients. The reason I don't tell people is because I don't want to be judged. Friends don't judge."

She rolled her eyes, hating that he'd made his point so well. Mika figured eventually Cain and Jen would end up in bed together. Did it really matter that he knew her condition? "I have an autoimmune disease. I was born with it." Her lips parted, and then she paused, gathering her thoughts. "Right now it's in remission, or I should say suppression, but when it comes back—" Her gaze flew to his. "It's a severe case, and that's why I take the injections."

"Okay, what happens when you're not in remission?"

She toyed with the ice in her glass. If Cain was really her friend, he'd eventually treat her with the same polite indifference as the rest of her buddies. He'd pretend not to see the lesions or the scars, and she'd love him for the lie.

"I take cover one way or the other."

"Why?" He moved the glass away from her absent ministrations and his thumbs brushed her knuckles.

"Because it's ugly. Can we talk about something else now?"

"Maybe you'll be in remission for a long time."

She shook her head. "Sometimes, but not often and not someone like me."

His brow furrowed. "Will you tell me what it is?"

He stared so poignantly at her, she stopped breathing. "Turns me into someone no one would want to touch. At least, that's what I thought until tonight." She picked up her fork and poked it into the red pepper the waiter delivered. She paused. "You're lucky, you know. People like you and that blonde in the bar can walk freely, never having to deal with looks of disgust from people. You can stand confidently in front of a mirror and see perfection looking back."

"Nobody is perfect, Mika. Nobody." He gripped her wrist. "Believe me, Ben wanted you."

"No one wants a monster."

"Stop calling yourself that," he said harshly. "Whatever it is, I can see it's a challenge for you, but I also see the strength in you."

Mika used her knife to push the pepper off her fork. She stared down at it. "When it's bad, you either find the strength to ignore it or kill yourself, and many have."

Without directly voicing the worst moments of her life, she just admitted she'd contemplated ending her life. She'd never admitted that to anyone.

When she was seventeen, and a flare had covered seventy percent of her body, she'd stood in the bathroom with a bottle of pills in one hand and her long-sleeved full-length dress in the other. Grade twelve graduation wasn't just about taking a step closer to legal drinking age, it was about the dress, and the night, and a girl's date. Everyone had a date for prom. Everyone but her. Behind her back, the mean girls and callous boys used to call her Snowflake, but it wasn't an endearing term. Since then, it wasn't the only time she'd contemplated the struggles of living with her disease.

Cain pulled the appetizers to the center of the table. "Mika, tonight when I saw you dancing in that dress and smiling up at Ben, I had a thought."

"If this is the part where you're going to lie to me and say something nice to make me feel better, don't."

"That's exactly what I'm going to do, but it's not a lie. Because of my profession, oldest on record according to you, I've seen a lot of women. Some more beautiful than others, but it's not beauty that attracts a man. It's her essence, and I've never seen a woman glow as beautiful as you. You stand out on a crowded dance floor. You didn't notice, but there were several men who watched you tonight, because they saw it too."

Mika peered at him from under her bangs, her eyes misted with tears, and she bowed her head. "Thanks, Cain. You're a good guy."

His gaze shot to the table, and his jaw edged into a rigid line. "I wish that were true." He lifted her hand and kissed her fingers. "The Wyatts and Bens of the world don't deserve you. Even as a booty call." He waited until she looked into his eyes. "I love my friend, Mika. She deserves the best."

Two hours later, they rolled into their driveway, and he parked the car.

"Thank you for dinner and bringing me home, Cain."

He walked her to the door of the cottage, his expression curling with concern. "I need to tell you something. You're going to be angry at me, but I hope you'll forgive me."

"Why would I be angry?" She dug in her purse for her keys. "Oh, shoot," she exclaimed, pushing the key into the lock and leaving him on the stoop.

****

"What's wrong?"

She dropped her purse on the table and aimed for the fridge. "I forgot. I didn't take my injection today. It's Saturday."

He edged his way inside and watched her as she pulled a box from the fridge, setting it on the counter. "What did you want to tell me?" she asked, opening the cabinet, retrieving a cotton ball and a small Band-Aid, placing it next to the injection.

"Can I help?" he asked, staring at the little pile of supplies.

She smiled warmly at him. "Thanks, but I can handle it. I inject into the stomach. Easiest place to reach. It would be better in the arm, but it's awkward to do that."

"You gave yourself an actual needle last time."

She nodded. "Yeah, sometimes they mess up and send the syringes. I like these pens better."

He stepped up to the counter and looked down at the plastic tube. "Humira" was written along the side. "I want to," he said, and his gaze rose to meet hers. "Show me what to do."

"Why?" she asked, her brows puckering together.

He didn't know how to answer that. He'd never been responsible for anyone but himself and Breeze, who chose that moment to nudge open the screen door and trot in, wagging her tail. She bumped against his leg for attention, and then Breeze went looking for a caress from Mika.

She gave the dog a pat. "Hey, girl."

Breeze's tail swooshed back and forth, thumping against the island as she stared up at Mika.

Natasza Waters

"Crazy dog, she does this all the time."

"What?"

"She sits beside me when I take the injection."

He picked up the package with the alcohol swab and tore it open. "Now, you have us both watching."

"Now, you're being crazy," she said, removing her shawl and draping it over the kitchen chair. "I'll just go in the bathroom. I'll be right back."

He placed a hand on her bare shoulder. His heart thundered and Mika stilled. Slowly, very slowly, he slid the neckline of her off-the-shoulder dress down her arm, seeing the discolored skin for the first time. Beneath the red dress, she wore a strapless red silk bra. Cain bit his lip, his pulse raging.

He thumbed the dark scars on her arms. Mika stood stalk still. Twice he'd seen her in off-the-shoulder clothes. He'd assumed the rest of her lovely, smooth skin covered her body. Cain stared at the large circles, which reminded him of a burn victim. They rounded her entire elbow and crawled up her flesh. What had done this to her?

Mika tensed with his gaze. "Ugly, I know, but you'll get used to it. Believe me, this is nothing."

She tried to take the medication from him, but he held on. His thumb caressed her elbow. The urge to kiss her hard labored his breathing.

"Show me," he said, rubbing the sterilized swab against her upper arm, the alcohol assaulting his nose. Mika took the pen,

242

gently tipped it back and forth a couple times, then pulled a cap off both ends.

She depressed the plastic tip at the end of the tube. "You hold this against the skin, then press the top like a Bic pen, keeping contact with my arm. The needle auto ejects. Count to ten, and it's done."

She handed him the injector, and he lined it up over the area he'd swabbed. He watched as she took a deep breath in, then let it out, nodding at the same time. He pressed the button and heard a *click*. Her expression flinched, and he flinched with her.

"Sometimes you get a good spot, sometimes not," she said, five Mississippi, six Mississippi, she counted all the way to ten. "Pull it back straight."

He did as she instructed, and she put a cotton ball over a tiny bead of blood. When she removed the ball, he gently placed the round bandage over top. Quickly, she gathered the bits and pieces and threw them in the garbage, except for the injector which she shoved into a brown plastic container. It clattered with other empty pens.

"So, there ya go. You can stop bugging me. You know my nasty secret." She adjusted her top and smiled up at him. "It's not contagious."

The urge to give Mika a hug made him step closer. "Come here." She rested her head on his shoulder, and he nestled her in his arms. "Don't assume because of my ill-chosen profession that

I would judge you against anyone else." He tipped her chin so she'd look at him. "Unlike me, you have nothing to hide from the world."

Tomorrow was another day, or maybe the day after would be soon enough to tell her how he'd called Sofia, a woman who shared the same profession as him, and did quite well at it, being very particular about her clientele. He'd told her to use everything in her arsenal to intervene at the Bard, and draw Ben's attention.

Long ago, he'd saved Sofia from the streets. She'd been hooking and had a bastard of a John. He gave her the opportunity to get away. She took it, but didn't leave the profession, she just got better at it with a little help from him.

"I have a meeting in San Francisco next Saturday, but I don't leave till noon," he said.

"Cain, you don't have to do that. Seriously."

He did. He did have to because he needed her, and she needed him. "Maybe I like watching your cute little face flinch in pain. Payback for calling me Hooker Boy."

She snorted and gave him a poke in the stomach. "Sheesh, that's hard," she said, then walked over to the sofa with Breeze on her heels. When she sat down, Breeze hopped up and laid her head in Mika's lap. "You're just a big goofy girl, aren't ya?" she said, running her fingers through Breeze's fur. The dog whined and her tongue snapped out and caught Mika on the cheek. Lying down, she pulled the blanket over her legs, and Breeze stretched out beside her.

"You're teaching my dog bad manners again," he said good-naturedly, sitting in the chair across from them.

"Maybe in your house because your pompous Italian sofa can't handle it." Mika wrapped her arm around Breeze, and they both closed their eyes. "No hoity-toity in this house." She kissed Breeze between her ears, and he could have sworn the dog smiled.

"That damn dog gets more attention than I do."

"Yeah, right. I've seen women slobber all over themselves walking by you. I should stick a 'lookin' for girlfriend' sign on your back." She snuggled against the pillow. "Just make sure your health insurance is up to date. After the riot, there won't be much left of you." She giggled and peeked one eye open.

He slowly shook his head at her. "Don't need a girlfriend."

Both her eyes snapped open. "Why not? Oh, right. I forgot."

"Not that. You two are enough of a handful."

She tsked. "I'm easy."

He wished.

"I'm going to visit Mom tomorrow morning."

"I'll come with you."

She snuggled the blanket up to her chin.

What he wouldn't give to be a dog right now. He basked in the warmth of the little cottage and watched them, the silence comforting. The only reason he needed to leave was because he had the last piece of the puzzle.

"I better get to bed. Good night," he said and walked to the door.

As he closed it, he heard Mika say to Breeze, "I'll still have you when it comes back, won't I, Breeze?"

An icy chill bled through him with her words. Did she think he'd abandon their friendship? Abandon her?

He ran as fast as he could back to his place. Tossing his coat, he sat down at his laptop and Googled *Humira*. He found the home page for the drug and clicked on it. Pictures of smiling people sat beside the uses for the drug. Rheumatoid Arthritis, Crohn's disease, Ulcerative colitis, Psoriatic Arthritis, and then his eyes landed on the only thing that would be truly visible to the eye. What she thought made her a monster. Moderate to severe Plaque Psoriasis. He clicked on the arrow.

HUMIRA is a prescription medicine used to treat adults with moderate to severe chronic plaque psoriasis who are ready for systemic therapy or phototherapy, and are under the care of a doctor who will decide if other systemic therapies are less appropriate.

His eyes coursed down the page.

Remember, HUMIRA is a treatment, not a cure.

In other words, it meant there was no cure.

The more he read, the more he became sick to his stomach with the possible side effects, but it was also her last hope.

Psoriasis sufferers took it only when their symptoms became severe. He Googled stages of Psoriasis and found a site with pictures, but he hesitated before selecting it. Would he see her differently if he looked at these? What if it was really bad and she wasn't exaggerating?

He scrubbed his face with both hands, then rested his palms on the table top. Jen implied he was a shallow prick. Mika meant something to him. When he called her his fair lady, it was the truth.

He'd become accustomed to her face and her presence. He liked to watch her run with Breeze on the beach and when she worked in the garden. Standing on the edge of a desolate wasteland, he wanted to step into her world of warmth and color. He never wanted to go back. Karen's email echoed in his mind. *My husband is being horrible lately, but how can I blame him. I can't even look at myself.*

"No," he said fiercely. He was better than that. No matter what this disease did to her, he'd still see her the same. He clicked on the site, and the words stalled in his mind. He shook his head. No way, he thought. She could never look like this.

He clicked on the slideshow, and his guts churned. A picture of a man's feet covered in white scales and bloody cracks filled the page. He hit the forward arrow, and a picture of a woman facing away from the camera showed her red lesions. There were

247

so many of them it formed one enormous patch covering her entire back and ass.

He sucked in his breath, and kept clicking. An enormous patch of inflamed skin covered in white lesions, from her hairline to her shoulders, coated an otherwise beautiful woman. He clicked on the next picture. *A distinct, thick round yellow crust over a circular lump of skin.* He read the blurb beside it.

As the photos show, plaque psoriasis is an unpleasant condition. Unfortunately, common misconceptions can make people with psoriasis feel isolated, unwelcome, and even ostracized. Anyone can develop psoriasis, but it is not spread from person to person.

Awareness and visibility are important for bringing psoriasis into the public eye. Do your part by sharing this slideshow with friends and family. Together we can help encourage research, advocacy, and a world that is more welcoming to people with psoriasis—no matter what it looks like.

One more site caught his eye, and it was the one that scared him the most. "Beautiful and vibrant woman takes her own life because she couldn't live with Psoriasis," he read out loud.

He closed the website and slowly lowered the lid of his laptop.

"Mika," he said to the darkened room. "I won't ever let you feel ostracized or let you isolate yourself." *I become a monster.* Her hushed words carved through his heart. No wonder she thought no one would want to make love to her. He opened the patio door and looked over the water. *People like you are lucky. People don't stare at you, sickened by what they see.*

He ran a slow hand through his hair. It all made sense now. Why she wore the baggy clothes and covered herself. The reason she didn't want to get in the hot tub the night of his birthday. Was it fair that he'd orchestrated the plan to keep Ben away from her? It was the same reason he'd kept Wyatt away from her.

The same reason he'd closed his escort business. Of course she didn't know he didn't accept clients any longer. She assumed, incorrectly, that his business meetings were with women.

Cain stared up into the heavens. The stars brilliant. Could he actually step back and bite the bullet the next time some asshole came sniffing around her?

Chapter Sixteen

Every Saturday morning he ventured over to have coffee with Mika, and every Saturday he pulled her injection from the fridge. She'd say he didn't have to help, but he did.

They ran five times a week before dinner and jogged the trails with Breeze panting alongside them.

"Gotta stop," she said and flopped down on a large rock.

She seemed more out of breath than usual. Wasn't that one of the side effects? Maybe she should see a doctor. Mika yanked the bottle of water from her belt and drank it down in gulps.

"I've made a decision," she said once her heavy breathing receded.

"About Greece?"

"No, I can't afford to go to Greece. About running the Victoria Goodlife half marathon."

He smiled at her. "You're doing eleven now, you'd have to work up to twenty-one."

"I can do it."

That's all it took for him to commit to her, and each day he pushed her harder. He took her sharp retorts and every colorful word she threw at him, but he kept pushing.

Two weeks later, and up to fifteen kilometers, she tripped, landing face first in the sand. He lay beside her, looking up at the sky, and grinned until she stopped swearing at him and herself. She rolled over and they both looked into the heavens.

"One minute," he warned, and she blew out her breath. "By the way, I hope you got your vacation time planned with your boss."

She rolled her head to stare at him. "I told you, I can't afford it. We're not all hookers, ya know."

He spit out a laugh. "I've got your ticket already, so pack your things. We leave next Saturday. Do you have a carrying case for the biologics? You have to keep them cold."

"You expect me to just wing my way to Greece with you?"

He rolled onto his side, and she did the same. "Yup, I need my best friend with me when I tell my dad I'm his biological son."

She sat bolt upright. "You knew?"

"I had the test done the last time I was in Greece. Stole Dad's toothbrush. I wanted to know for certain even though I was pretty sure."

"Why didn't you tell him?"

"I knew there was a time and a place. Maybe now is the time."

"And what if he refuses the truth? You have to be ready for that. If he's as much of a jerk as you say he is, he might."

"I'm prepared for that. My conscience is clean." At least about that, he thought.

251

She rolled to her knees and gave him an odd look. "You,"—she pointed a finger at him—"Most definitely don't have a clean conscience. Have you forgotten what you do for a living?" Standing, she brushed the sand from her clothes.

She reached out to him, but instead of letting her pull him up, he yanked her down, and she landed on him with a *thunk*. Sitting up, she straddled his hips, and he allowed himself to accept that his fair lady and friend was completely and utterly out of this world desirable.

What he felt for her had always been there, but he'd placed a wall between his lust and her innocence. His blood boiled and his shaft pulsed. The crown of her mons nudged against his hardening need. It had been five months since he'd taken a client in his escort capacity. All his energy had been poured into the charity website.

He placed a hand on each of her shoulders. "Come with me."

She pressed her lips together as she often did when she considered things. "What about Breeze? I don't want to leave her in a kennel."

"I have a sitter."

He just had to make damn sure their paths didn't cross, because Mika would put two and two together when she saw Sofia. He wanted to tell her what he'd done that night, but once he'd learned about the psoriasis, and he'd done a lot of research since then, he knew stress was extremely bad for someone with

252

her condition. That's the excuse he'd used, but he'd hid behind it because his feelings were growing in leaps and bounds for the little lady sitting on his damn crotch giving him the hard-on of the century.

"Okay," she said.

He sat up, and she shimmied off him. They both jumped to their feet. "Really?"

"Psst, I've always wanted to visit Greece. It's my heritage, too. Least half of it. We can overdose on souvlaki," she said, grinning from ear to ear. "My credit card is going to take a hit, but it's worth it."

"You can leave your cards at home, and you're still in training. We run every day while we're there. And, it's going to be harder because it's nothing but hills."

"I hate hills," she complained.

He glanced at his watch. "Stop stalling or I'll be smacking your ass."

She pranced away from him. "Hey, guess what?"

He gave her a raised brow. "Since I started all the torturous running, I've lost thirty-five pounds." She lifted her arms and did a twirl.

"I've noticed," he said under his breath and cleared his throat. "Let's finish this run." She trotted beside him. "Faster."

She picked up the pace, determination on her brow. He pulled ahead, and she kept up. They finished the last five

253

kilometers in record time. She bowed at the middle when they got back to the house, then flopped down on the grass. Breeze lay down beside her and panted, drops of water dripping from her tongue because she beat them home and slurped her dish empty.

"You have a passport, right?"

Her head sprang up. "No." She curled around onto her knees. "There's no way I can get one that quick."

"Call in sick tomorrow morning, and we'll go down and drop off the paperwork and get a picture on the way."

"You're gonna get me fired."

He didn't respond because buried deep inside him, he wished she would, and he'd be right there to take care of her.

****

The knock on her door had her flying into overdrive. She'd woken up late because she'd stayed up late last night. It was Sarah's birthday party, and the girls had gone out to celebrate downtown. Thank God, she'd almost finished packing before she left, and just had to add her toiletries. Her hair was still wet, but that was tough.

"You ready?" Cain called out.

Did that man not understand the Landlord-Tenant thing about privacy?

"Just about," she yelled back, flipping the top shut on her suitcase and zipping it closed. She jumped into her black pumps and rolled her case into the living room.

"You slept in," he stated, taking the case from her and heading for the door.

"Sorry. It's okay, we still have time."

His car was about the sexiest thing on the planet, and it always smelled so darn good, with a mix of his fancy aftershave and leather. Cain hopped in beside her.

"I know it's the crack of dawn, but we have to make the connector in Vancouver, and this was the only flight."

She saw a car parked in front of his place. "Is that the dog sitter?"

"Yup," he said, snapping on his seat belt and shoving the stick into first gear.

"Wait," she yelled out. He slammed on the breaks when they were beside his house.

"What?" he said startled.

She jumped out. "I gotta pee. I'll never make it." She ran for the front door and he lunged, choking himself on his seatbelt.

"Shit. No, Mika, we'll stop on the way." He chased her and almost bowled her over when he rushed in to see Sofia and Mika face to face.

"Hi," Mika said weakly.

"Hiya. Nice to meet you, this time," Sofia stretched out her hand. Mika just stared at the other woman. "You're the sitter?"

Sofia's long blonde hair swayed as she bobbed her head. "Friend, sitter, you know, you know." She gave him a wink, and he wanted to die right there. "By the way, that guy, Ben—he was an asshole. You were right to dump him there and then."

Mika stared, her mouth open a little. "Yeah," she breathed. "I just have to use the bathroom." She bulleted from the room, and Sofia watched her go, then her eyes narrowed.

"You didn't tell her, what you did, did you?"

He stretched his neck, considering what would happened next.

"Now, you're getting on a long haul flight to Greece with her?"

He closed his eyes and breathed out a sigh. Mika stepped carefully into the room and skirted the edge with a wary expression.

"Have a good time," Sofia said and darted a look between them.

Mika bolted out the front door, and he felt the cold wind that followed her. "See ya, Sof."

"Good luck," she sang out.

Mika stood with her hand on the top of the car, staring at the roof. He rounded it like a big chicken, as if the car could protect him. "I'll explain everything on the way."

She looked left then right, but not at him.

"I promise you, I had good intentions."

She cracked the door slowly and got in. Without a word, she pulled the belt across her body and shoved it into the latch.

He wasn't sure talking right now was a good idea, but neither was saying nothing and letting her mind go in all sorts of wrong directions.

"Sofia is a friend of mine. We've known each other for a few years."

"If she's your girlfriend, why isn't she going to Greece with you?" Mika crossed her legs and stared straight ahead.

"Not my girlfriend. Not in the sense that she and I have ever been involved. I helped her a long time ago. We became professional peers, you might say."

"She's a prostitute?" Mika stammered.

He nodded. "Yes. A very well-paid escort."

He drove out to the roadway and turned left toward the airport located in Sidney.

"She was with you that night? That was your business meeting?"

"No, Mika, I called her when you left on your date."

Mika's eyes rounded with questions when she looked at him.

"Listen, I…I called her to…to…" He gripped the steering wheel tightly and blurted out, "I didn't want him to take you home. I asked Sofia to intervene, hoping he'd do exactly what he did, and you'd see he wasn't worth your time."

He squinted, waiting for her to go nuts on him, and he'd deserve every nasty word she threw his way.

257

His heart raced. She didn't say anything, but her warm, soft fingers covered his, and she gave him a squeeze, then placed her hand back in her lap. Call him gutless, but he was afraid to look at her. He wasn't certain if she was so angry she couldn't talk or whether she understood.

Within twenty minutes he pulled into the airport. She got out. He rounded the car and snagged her in his arms. "Are you mad at me?"

Her big eyes gazed up at him from beneath her curls. "No."

He pulled her tighter. "I didn't do it to hurt you. I wanted to save you from hurt."

"I get that," she said. "I hope Ben learned a lesson when she told him what her fee was, whatever it is."

"She left as soon as I had you safely out of there."

Mika gave him a smirk. "Just meant another night with the battery operated boyfriend. No big deal."

He sucked the air in through his teeth. "About that...umm, you're kidding when you say that, right?"

Mika didn't answer him. She nudged him to retrieve her bags. After wrestling her overweight luggage and his smaller case out of the trunk, they walked all the way into the terminal.

Just as they were stepping into the First Class lineup, she answered his question. "No."

"Your passports, please. Oh, Mr. Sallas, nice to see you again," the attendant said, flicking a glance at Mika.

"Good Morning, Angela," he growled.

The last straw. The last camel, and his resistance broke.

No more B.O.B. No more fucking around. Three plane rides. One boat ride, and Mika was about to find out what he'd been suppressing for months. He was taking her home. Taking her back to the starting line. Back to the place where he'd taken the wrong turn in his life. Their paths had crossed for a reason. She had refused love because she saw herself as damaged on the outside. He had abused himself until he was damaged on the inside. Mika and Cain were going to start again.

****

Thirty hours later, he heard her say "Wooow!" for the fiftieth time. The first time was getting off the plane in Athens. Then a few times on the ferry ride to his parents' small, picturesque island. When they arrived at his family's massive estate, her eyes nearly popped out, and she said it over and over again as he led her through the villa to her room.

"Jaw dropping beautiful," she murmured. "Greece is amazing. I love the smell of the sea and the scent of the flowers. There are flowers blooming everywhere," she gushed.

But the biggest wow came when he opened the door to the suite. She wandered in, trying to see everything at once. White stucco walls and high arched ceilings graced the guest room. There were no windows, only passages onto a large patio with vines dripping from the railings and a view that went on for miles across a crystalline sea. The breeze wrapped invisible arms of warmth around him, sweeping intoxicating thoughts into his mind, while she seemed overly enamored by the thick, chunky furniture cluttering the room and a massive king bed sitting in an alcove.

The maid, who had greeted them when they arrived, said his parents were on the mainland, and would be back tomorrow night.

"When is your brother getting here?" she called out, still staring out at the sea from the balcony.

He joined her and took a steadying breath. "Later on today. He'll be here for dinner."

"Is he bringing anyone with him?"

"Probably. Whatever his current flavor is."

"That's not nice."

"True, though."

She turned and leaned against the half wall, staring at him with a thoughtful expression. "I can't believe I'm here."

The wind played with her hair, her warm, expressive features smiling at him. He gripped the ledge, trapping her within his arms.

"Yes, you are. With me," he said in hushed words. "Do you know why?" He wound his hand to the back of her neck, her silky curls tickling his fingers.

"To tell your dad you're his son?" Her expression creased with confusion.

"That might be one reason, but not the one that matters."

She smiled. "That's pretty important."

Cain shook his head. "I wanted to bring us both home. Your heritage. My birth place. I wanted to be here when I tell you, I've looked in your eyes at least a thousand times, and every time I've kissed you with my gaze." Her chest rose with a deep inhale. "I can't live with the thought that one day someone will take you away from me, Mika." He pressed closer, leaving only a sliver width between them.

Her eyes widened with surprise.

Cain's heart thundered as he brushed her mouth with a gentle kiss. His tongue teased her lips until she responded, and his world teetered with her acceptance. Her kiss was hungry and deep, not like a scared rabbit the night of his birthday. When her arms snaked around his neck, he poured every ounce of his experience into the moment. Finally, they both needed air, and parted.

"Okay," she whispered looking down. "Okay, that was stupid."

"Why?" He buried his face in her hair, loving the silky curls.

She squirmed to get away from him, and he reluctantly let her go. "It's not your birthday…I…I think you better go to your room."

A small twitch at the side of his mouth made her take another step back.

"I am in my room."

He reached for the button on his shirt, and she took another step back. With each button he released, he took a step forward and she took one backwards, until the bed stopped her retreat. Exactly where he wanted her.

<u>Chapter Seventeen</u>

"What are you doing?"

Cain stripped his shirt from his shoulders and noted a flash of raw hunger lit Mika's eyes. With a toss, his shirt landed on the bench at the foot of the king size canopy bed.

"Calling your bluff," he answered and released the button on his jeans, but kept them on—for now. "I seem to recall you saying I don't affect you."

She didn't blink, her expression stunned.

All her fears stood in the way of their bliss. He'd have to talk his way through each hurdle.

"Mika, you told me you had a small window of opportunity, and that's why you accepted a date with Ben. You're worth so much more than a one-night stand. If someone is going to give you pleasure, it's going to be me."

"I...I can't do that." Her eyes grew wider as they skittered a look across the bed, then back at him.

Mika seemed genuinely surprised. "Why not?"

"I think it's pretty obvious, Cain. You're an escort." He advanced and she sat with a plop on the bed, her face flushed.

He chuckled. "Sweetheart, I haven't seen a client in months."

"What?" she squeaked? "But your business meetings—"

"Were for the web-based business. Soon after you moved in, I realized I needed to focus my efforts on something real, and I resurrected the idea for an organization I'd created over two years ago. I've been working non-stop to bring things together. The trips I've taken were to meet with philanthropists interested in buying the website."

She huffed. "So, you're in a dry spell. I'm sure you'll get a request soon."

Mika looked like she was going to scramble away, and he leaned closer. She, in turn, leaned back.

"Can't request what isn't there. My other business site is permanently closed." With a light touch, he followed the contour of her cheek. "Now, let's discuss B.O.B," he teased, wanting her to calm down.

She sputtered. "Let's not."

Mika tried to sweep his hand from her face, but he hooked their fingers together. "I bet you brought one with you." Her eyes swung to her suitcase.

Busted.

"From this point onward, the only time B.O.B will make an appearance is when he's in my hand, and believe me, I'm going to use it on you."

A little whimper erupted from her, and she shook her head.

He lowered his chin. "But that will come later. First, and most importantly, is making love to you, and when you come,

I'm going to be deep inside you. Watch you come undone in my arms."

Her pretty lips parted for a second then snapped shut. "Listen, sleeping in the same room is not a good idea. I'm sure in a house this large there's another room. I'll go find one."

"I don't want you to find another room."

"Stop kidding around." She quickly got to her feet and unzipped her suitcase. "I need a refrigerator. Can I put this downstairs?" she asked with a nervous flutter in her voice as she pulled her injections from the case.

Taking the carrier bag from her, he walked to the bar and placed it inside the mini fridge. For a second, he considered plying her with alcohol to soothe her nerves. Nope. He wanted her clearheaded. This wasn't just about sex.

He retraced his steps, and stopped within reaching distance of the woman he loved. "We're staying in this room—together."

Her head shook emphatically. "I don't expect you to understand, but you of all people...I just can't." Mika inhaled a shaky breath. "I was drunk the night of your birthday party." She palmed her hands as if praying. "Loose lips. Stupid dreams."

Cain's gut tumbled with excitement. "Dreams of what?"

"Nothing."

She gripped the handle of the suitcase and swept it off of the bench. In a hurry, she forgot it was open. The contents spilled to the tiled floor and she swore, stooping and hurriedly tried to stuff everything back inside.

He bent to his haunches to help her, but when she tried to zip it shut, he stilled her shaking fingers. "Do you know what happens when two people have the same dream?"

She bowed her head, unwilling to share.

"Do you have any feelings at all for me?" he asked.

"Of course I do," she said, sweeping a strand of hair behind her ear. "Who wouldn't? Better yet, who hasn't, but—" She looked up and bit her bottom lip. "Let's just change and go to the beach, okay?"

Palming her arms, he drew her up. "You said you loved me."

"I do. As a friend!"

He paused and smiled. "Look me in the eyes and tell me what you feel is one-hundred percent platonic. Because I can't look at you and say the same thing. It would be the biggest lie I'd ever uttered."

"You're going to give me a heart attack." She blew out a breath and offered him a nervous smile. "You'd feel bad if I died. You'd have to ship me home in a cypress box, and think about all that paperwork." She plucked a shirt and a pair of white pants from the case.

He tugged the clothes from her grip and dropped them on the bench. "Mika, please stop. I don't care about your scars." Slipping his fingers to the top of her blouse, he freed the top

266

button. "Why do you think I called Sof that night? I couldn't let Ben touch you." Another button came free, and then another.

"Why are you undressing me?"

He grinned. "Because I'm going kiss every square inch of your gorgeous body."

Her words choked in her throat before she said, "Seriously, why do you want to ruin everything?"

"Not ruining anything." He smiled. "I'm admitting that your sister was right."

Her pretty eyes widened with total shock and she barked out a laugh. "Are you high?"

None of her wit or sharp words would deter him. "You're the one and only woman in my life, Mika."

With slow, practiced movements, he brushed the fabric of her open blouse aside. Distracting her with a kiss, he slipped the shirt from her shoulders. It was quite possible *he* was going to have the heart attack. With a flick of his fingers, her bra came undone, and a little moan escaped her throat. Her fists clenched, and he paused. If he stopped now, she'd think it was doubt and never trust him.

Keeping her locked in his gaze, he peeled the bra straps from her shoulders. "What we have, I cherish, but I want more." Grazing her nipple with his thumb, her sweet lips parted.

Mika's eyes snapped shut.

Cain slid his hands down her sides to her hips and drew her pants to her ankles, appreciating the firm tone and curves of her long legs on the way down.

Before he rose, he tipped his head back. Her breasts rose and fell with heavy breaths. "Do you have any idea how often I've wanted to make you come."

Mika licked her lips and shook her head. He placed a gentle kiss and a slow tantalizing lick across her shaved mound. His heart spiked, wanting to grip her ass and devour her, but he exhaled and rose.

Face to face, he threaded his fingers through her thick hair and teased her with his mouth. "Easy," he breathed on her lips.

"This…this is not easy," she said, pinning her arms to her sides.

Gripping her wrists, he coaxed her hands to lay on his chest. "Touch me." His words sounded more like a plea than a command. With her eyes closed, she shook her head like a petulant child. "Mika, I want this. I want us." Now his voice held a tremor, too. "Please."

Her eyes slowly opened. Releasing Mika's hands, he captured her sweet face between his palms.

"I need you to understand."

She tilted her head, her gaze zig-zagging across his face.

"Can you imagine what it was like fucking all those women? Money fed their desires. I fed their lust, and they drained me. When I realized I'd walled myself inside an empty wasteland of sex, I was already lost." He pursed his lips for a moment, considering his words. "I was bitter. Hated myself. And then you arrived at my door. You didn't want anything from me but friendship."

Her brow creased with concern. "I still do, but you want to ruin everything."

"You ruined my dog."

A curl of a smile lifted her lips.

"As much as I hate what I was, I love what I am with you. *'Mika is mine.'* That's what I said when I watched you leave with Ben." He swept a strand of hair from her cheek. "You were never supposed to find out about the donation for the healthcare facility. I feared you'd think I was doing to you, what all those women did to me, buying your love."

Her palms slowly slid down his chest, and his pulse beat faster.

"I never thought that. But Cain, I'm not Jen, I can't have random sex with you and then pretend it never happened."

"You were willing to spend the night with Ben." His temper spiraled just thinking of another man touching her.

Her brow creased, but she smiled. "Because he meant nothing to me."

"Do I mean something to you?"

She swallowed thickly. "I'm standing completely naked in front of you. What do you think?"

His thumb turned gentle circles on her cheek. "I think you're afraid to admit you love me." Her brow crunched together. "How many men have touched you, Mika?"

"Intimately—one," she said, barely above a whisper.

There was so much more, and he spoke what he thought were her fears. "And because he was a shallow man, he only saw the surface, but he wounded you. You erected walls of humor and a fiery tongue. A warm smile and high gates with a sign reading, *you'll only find a friend behind these bars I protect myself with.*"

A tear formed in her eye, swimming against the rim, then escaping down her lash.

"You watch your friends who are deeply in love, and I see the joy, but I've seen the longing, too. With your fingers wrapped tightly around those bars, peering through them, you think you'll never have what they have."

A gust of anguish, propelled by the truth, released from deep within her. Her lips parted but the flippant remark, the fiery comeback died before given breath, because he saw through her ruse and once bared—her hiding place revealed, she had no choice but to face him. Like her tears, her fears had to surface in order to wash them away.

"Unfurl your fingers, and step away from your prison, Mika. I want you to let me in."

"I don't have any experience in bed. You're just going to be disappointed," she spouted.

He crouched, placing his hands on the back of her toned thighs and hitched her up to his hips. She clung to him as he laid her on the bed. Beautiful brown eyes gazed up at him.

"Take a deep breath, and when you let it go, you're going to release every doubt." He trailed kisses down her soft neck and closed his eyes when he twirled his tongue around her taut nipple. Mika's hands flew to the waistband of his pants and curled the fabric in her fingers. "Take them off, baby."

She hesitated and his heart shuddered to a stop when she released her grip.

One misgiving or sign of hesitation, and she'd back into the corner from which she'd just risen. His hand glided down her outer thigh. He bent to kiss her naval, her hip, and then her knee. He put his gaze on her lower leg, the discolored patches of skin covering her shins. Mika instantly placed one leg over the other.

"Shhh, it's nothing." He kissed her all the way down to her toes.

"This is a bad idea." She sat bolt upright. "I'm going to get dressed."

He placed his hands on either side of her hips and hovered inches away from her lips. His pulse leaped and doubt bit at his intentions. He closed his eyes with her refusal stilling his heart.

"You're the only person who's ever made me feel like I was worth something. I wanted—" He shook his head. "This isn't

271

about your scars—it's about what I used to be, isn't it?" He needed the truth as well, and if this was hers, he had to accept it.

"No, it's not," she said harshly. "Look." She stuck her legs straight out and pointed, then shimmied off the bed, turning her back to him.

Small and large circular discolorations covered her back, her ass, and around her legs. A large, oblong patch went from hip to hip in the sensual sway of her back. He saw them all, but at the same time he didn't.

"All I see is a beautiful woman," he said and dropped his gaze. "The scars will fade with time, but nothing will change what I was." He swallowed thickly and sat on the edge of the bed. "I understand, Mika. My brother said no woman in her right mind could trust someone like me. Even if I believed him, my heart didn't want to listen."

She kneeled on the floor between his legs and stared up at him. His brow tightened, twisting a dark brunette curl around his finger.

"Cain, you are an incredible man. I'm the reject. Ugly and inexperienced. That's the damn truth." She shook her head. "You're…you're 007 and I'm Young Frankenstein."

"Oh my, God, woman." He palmed her face. "You are Aphrodite, Athena, and Mary Poppins all rolled into one beautiful human being." He kissed her hard, wanting to incinerate every critical word she'd ever heard. "If the only thing you're scared of is what I think when I look at you, then you need to know I've never desired a woman more."

She gazed at him for the longest time. "You really believe that, don't you?"

"Yes," is said emphatically.

When her fingers traced the muscles on his bare chest, his blood sparked and so did his heart. Without his prodding, she touched him.

Quietly, she said, "The last time I was with someone, it was a disaster."

"Did he hurt you? I mean physically."

A flush radiated across her cheeks. "I don't really remember. I mean, I was drunk, and I felt some pressure, and then he...he saw my P. It was bad at the time, and he freaked out, and that was that."

His thoughts settled on an idea, suppressing his rampaging desire for a moment. "Mika, you felt pressure, but no pain?"

"I don't remember any."

Holy shit, it couldn't be, but maybe—"What kind of vibrator do you use?"

"Have you no shame at all?" she squeaked.

Happiness overwhelmed him. Was he about to become the luckiest sonofabitch alive? "Mika, do you insert your toy?"

She flushed red from her forehead to her chest. "No, it's, it's uncomfortable, I just..."

He kissed her, probing her sweet mouth. "Sweetheart, there shouldn't be any discomfort. Have you never talked about this with the girls?"

She shook her head. "They go on and on about sex. They all love it." Mika cleared her throat. "Inserting—hurt, so I bought this little—God, this is embarrassing. Why am I talking about this with you?"

He raised a brow at her. "You stimulate your clit, and that's how you orgasm."

Mika's palms slid down his forearms. "Do you think there's something wrong with me?"

"No, baby, there isn't, but it's going to be a little uncomfortable for a couple seconds." Cain stood up and grinned.

She narrowed an eye at him and stood. "What?"

Biting on his bottom lip, he gently coaxed her hand against his erection. "These jeans are getting extremely uncomfortable, sweetheart. Would you mind taking them off?"

Mika rolled her eyes. "You're enjoying this, aren't you?"

Slipping his hand to the back of her neck, he said, "Definitely." Her breasts brushed against his chest when he kissed her. True pleasure made him groan as she released his zipper. Crouching, she slid his pants to the tile floor. God love her, when faced with his aching, stiff cock, she didn't look away from his eyes.

Cain sat on the bed and shifted backwards. "Join me."

"We're naked."

He grinned. "Yes, we are." He paused. "I know you hate your scars, but I'm proud of what you've accomplished. Your body is taut, sexy and perfect. I want you to feel comfortable like this with me. Because, baby, I love looking at you."

Mika eyed him from beneath her bangs, then straddled his legs. He couldn't resist, and circled her breast, sucking gently. Her nipple stiffened beneath his tongue and her fingers squeezed his shoulders.

A little gasp escaped her mouth and his heart soared.

Supporting her body, he rolled her onto her back. "Will you trust me with your innocence?"

Her chest rose and fell with shallow breaths. "You really want this, don't you?"

She sounded so surprised, it made him chuckle. He had a thousand yesses lined up, but it'd take too long to say them all. "Not just want—so much more than that."

Her finger traced his jaw. "You make me feel—sexy, but I know I'm flawed at the same time."

The pout of her lips drove him to lean forward and follow the pillowy outline with his tongue. He kissed her, nibbling on her softness.

"Unique, sweetheart. Not flawed. The scars are part of you, but I want all of you." Being a professional in the trade didn't mean he could subdue nature. His control was slipping fast. "*Agapi mou.*"

Natasza Waters

"Did you just moo at me?" Her brows rose.

He rubbed his cheek against the enticing curve of her breast. Molding his hands to her thighs, he urged them open. "No, it's Greek," he said, gazing up the length of her body.

He'd let her search out the meaning and lowered his mouth to her sweet sex.

Sliding his tongue slowly across her moist slit, his erection ached to be inside her. With rhythmic strokes of his tongue, her passion grew before his eyes.

"Oh my God," she cried out, her hips rising from the bed with his ministrations.

The alphabet was an old technique he'd used for years, and she loved the "I," when his tongue teased the entrance to her core. With "T" her body melted, the cross made with the pad of his thumb and a stroke of his tongue. "O" made her stomach tremble when his mouth covered her nub, and sucked with quick little pulses until her fingers twisted the bed cover into a ball.

He leaned over her body. Against the Egyptian sheets, her rich, dark curls surrounded her head. Grinning down at her, he kissed her nose and then her mouth.

"You don't have to be experienced, Mika." Her labia wet with desire, he slid his shaft against her folds, gently rolling his hips. "You are all I need, and we're going to savor every second."

"You come well-equipped for your profession," she whispered, her eyes glinting with flickers of mirth between little gasps of desire.

A hearty laugh burst from his mouth. Tipping his forehead to hers, he loved that they laughed in each other's arms. "My cock is yours, my fair lady. No one else's."

Rotating his hips, her moisture covered his throbbing head. Friends first, now lovers. The way it was supposed to be.

The embers died a little in her gaze. "You'd tell me the truth, right?"

He nodded. "I will."

Her one eye narrowed. "Is this pro bono work or should I say, pro boner?"

His shoulders shook with laughter. The desire didn't die, it strengthened, knowing her first lover would be him.

Still a little nervous, she said, "Does this mean you accept my request form?"

Laying on his side near her hip, he thumbed circles around her bundle of nerves, barely touching, creating a fire of need inside her. "Tossed them all out, except yours."

There was something so fucking erotic about this moment. Cain licked his lips, gazing at her firm, flat stomach and sexy naval. The more he strummed her pretty clit, the wetter she became.

Natasza Waters

Quick little gasps escaped her mouth. "Oh, God this is torture."

"Making love isn't a sprint, it's a dance," he said, shifting between her thighs and leaned forward. He teased the tip of her breast with his tongue. Lifting his head, he gazed into her incredible eyes. "And I've been waiting all my life to dance with you."

"Have you taken someone's virginity before or were they all amazing lovers?"

He grinned with understanding. She was throwing up diversions left and right. He wished he could tell her he hadn't, but there wasn't much he hadn't done in bed. He brushed her nose, giving her the time she obviously needed.

"I was hired a couple times to do that." She smiled meekly at him. And he understood. Just as he would be her first, she wanted to mean something to him. "There's a difference, Mika." Touching her tenderly, he signaled to her subconscious she was safe in his hands. "I want to swallow your gasp when I enter you. Every beautiful thrust will bring us closer. I'm going to treasure the moment you come with me. I haven't done that with anyone." The fear receded in her eyes, replaced with a lick of desire.

Speaking to her in calming tones, he toyed with her clit and gently probed the entrance to her channel. Plenty of myths surrounded the tissue known as the hymen. He wanted to make this as pleasant and easy as possible for Mika. He kissed a trail

278

down the middle of her body, ending at her mons, sucking the sensitive tip gently. Teasing the delicate nerves, her thighs relaxed.

"I want," she whispered shyly.

"I know, baby," he whispered back, kissing her deeply. Desire swarmed through his body.

With little fanfare, he retrieved the condom from the bedside table. He was safe, but until he could explain what she truly meant to him, he'd wear the damn thing.

Relaxed, wet, his touch prepared her.

They stared into each other's eyes and she smiled. "Sweet, Mika. I love you so much."

With one quick, deep thrust, Cain swallowed her gasp of pain.

He kissed her again and again. It was torture not powering into her warmth, allowing her time to become accustomed to him. His heart bloomed when her arms circled his neck.

"Stings." She blinked back a tear. "Just kiss me."

"Sweetheart, I'm going to kiss you for the rest of your life."

Slowly, carefully, he began to rock his hips, teasing her pearl with his thumb.

"That feels…." She sighed and her eyes opened. "Full."

Oh God help him, she was so fucking tight, he was going to lose it, and withdrew from her heat. He rolled them over and positioned her on top, tucking his arms behind his head, and gazed up at her.

"Explore, Mika." Suddenly, she looked a little fearful. "No, no." He drew her down and soothed her worry with a tender kiss. "Touch. Taste. The worst is over." He palmed her breast, rolling the pebbled berry with his fingers.

Curiosity replaced trepidation. Her hands trailed down his body. Along his sides, she turned her fingernails into teasing little weapons, and a wicked smile broke out on her face.

"Yes, I'm ticklish."

Her eyes twinkled, and his heart exploded with warmth. Leaning over, she pressed her mouth to his. "You're all mine," she whispered with a tone of disbelief.

"Completely." Her thick curls fell around him, and his fingers threaded themselves within the silky nest.

"This feels so wicked, and hot, and crazy."

He grinned up at her. "Are you going to make me come?" he asked, trying to keep his control when she straightened, straddling his hips.

Before him was the image he'd always remember. The gentle curves of her body, her taut stomach and smooth, olive skin, mesmerized him. Rising on her knees, she swayed her hips and lifted her hair to the top of her head. *Oh, fucking hell, she was incredible.* His shaft strained with her moist clit feathering across his crown. Mika's gaze deepened, the laughter gone.

"Show me, Cain. Show me what it's like to be loved."

"Oh, shit, Mika."

It was like dropping ten floors in an elevator without brakes when her hot, wet core slid over his shaft. Love trampled over lust. His passion raw, wild, and hungry.

A torturous game ensued. So much love. So pure. He stroked slowly at first, reading her body, watching her unravel in his hands. Deep inside her, so fucking deep, his cock swelled, his body taut.

"Cain!"

His eyes slammed shut, every thrust a spike of ecstasy. "Jesus, you feel so good, baby."

Their palms slapped together. Fingers forking. Her inner muscles milked his cock. He pistoned into her moist heat. The sounds—fuck, the sound of her wetness as he plunged from root to tip—drove him insane.

She came apart, her head rolling back, exposing her graceful neck, and he followed her into the beautiful plane of release.

It took a few seconds to come back down to earth, and then he was all over her, kissing her madly, smothering her as she lay panting, her body languid and her arms stretched out.

"No wonder they're all nymphomaniacs," she said, breathlessly.

He trapped her thighs with his leg and went for her neck, getting in a little revenge tickle.

Natasza Waters

She squeaked and slapped him away playfully. Grasping her jaw, he left one more enduring kiss on her inflamed lips. "*Omorfi*," he murmured, tracing her mouth with the tip of his tongue.

"What does that mean?"

"Beautiful," he explained. "Tonight after we ditch my brother, I'm going to make love to you till the sun rises again."

"Beach?" she asked.

"Hey?" His head lifted with a jerk.

"What?" She shrugged with an impish look. "I had you. It was okay, I suppoooose," she drawled.

With a heave, he turned her over and swatted her ass. She shrieked and tried to wiggle away, but he had her nailed down, and her bare ass was just too sweet not to bite.

"Y'ouch!" she screeched.

When he soothed the nip with his hand and added a kiss, she mumbled into the bed sheets. "What was that?" he asked.

She lifted her head because it was the only thing she could move. "I said!" she yelled. "You weren't half bad." And laughed her fool head off.

The smack echoed in the room, and another screech followed.

"All right, all right, geez."

He curled her into his arms and saw the glint of tears in her eyes. "Aw, sweetheart," he crooned.

"That smarted."

282

She gave him a huge boo-boo lip, and he sucked on it gently and caressed her soft ass.

"Should we head down to the beach and take a walk?" he suggested.

"I need coffee," she said, then sighed, relaxing against his chest.

He lay back against the pillow, holding her tight. He wasn't ready to let go. "How about a power snooze?"

She purred her assent like a satisfied kitten.

Cain waited until she drifted off before he strolled to the bathroom and removed the condom. Returning with a warm, wet hand towel, he gently cleaned her. She sighed with relief and snuggled into him. As he folded the towel he paused, seeing the blood. For him, sex had filled his bank account and quenched a layer of lust, until now. This moment seemed almost biblical.

Cain placed the cloth on the table and kissed her forehead. A warm and languid sensation kept him close to Mika. He closed his eyes. "Thank you for being brave," he whispered.

She nuzzled his cheek. "I'm happy."

No matter how close she was, she wasn't close enough. "So am I."

He plucked his phone from the side table and set the alarm for an hour. Mika had drifted off again, and his eyes drooped with sated exhaustion. Those delicious breasts of hers pressed against his chest, gave his cock a reason to rise again. With the lightest touch, his thumb swept the tip of her nipple. Small pebbles of need formed across her soft, tawny areola and the berry-colored tip puckered.

A sublime smile pulled at her lips. "What are you doing?"

His arms wrapped protectively around her. "You're a healing balm to a dying man."

Her lids flashed open. "What?"

"Little by little, I died with each client. I almost lost something, something that belongs to you, Mika." Her leg caressed his shin, then she draped her sexy thigh across his hip.

"What belongs to me?"

Instead of answering, he reached for his iPhone, selected a song and hit play. Mika's eyes remained closed, but her smile stretched her lovely lips, and he kissed her back to sleep as John Legend sang "*All of Me.*"

Chapter Eighteen

Cain tried to convince her to wear her bathing suit with just a throw to cover herself. She balked at the idea and reached for the one piece she'd bought the day they'd gone shopping together.

"Not that one. I bought you something else," he said, and turned with a piece of string hanging off his fingers.

"Are you nuts?" she squeaked. "That isn't a bikini, that's floss."

He snatched her one-piece and threw it across the room. She succumbed to the bikini, but put her lightweight white pants on, covering her legs.

His eyes simmered with heat when she tied the bikini strap around her neck. He bit the edge of his lip. "You can take this as gospel coming from a professional. You have the most fucking beautiful breasts I have ever seen."

"I do?"

"Let's get going because I have other ideas that might take precedence over a walk on the beach."

Cain held her hand as they strolled down the cobbled road toward the ocean. They passed through a small market with vendors selling beautiful pottery and handmade sandals. Slipping into a small coffee shop, they ordered two cappuccinos and spoke to the island residents. Actually, Cain spoke to them, and she adored listening to him. For some odd reason, he became ten times sexier being able to speak the language fluently.

A young woman with brightly colored blankets hanging from her cart beckoned them. Cain placed one of the hats the gal sold on Mika's head, a big floppy thing. His mouth spread into a huge, cheesy grin, as if he'd accomplished something grand. The warm breeze made her feel weightless, and Cain's arm around her shoulders, like she was someone special.

Fishermen worked on their boats down at the wharf, while kids played in the street, kicking a ball between each other. The crystal-clear azure water tempted her to run screaming like a little kid into the surf. They passed whitewashed buildings with bright blue shutters exactly like the pictures she'd seen.

"Let's walk that way. We'll eventually get to my parents' private beach, and then we can take the stairs up to the villa."

"Lead the way."

Children played in the water while beautiful young women sunbathed on the shore. A family, more than likely tourists, relaxed on a colorful blanket next to a sandcastle with an abandoned yellow pail and plastic shovel laying nearby.

As they strolled along the water's edge, she couldn't help but dart glances up at the man who walked beside her. He'd put on a white shirt that rippled in the wind and a pair of shorts. His dark, silky hair and a pair of shades covering his sensual eyes taunted her to yank him behind a rock and maul him to death. He caught her staring, and his perfect white teeth gleamed with a broad smile as he drew her into the crook of his arm. She'd never seen him smile so much.

"You're pretty proud of yourself, aren't you?" she teased.

He shrugged his shoulders and grinned. "Yes, I am."

"Because you took my virginity and made me scream like a crazy woman?"

Cain's head thrust backward with a laugh. "Something like that."

They reached a piece of pristine beach, the sand blistering white, and empty of inhabitants. Cain stopped, taking the bag from her shoulder she'd carried from the house. They laid out their beach blankets, weighing down the edges.

"Is this your parents' beach?"

He nodded.

They sat back to back and soaked in the sun. "This is paradise, isn't it?"

"It is now," he said.

"Why now?"

Cain laid her down. The tip of his finger traced her cheek. "We shouldn't have waited this long."

"Don't good things happen in their own time?"

He kissed her tenderly. "Maybe, but I don't think I could have waited another day." He brushed the tip of her nose. "Want to go swimming with me?"

Natasza Waters

Rolling to her knees, she unzipped her pants and wiggled out of them, while Cain tucked his shirt into the bag. As they stood, his phone beeped.

"Abel's here. They're settling in. I'll let him know where we are."

Before leaving the blanket, planning on a speedy run to the water because the sand was hot, he curled his hand around her waist and drew her in for a luxurious kiss. He had fast fingers, and she felt the strings at her neck come undone.

"It's a private beach," he growled into her ear.

She started to do it up again. "No way." But he had the rest undone and tossed the floss to the blanket.

"I want you to feel as irresistible as you are to me."

His gaze alone made her nipples pucker. She took a big, brave breath and didn't shy away. Cain's mouth was lethal when he kissed her, his tongue caressing, as if praising her. With gentle circles, his thumb teased her nipples. A moan erupted from his throat, and her thighs squeezed with a needy ache in her core.

He pulled away, leaving her breathless, then winked at her. He knew exactly what he was doing. "Sex might be old hat to you, having done it a million times, but I've only got one under my belt. Teasing me is evil."

Cain chuckled and slid his hands down her bare arms. "You need a little time, sweetheart. Believe me, if that hadn't been your first, we'd still be in bed." He kissed her, and her heart spiraled. "I promise, we will catch up."

288

Holding her hand, they waded into the warm water and she sighed, wanting to fall face first—so she did. She came up for air when Cain's arms wrapped around her from behind, and her core clenched as his hands cupped her breasts, and he whispered in her ear.

"Sorry, but I've wanted these in my hands for so long, I can't stop." He gently massaged them, and she felt his shaft harden against her ass. Before things got too out of hand, she turned and wrapped her thighs around his hips as he waded into deeper water. His kiss was mind-numbing, and he ended it by licking the saltwater from her neck, giving her goose bumps.

He slowly swayed her back and forth in the tranquil surf. "Tell me about your business."

"It's the past. I don't want to think about it anymore."

She grinned. "Not that one, the one you've been working on."

"Oh, yeah. Of course. It's an internet-based company that brings together charities and benefactors. While setting it up, I've been searching for philanthropists and families with healthy bank accounts, who can create a relationship with a charity of their choice."

"That's a fantastic idea. Hasn't anyone done that before?"

"Not like this. I hope I can sell the program to a group of individuals who will nurture and keep it growing for a minimum of thirty years. It's one of the stipulations. In the last few months, one organization in particular became a benefactor from all the investors. Kind of like the core that would always receive support."

"What is it? Does someone need help in your family?"

He leaned in and kissed her, licking the salty water from her lips. "No, but you're important to me. It's a research lab with the primary focus of finding a cure for psoriasis. Not a cream or an injection that will subdue it, but rather cure it."

Overwhelmed, her lips drew apart, but nothing came out.

"I expect to sell the company soon. Two of the largest benefactors have incredible wealth."

"Thhh…" She was lucky she got that much out, but tried again. "That's wonderful."

"Each year, I'm going to personally support the lab with ten million dollars."

"Be-be-because of me?"

Cain's brows came together in a curious smile. "Because I love you."

"You really do?" She covered her eyes. "Wait, no you can't."

"Are we doing this again?"

She was so shocked. "I'm overwhelmed. I'm grateful."

"I don't want you to suffer, or anyone with pso—"

She covered his lips and shook her head. "We, we just call it P."

He nodded. "Or anyone to have to deal with the shame and the pain of P."

She grabbed his hand and waded toward the shore. Reaching the blanket, she pointed. He sat as she plucked her suit top from the bag and paced while doing it up. Two steps turned into three, turned into four, and then she rounded back, kneeled in front of him, and forked her fingers through his.

"What we have isn't going to last." She squeezed his hands. "You don't understand. You've never seen it—"

"I have, Mika. I've been researching it ever since I figured out why you take Humira. It doesn't change anything."

"It does," she said sharply. "It changes everything. You have to believe me. We're on our first day of vacation in this beautiful place." Ruh-roh, the lump in her throat thickened, but she kept talking. "I don't want anything to ruin that. The same way I don't ever want to see disgust in your eyes, and I guarantee there will be." Tears threatened, but she held them back. "I will forever be your friend, but what won't be forever, is us." The salty tears streamed down her face, and she let them fall. "This time *you* have to be brave and promise me when the time comes, you'll walk away and not feel guilty."

Cain began to shake his head.

"Hey, look who I found."

She glanced up to see a man as handsome as Cain walking across the sand. Strolling beside him, all wiggling curves and blonde luscious hair, was one bombshell of a beauty in a string bikini.

"Gaaawd," she muttered under her breath, swiping the tears away.

Cain's brow rippled at her. "Told ya," he said, just as quietly, and then pushed to his feet, curling an arm around her waist. "Abel. Hey, man."

The brothers embraced each other, and added a manly pat on the back. Abel turned his dark, almost black eyes toward her. His complexion was swarthier than Cain's, but their features were very similar. "Welcome to Greece."

She held her hand out, and he came in for an unexpected hug. She kinda patted him on the arm, and he released her.

"This is Brandi," Abel said, introducing the luscious blonde.

"Hi, y'all," she greeted in an ultra-high pitched voice and waved her fingers. She swayed her ample hips toward Cain. "You're very handsome, too. Abel told me all about you." Her eyes slid up and down Cain like she was licking him with her tongue. Ugh.

"Hello, Brandi. This is my girlfriend, Mika."

"Oh, wow. What a cool name. Are you Greek?"

Mika pasted on a toothy half-smile. "Thanks. And, uh, no, I'm Canadian. My father was Greek."

"Oh, wow. I couldn't live in the snow all the time. You must be really outdoorsy. Baby, I'm going to go for a swim. It's so hot," Brandi said, fanning herself.

"Be there in a second," Abel answered.

When Brandi set off for the water, Abel raised a brow then shrugged good-naturedly. "What can I say?"

Cain's jaw grew taut. "Think I've seen turtles with higher IQs."

Mika slapped her hand over her mouth, but couldn't stop herself from laughing. Cain joined her, and then they cracked up.

Abel watched them and shot a glance toward the heavens. "Ah, man, I had a feeling you'd found your match when you told me about Mika. And I'll say, it's good to see you laugh, brother."

"Helluva lot has changed in the last six months."

"I'd have to agree," Abel said, settling on a blanket, and they joined him. "You know something…you're exactly who I pictured my brother would finally give up his service for, Mika."

"How did you know, he—" They both gave her a funny look. "Brothers talk. I get it."

"We do. Don't know about other brothers," Abel offered. "I've been badgering him for years to join the family business, but he kept shooting me down. I figured he liked being spoiled by rich women. When he told me he had a new tenant staying in the cottage, there was something in his voice." Abel flicked his fingers. "Then it dawned on me. He wasn't an angry prick anymore."

"Aw, man," Cain groaned.

"Seriously, I hope when the old man hears about your new business venture, he's going to ease up."

Mika sat quietly, wondering whether or not Abel knew Cain had the DNA test done.

Cain swept his arm across her shoulders. "I've got a support group now. I don't care what Dad or anyone else thinks. I am what I am. He can take me or leave me."

Nice, Cain, she thought, not missing the double meaning. It was then that Abel's gaze fell on her arms and moved down to her legs. Normally, clothing hid her imperfections, but Cain had seduced her into being brave. For a short while, she'd forgotten about the rest of the world and the uncertain gazes.

"Those scars look like they're from one hell of a bad burn. Were you in an accident?" Abel asked.

Cain stiffened beside her, but she was used to questions. "No, they're scars, but not from a burn," she said and gave him an understanding smile. She rose. "Think I'll go join Bambi for a swim."

"Brandi," Abel corrected.

Cain snorted. "She knows her name."

****

As soon as Mika was out of earshot, he glared at his brother. "Were you born under a rock? What the fuck is the matter with your manners, man?"

"What?" Abel raised his hands. "Because I asked her about the scars? They look fucking awful. She seems like a nice gal,

294

but hell, man, you've had top shelf for years." He winced. "Sorry, but her skin looks like she's been cooked in a radiation chamber."

His anger vaulted to the red zone. "Shut—the—fuck—up. I love Mika for who she is. How brave she is and how good we are together. I don't give a good goddamn whether her entire body is covered in scars."

Abel blinked and jerked his head. "Take a breath, I'm just making an observation."

"Make it to me if you feel that inclined, but not to her. She's used to rudeness, people gawking at her, but it doesn't mean my brother gets to be an asshole." He flicked the sand with his toes and folded his arms around his legs.

"You're serious about her. I mean, holy shit, you just said you love her. You're going to spend the rest of your life with that woman, aren't you?"

He nodded and shoved his shades up onto his head. "That's what I want." He paused. "I just have to convince her."

Cain rubbed his neck and remembered her plea before Abel arrived. He didn't agree to the promise. Nor would he.

"What happened to you? Are you sure you're not just bored with fucking random women, and this is some kind of reality check?"

Abel was a good guy. As brothers, there were similarities, but not when it came to women. Cain appreciated Mika's intelligence, his brother dated gals specifically based on bra size.

"Definitely a reality check. For both of us."

Abel didn't look convinced. "So, she's close at hand and sex on demand, is that it?"

"Nope. The first time I made love to her was this afternoon."

Abel's mouth gaped open wide enough to shove in a goat. "Fuck off."

He shrugged. "It's the truth, and it wasn't easy for her, but it was worth it. Worth the wait. Revealing the things that make her laugh. Most of all," he said, turning on his hip and watching Bambi, as Mika called her, prancing in the water like a seven-year-old while Mika swam out to the farthest buoy marking the cove. "It's her brave heart." He cleared his throat. "She has an autoimmune disorder, that's why she has the scars. But I don't see them. Can't see anything but her amazing soul. She's the reason I closed my business." He swayed his head. "And between brothers, she's got the hottest fucking rack and the best hips I've ever seen."

Abel chuckled. "Now, that's the brother I know, and I agree."

They bumped fists.

"But really, what you're saying is you love her because she's flawed and real." Abel leaned back, resting his elbows in the sand behind him.

"She's not flawed at all. And she keeps me real. Still calls me Hooker Boy." He grinned, loving her tenacity and her smart mouth.

Abel barked out a laugh. "She really calls you that?"

"She does. That's what I mean. She just comes out with the funniest shit. I wasn't in a very good place when she leased the cottage, but when I opened my eyes, I realized I had something to look forward to. Breeze started hanging out with her. Before long, I had to hoof it over to the cottage to find my dog. There she was on the couch, her head in Mika's lap while they watched TV together."

Abel listened without interrupting.

"I'd take Breeze back to my place, and the second I stepped in the door, I realized how cold and empty it was. Breeze would lie at the door and whine, and I felt like doing the same. The next night, it happened again, and all I wanted to do was sit in the cottage with them."

"So, kinda like eating home cooking instead of take-out."

Cain paused on that analogy for a second. "I wouldn't exactly put it that way. Mika claimed me as her friend. I thought that would be enough for me. But it wasn't." He strayed a look at his brother. "Pathetic, huh?"

"I don't think it's pathetic at all. When you told me you stopped the escort service, the first thing that crossed my mind was you wanted to be a man she could trust." He paused. "So, um, you moving into the cottage when you get home?"

He rubbed his forehead and laughed. "Don't know. Haven't thought that far ahead, but I know she hates my house."

"Seriously? I know women who'd kill for your digs."

"So do I, but I didn't fall in love with any of them."

"Babeeee." Brandi's call sent a few birds flying from the trees. "You forget about me?"

"Don't say it. I know, and don't worry she's not gonna be your sister-in-law."

"Sure as hell hope not," Cain said, scanning the water. He jumped to his feet. "Where's Mika?"

Abel looked out and shook his head. "I don't see her."

Cain hit the water at full speed, powering his arms through the ocean. He reached the buoy and looked around. "Mika!" He tread water in a circle. "Mika, answer me?" He dove under the water, swimming toward the rocks. Something grabbed his ankle, and he kicked to the surface.

Abel swept the water from his eyes. "You search that side of the cove, I'll go this way."

"Mika!" he shouted. He swam hard for the east entrance to the cove. God, why hadn't he warned her? The riptide could be harsh out here. "Mika!" He listened between his heavy breaths.

"Over here," Her voice was barely audible.

"Where are you?"

"Don't come over here. The current is really strong. I barely got out. I'm on the rocks. I'm coming."

He treaded water, the swell of the sea lifting him. His pulse receded, seeing her stepping carefully on the rocky outcropping of the entrance. With long strokes, he reached the ragged cliff below her, but stayed far enough away not to let the incoming tide push him against the sharp edges. "Are you okay?"

She stood about twenty feet above him. "Just scratched up a bit. Shoot that scared the hell out of me."

"The current isn't strong here. Jump."

"Pooh on you, buddy."

"We used to do it all the time as kids." She gave him a quick jerk of her middle finger causing him to suck in a mouthful of water. Sputtering, he cleared his air passage. "Sweetheart, you're bleeding. Get down here."

"There might be sharks," she yelled back.

"There are no sharks."

"Oh, yeah, what's that fin behind you, Flipper?"

He whipped around and she hooted. "Get your ass down here, woman."

Mika took a running jump and whooped as she fell to the water. As soon as she surfaced, he flung an arm around her narrow waist. "You scared the shit out of me."

She brushed hair from her eyes and blinked the water away. "You try being thrown against those rocks. That hurt."

Back on the beach, he inspected her cuts. They weren't deep, but there were plenty of them. He patted them dry with the towel. "Let's go back to the villa. Salt water is good for wounds, but we'll find some antiseptic just in case."

"It's fine. You'll be sick to your stomach when you see what happens to me."

He ignored the jibe she gave herself. "Abel, we're heading back," he yelled. "We'll meet you later for dinner."

Abel waved from the water, more interested in the fact Brandi had lost her top. She jumped up, waving. "See you guys!"

"Seriously?" Mika said and flung the beach bag over her shoulder.

"Don't worry. Abel assured me, she's not going to be our sister-in-law."

"Good." She stopped dead in her tracks. "What do you mean, our?"

"Hmm?" Oh shit.

"You said, our."

"Did I?" He quickly shook out the towel. "Ready to head back? The stairs are steep, you okay to do that?"

"Think so."

When they reached the steps, she looked up. They took four turns. Thirty steps before a turn. Mika ran them at a fast clip, and he kept pace. By the time she hit the last stair, she was really panting.

300

She shouldn't be breathing that hard. They'd done hills and fifteen kilometers before they left. This was the drug, it had to be. She leaned over to get her breath back, and he rested his palm on her back. He hadn't noticed it before, but the skin beneath the scar across her lower back felt rough, instead of soft.

"Sweetheart, is there any other option other than the Humira that you haven't tried?"

She shook her head. "No, it's a lifesaver for me. I've tried everything else." She stood up and breathed out deeply. "That's the problem with P, it's smart. It learns a workaround every drug."

They walked along the path through his mother's garden filled with red blooms and twisting vines. "What would happen if you stopped taking it?"

Mika halted. "Remember, I told you I'd become a monster."

He nodded.

"The drawback with biologics is something that has to be considered before starting them. The side effects are bad enough, but the worst problem is when you stop or when the drug stops working. It acts as if it's angry you suppressed it, and comes back with a vengeance. Far worse than before. I just bought myself some time."

He drew her into his arms. "You're talking from experience."

"Yes."

"You told me the night I swept you away from Ben, you had a severe case."

She nodded. "That's why I made you promise me we'll go our separate ways." She carried on without him.

"I didn't promise that," he called after her.

Mika spun around.

"I didn't promise that, Mika. Nor will I. I'm going to have faith that for a long, long while this drug will work for you, and by that time there will be something else. If the stars align, maybe even a cure."

A sympathetic smile wrinkled her forehead, and she reached for a beautiful red bloom next to her. "Beauty is only skin deep, Cain, but ugly can't be ignored."

He pulled the bloom from the plant and gently settled it behind her ear. "Love is blind, Mika. Haven't you heard that before?"

She took his hand and pulled on it gently. "You're such a mush, come on."

That evening, after tending to Mika's legs, and a long, drawn-out home-cooked meal of everything Greek, he and Mika retired to their room. They shared a glass of wine on the balcony cuddled in a wide lounger built for two, staring up at the stars, sometimes talking, sometimes silent.

With slow, gentle circles, his thumb caressed her arm. He considered her words, and what might happen. Could he really handle it? He'd spent his entire adult life escorting women. Not all were beautiful, but many were. A multi-billion dollar industry relied on good looks. Beauty was everything to a woman who had it, and didn't want to lose it. What did it mean to Mika, who had it, and knew for certain she would lose it?

When he carried her to bed, he didn't do what he had promised earlier. Instead, he held her and caressed her curves with his palm until she fell asleep. As her breathing deepened, he got up to go to the bathroom and stopped in front of the large oval mirror.

He worked hard to keep himself fit. Staring, he imagined if it were his skin covered in lesions, and what that would be like to see every day. How much inner strength would it take to be brave enough to face the world with her disorder? He cast his gaze to Mika, curled up in their bed.

Tonight she'd told him about the time when she was only four or five, and it attacked the area around her groin. To seal the deep cracks, the doctor prescribed a liquid that burned like iodine. They'd applied it to the raw flesh and held her down while she screamed.

P sufferers lived with the shame of the disease. They endured hurtful words from callous people, but now he understood they also suffered with the pain of the symptoms and of the cures.

Natasza Waters

After relieving himself, he slid under the light cotton sheet, and she snuggled up to his side. He wasn't a vain man, but was he sure he was strong enough for her?

Chapter Nineteen

Mika enjoyed the wind in her face. She could even put up with Brandi's chatter sitting in the back of the speedboat. The brothers sat up front. Cain had the wheel and said they were headed for another island.

"Everything is so rocky here. The hills. The houses. We're surrounded by water, but the air is dry. It's so hard on the skin," Brandi said with a whine. "Don't you find that?"

"Ah, yeah." Cain shot a look over his shoulder. Even though he wore shades, she was sure he rolled his eyes.

Thirty minutes later, they arrived at a little dock. Beautiful white homes nudged together created an eclectic jigsaw puzzle across the hillside of the island.

"More hills?" Brandi exclaimed as Abel helped her out of the boat.

"But it's beautiful, and we're going to the winery," Mika added.

"Oohh, I like those."

She and Cain waited for the other couple to walk up the dock a little ways before they jumped off the boat.

"Oooh, my poor legs. My poor skin," she mimicked Miss Brandi, the airhead. "Her name really should be Bambi."

"Be nice, darling," Cain admonished. "It's not her fault she was only born with a single brain cell."

They both snickered like rotten teenagers. "You want to run it?" she asked, seeing the road rise toward the winery tucked on the top of the hill. Perfect rows of grape vines covered the slopes.

"Let's do it."

They reached the top, and she restrained from pushing herself to the panting stage. It could be the change in geography that affected her yesterday, but after a good night's sleep and the luxurious kisses Cain prodded her from sleep with this morning, followed by his talented hands, she was powered up.

It took Brandi and Abel twenty minutes to walk up the winding road that led to his family's winery. One of many, apparently.

"I need water," she said, blowing out her breath.

"Let's get out of the heat," Cain suggested, opening the thick, arched door.

The smell of oak and wine scented the air. A large bar and cobblestoned walls offered a quaint and cool place to while away some hours.

"Cain?" A dark-haired, dark-eyed beauty came running from the bar and flung herself into his arms, kissing him square on the mouth.

She spoke Greek at a hundred miles an hour. Mika couldn't understand a word.

"Daphne!" He responded to her with a few sentences in Greek, and then said, "Daphne, I'd like you to meet Mika."

"Hello, you are here with Cain?" she asked with a thick accent.

Cain spoke to her again, and this time her expression wasn't as friendly. "I see. How lovely for you. Please, come." Daphne's thick locks swung around her shoulders. "In fact, I have some business we need to discuss. Mika, why don't you go with Dimitri, our host? He can show you the winery, and I will speak with Cain."

"Abel and his friend are right behind us," Cain said. "I'm not really part of the business. You should speak with him. I'll give Mika the tour."

He quickly led her from the tasting room and headed toward a set of stairs. "Old girlfriend, huh?"

"Why weren't you born with one brain cell?" he muttered, leading the way.

"I wouldn't have come up with Hooker Boy, if I had."

"Very funny."

The winery was incredible and very old. Cain shared his family's history as he led her into several caves—actual caves—and they tasted a few very good wines.

Wandering toward the stairs, she asked, "Tell me about good old Daph."

Natasza Waters

"Why do women purposely go there? It's like self-torture, or something. I don't love her. I love you. Nothing else to say."

"High school sweetheart?"

He blew out a breath. "Yes. Anything else?"

She was kind of enjoying his edgy mannerisms. "First kiss?"

"No."

"First, ahem?"

He rolled his eyes. "Second, now get up the stairs."

She chuckled. "She's still hot for you."

When they entered the tasting room, he wrapped his arm securely around her waist and led her toward the balcony. "It's lunchtime. Maybe if I fill your mouth, I won't have to worry about the third degree."

"Ohooohooo. Testy, aren't we?" She took a step and..."Ouch," she squeaked when his hand clapped her behind.

She lifted a finger at him. "Ya know, I can dole out the same, buddy."

"You won't be sitting on it, if you keep it up."

She chuckled evilly. He leaned over and planted a long kiss on her mouth. "I think I'm going to get you drunk and take you for a little walk in the vineyard."

They stepped onto a balcony with a breathtaking view. Tables and chairs lined the deck, with flowers clinging to the posts. Greece had to be the most beautiful place on earth. Brandi and Abel joined them, and they enjoyed lunch with a few bottles of the special reserve wines.

"Oh goodness," she said and sat back in her chair. "I'm going to have to run more if I don't want to gain ten pounds, but everything is so good here."

Mika let the dreamy feeling of the wine and lunch have its way.

"Greek women aren't big because of hefty bones," Abel commented.

She flipped open one eye. "I'm half Greek. Still want to tango with me?" she asked Cain.

He slipped his shades off and laid them on the table, then gripped her wrist, drawing her right into his lap. "Fat ass or not, we'll always tango."

His hand fanned across the back of her head, and his lips melted against hers. Or was that her melting?

"Hey, lovebirds. We have to head back," Abel interrupted. "Mom and Dad are gonna be home in a couple hours."

Mika felt Cain tense. It was an automatic reaction, and she realized even though he talked a good game, his dad's opinion meant something to him.

They left the winery, but not before she had to endure Cain receiving a goodbye hug and too long of a kiss from Daph.

****

As four o'clock struck, the villa's front door opened and a woman called out in Greek. Cain and Abel met on the walkway above the entry and answered in Greek. She and Brandi took their time coming down the stairs to give the brothers' mother a moment to greet her sons. It looked like a happy homecoming with big hugs and kisses for each of them.

Tall and voluptuous in figure, Mrs. Sallas' beauty reminded Mika of Sofia Loren. Standing beside her was obviously their father, a brooding, severe-looking man. As she and Brandi reached the last step, Cain guided his mother to them.

"Mama, I'd like you to meet Mika Makris." He rolled into Greek once again as his mother surveyed her for a moment.

"Mrs. Sallas, I'm pleased to meet you."

Cain's mother paused, looked at Cain, and then back at her. "My English is not as good as it should be, but I welcome you, Mika, to our home."

"Thank you, Mrs. Sallas." She attempted to put the same inflection that she'd heard Cain use since he'd been here.

"Please, I am Leda to you."

Mika wasn't bilingual like Cain, and she thought she'd slaughtered their last name, at least until Brandi took her turn.

Abel stepped up. "And this is my friend Bamb...I mean Brandi."

Mika tried not to let her eyes pop open, and Cain dropped his head to hide a grin. Whoops.

"Brandi, hello. Welcome," Leda greeted.

"Mrs. Sallas." But it came out more like salad... "Your son is so handsome, and I see where he gets it." Her eyes veered to their father, who stood stiffly at the door.

310

"Papa," Abel said, stretching out a hand.

Their father spoke in Greek to Abel, and Mika could only assume it was a welcome home. Cain's father turned a harsh stare in her direction, but she didn't glance away. If Cain and his father had a strained relationship, part of that would be transferred to her, and she was more than willing to stand beside him. She was his support group.

"It's good to see you, Father." Cain's greeting was formal, but polite.

In English, his father said, "We've had a long day. Shall we have dinner together at eight?" he asked, ignoring Cain's hello.

That just pissed her off.

Leda jumped in. "Of course, of course. We will have a family meal. I'll tell Alexandria what to prepare. Mika, would you join me for a refreshment?"

"Can I come, too?" Brandi jumped in.

With an expression that only the wealthy can pull off, Leda nodded gracefully, but her eyes said something else.

They followed Cain's mother into the vast kitchen with open shelves and colorful bowls lining the walls. Fresh herbs hung near the sink. They skirted a large butcher's block as Leda called out and Alexandria appeared. A middle-aged woman who wore a white apron.

They spoke loud and rapidly to each other. Greeks always seemed to speak with passion.

"Follow me," Leda said, and led them to a small patio off the kitchen. "One of my most favorite places." She waved her hand for them to sit.

Alexandria appeared with a large pitcher filled with a deep red liquid and ice floating on top. She also set a plate of cold meats and cheese sprinkled with basil and olive oil on the table.

Leda placed her gaze on Mika. "Cain tells me you have his heart, ah." She swirled her fingers. "You are the woman he loves. I am overjoyed to hear this."

"Mmm, this is delish," Brandi spouted, with a mouth full of cheese.

Leda gave her a polite smile. "Please, eat." She filled Brandi's glass with the juice. "My son has told you about our family?"

Mika nodded. "Yes. I know, although he says it doesn't bother him, his father's opinion means a lot to Cain. It hurts him to be denied."

"What's going on?" Brandi asked in her shrill voice.

Leda patted her hand. "Not to worry, dear. Please enjoy."

Brandi shrugged and dug in.

Cain's mother smiled sadly. "I made a mistake once. Amos forgave me, but it was too close to my affair when I conceived Cain. The truth is, my affair was one of the heart and of flirtation, but I did not commit adultery. It happened a year after we were married. Amos spent all his time at the vineyards, and I felt abandoned." Leda's hands rolled together. "You must

312

understand, Amos is a rigid man by character. He will seem, ah, cold to you, but he is a good man and a good father."

"Has he been a good father to Cain? Does he treat his sons the same?"

Leda's brow wrinkled. "No, he does not, but he would never shun Cain completely. I think he knows he is wrong, and now is too proud to admit it."

Mika tasted the cool, red concoction. It was very good with a mild taste of raspberries. "I hope Amos can find it in his heart to forgive and accept. It weighs heavy on Cain."

"My son has never brought a woman home to meet us. You must be very special to him, and I am glad he has found you." She tilted her head. "He has been honest with you, I assume?"

"If you're speaking about his previous profession, yes."

"This is rude of me, but, is that how you met?"

Mika shook her head. "No. I rented the cottage on his property. We became friends, and he told me about his other profession."

"You mean him being a gigolo?" Brandi spouted. "I sure wish I had the money, I'd buy a night with him."

Both she and Leda's gazes landed on the dimwit at the same time.

Brandi swished her hand through the air. "I know that sounds terrible, but I mean, don't you wonder, Mika? How can you trust him? He's been with beautiful women like me all his life."

Anger at herself more than Bambi, made her grit her teeth. "And he will be again, I'm sure."

"Why, because of those ugly scars on your legs?"

She said it so innocently, Mika ignored the crassness underneath. "Yes, because of those."

Leda's head tilted in question, but she decided not to explain. There was no point. Brandi's words delivered a reality check she needed.

Brandi finished all the cheese on the plate and chugged back the juice. "Does Abel bring girls home?"

"All the time, dear." Leda said swiftly.

"Oh."

Well, that wasn't very nice. Even if Brandi was a dumbass, she didn't deserve that, but Mika understood it wasn't meant to hurt. It was simply fact, and the Greeks had a tendency to say it how it was. Her father was like that. When she and her sister gained any weight their dad would yell out "hey girls, your butts are getting a little big, lay off the meatballs." They'd all laugh, but then they'd stare down the meatballs as if they were enemy number one.

"I should go find, Cain. Thank you for the refreshments, Leda."

Leda's big, dark blue eyes fell on her. "My son is very strong-willed. I'm glad he has found you. He has been sad for many years, and I can see he is happy now."

She paused. "What does agapi mou mean?"

Leda's eyes creased with a smile. "My love."

"Do you think Abel loves me?" Brandi cut in, turning an inquiring look on Leda.

Mika shot off the patio and through the kitchen before Leda hit poor Brandi between the eyes with a truth bullet.

"Cain?" She closed the door to their suite. He was lying on the bed staring up at the ceiling at the delicate artwork intricately painted with muted colors. She neared the bed and he opened his arm with invitation. Snuggling up to his side, she asked, "Are you okay?"

"Sure, just getting a rest."

"Did the run up the hill tucker you out, old man?" She barely got a grin. "Cain, I can't imagine what it would be like to go through life being shunned by one parent over an untruth, but your mother loves you, and so does your brother…and…and so do I." She brushed the hair on his forehead aside. "I think your father loves you, too."

He turned his head, his strong jaw a sharp edge, and his eyes shaded with hurt. "I don't know why I expect anything to change when I come home. Every time I hope it might be different."

315

"It is different this time. You know the truth, and I'm here with you. You're locked and loaded to do battle, if that's what you want."

He gave her a weak smile. "You being here makes a difference, and so does the fact that you just told me you loved me for the second time. Or do you only love me like a friend?"

"You didn't need me to tell you that. You knew it already."

"I may have hoped, but I didn't know. When?" He played with a coil of her hair.

"Think I should take a shower before dinner."

He stopped her. "When?"

"Cain, you know girls are sappier than boys."

"That's not an answer."

She paused, then decided to divulge her secret. "I'm pretty sure it was when you took me shopping for the dress. And then when you gave me my injection the first time, but I knew it for sure when I saw you leaning against the wall in the hallway outside of ICU, when they'd told me they were moving Mom to Golden Years. I was certain you had something to do with it. That's when I fell madly in love with you." She paused and took a breath. "Aside from all those moments, I think the truth is, when I showed up on your doorstep and looked into your eyes for the first time."

He blinked and sat up. "And yet you went out on a date with a man-whore prepared to get laid."

"Hey, no pointing fingers. You're out-of-this-world gorgeous and an escort for God's sake. I didn't have a hope."

He curled her into his arms and kissed her, his tongue teasing her mouth to open. He took his time, and when he drew away, he said, "You, of all people, should know better than to judge a book by its cover."

Cain peeled the clothes from her body, and she, his. This time he loved her gently with a sensual, slow passion. His mouth made her body sing. There was something so primitive and raw when his erection see-sawed in and out of her vagina. The flex of his muscles, the heat in his eyes drove her past the point of breathless. Later, they showered together, and he dried her off with a soft terry towel.

As he gently blotted the drops of water from her breasts, he said, "I won't make the promise you've asked of me."

She sighed and smiled at his naiveté. Running a finger down his jaw, she nodded. "Yes, you will, and I won't hate you for it. I promise that."

They joined everyone downstairs for dinner. The night passed swiftly, and although his father wasn't the life of the party, he did interact with both of his sons. They spoke in Greek mostly, and Cain translated. Maybe his father was on his best behavior because she was there, or maybe Leda had said something. Whichever way, she was thankful that when they all retired for the evening it was amiable.

That is, until they reached the steps. "Cain, Mika, I'd like to speak with you privately," Amos said in perfect English.

"Mika, why don't you head up to bed? I'll be up in a minute."

"No," his father said. "It concerns you both."

Chapter Twenty

Cain gripped her hand, and they followed his father onto the main balcony situated outside of the cavernous great room. She sat down, but Cain remained standing behind her.

"I must tell you, I'm shocked that you have brought her here."

Cain remained silent. Mika waited for the other shoe to drop.

"I believed your life of prostituting yourself would never end. That you were destined for an early grave because of it. Mika has intervened, but bringing a client posing as a decent woman does not change matters." Cain's father placed a harsh look on her. "If you think you will marry into this family and fill your pockets with money, think again. No matter what he has told you, he has no claim to this family's fortunes."

She smacked her lips and looked up at Cain. He was vibrating with anger. "And I thought it was going so well," she drawled.

Cain didn't take his blistering gaze off his father. "Yeah, comes out of left field with a knockout punch." Cain leaned his intimidating form toward his father. "It is one thing to spend your whole life doubting my blood and treating me like an outcast, but it is *not acceptable* to throw unfounded accusations

319

at Mika. She is the reason I want to be a better man, because it sure as hell isn't you."

Amos rose slowly from his chair, the two men glaring at each other.

"Let's go, Cain."

He placed a hand to her back, and they left his father. At the stairs, she said, "I'll be up in a second. I just want to talk to your mom."

"What about?"

"Girl stuff." She flicked a finger. "Warm up those cold feet of yours."

She waited until he was halfway up the stairs before she turned for the kitchen. With a quick peek over her shoulder, she saw the door to their bedroom close and darted for the patio, closing the doors behind her.

Amos sat with a distant, hurt expression. "If your son could see that expression he might believe you actually love him."

Amos didn't acknowledge she was there.

"In the end, this will be your loss, because of your stubbornness. You'll never know how smart your son is or what he's done to make the world a better place. By shunning him, you won't share his successes, and that is a shame because there will be many. Why you transfer your guilt to your son is beyond me."

"I do not," Amos said, which shocked her, thinking she would have a one woman rant, and get it over with.

320

"You have. You wonder why your wife strayed. Even if she didn't commit the final act, she strayed with her heart. Blaming her would only end badly, so you blame Cain, resolute in your lie. I think you know it's a lie. Cain is your son, although he possesses a warm heart, unlike you, who never nurtured him or was proud of him. You grind your axe in the wrong back, and I see how much it hurts him. How his own father rebuked him." She drew the paper from her front pocket. "You know the truth already, but facing it would take a strong man to admit he has done a horrible thing and turned his back on his own blood." She laid the paper on the table in front of him. "I hope you choke on this for what you've done to him."

She quickly left the patio and closed the door. When she turned, Cain stood there, a silhouette in the room with only a few candles burning on the shelves to break the darkness. His expression was unreadable, and for a moment she thought she was in a huge amount of trouble, until he reached his hand out to her. She gripped his fingers, and he led her to their room without a word.

****

The cool nip of the morning air brushed her cheek. She smiled, realizing it wasn't air at all, it was Cain. Leaning over the bed, he kissed her awake. She stretched her arms around his neck.

"Good morning."

He slowly massaged her to bring her from a deep sleep. "Morning, HB," she said sweetly.

He chuckled and nuzzled her cheek. "Just using letters doesn't make it any better."

"What if the letters stand for something else?" She opened one eye. "Is that coffee I smell?"

Cain's hand slid under the sheet and massaged her breasts lightly. Since he'd woken her up so nicely, he could have a grope.

"Yes, it's Saturday, and what does HB stand for?"

She tugged him down. "How...about...Hot Buns?"

He laughed. "So, we're starting the cute names now, huh?"

Kissing his clean-shaven cheek, she hung an arm around his neck while he brushed the sheet aside and nibbled his way to her breast. "You could be Hooker Boy if you want. I just thought I'd give you a choice."

"Hmm." He moaned and circled her areola, sending a spike of pleasure to her core. "Here's your choice," he said, kneeling on the bed and ripping the towel from his waist."

"That's a big choice," she said deadpan, and he broke into a grin. A lift in his mood was good to see, and his smile warmed her after all the drama last night. "Hard decision, I mean."

He laughed even more.

Cain's fingers skated down to her sex, and he circled the pad of his thumb against her already moist lips.

"Think you should sit on that hard decision before making your choice," he said, playing with her.

"Are you trying to distract me from my morning coffee?" She sighed with his gentle entry into her channel.

"My girl deserves special kisses." He palmed her thighs, urging them to spread.

His warm mouth and experienced tongue worked her into a frenzy. Her back arched, needing more. Just about at the brink, his thick crown plunged into her channel, and sent them into a quaking, beautiful mess.

After showering, they sat on the balcony and enjoyed their morning coffee. The sun warmed her, but so did looking across the table at Cain. His handsome, cut jaw and jet-black hair caused a gushy feeling inside her. She considered the moment and wanted to hang onto it forever.

"How about we move to another island today?" Cain suggested, pulling her from her thoughts.

"Sure—"

Shouting broke their conversation, and they both launched to their feet, running for the door. When Cain opened it, his parents' voices rose from downstairs.

"Maybe you should stay here," he suggested.

"No way. I'm your back-up, remember?"

They walked across the causeway and looked over the edge. His parents didn't notice them to begin with. Leda's face was

Natasza Waters

streaked with tears but so, surprisingly, was Amos'. The Greek flew in both directions.

"Mama," Cain called down. When she looked up, Cain shook his head. "It's all right. We're leaving."

"No, no," Leda said. "Both of you, come down here."

"What's going on?" Mika whispered to him.

As they headed for the stairs, he said, "Not sure. Mom was giving him hell, calling him every Greek name in the book."

They approached slowly. When they stopped, Cain wrapped his arm around her waist and held her close.

"We're leaving," he said to his father. "It upsets you that we're here, so we'll go."

His father's keen eyes, still watering, thrust the paper into the air. "It upsets me that you knew about this," he said, shaking it. His eyes fell on Mika. "It upsets me that I have been too afraid to admit I failed you and turned my back on my own son."

Cain watched him wave the paper in the air. He guessed what it was and turned a look on her.

"Where did you get that?" he asked his father.

Amos stilled for a moment, and Mika bowed her head, gnawing on her lip. Everyone read the moment for what it was. She had stepped out of bounds by taking the DNA test and giving it to his father. The only person who smiled was Leda.

"My future daughter-in-law thought it was important that I know the truth, and that I stop being a fool," Amos stated gruffly. "What I want to know is why you didn't give me this? I

324

can see she did it without your knowledge. She did it because she loves you, but mostly I think she did it because, as she mentioned, so I'd choke on it."

She flinched with that. Not to worry, she told herself. It wasn't like she would ever really be his daughter-in-law.

No one spoke for the longest time. The sounds of the village below filtered into the room.

"You're not leaving," Leda said. "I have hardly had a chance to spend time with Mika. Do not take her away, Cain." She dabbed a Kleenex against her cheeks. "And...your father has something to say."

They both stared at Amos. "I was wrong," he said, speaking in English. "I have been very wrong. As Mika pointed out, my heart, although I don't show it much, was broken when Leda left me. I denied you because doubt kept me angry. Then I became more so when we found out what you did with your life. I knew I had a part in that. I made you feel unworthy. Again, it was my fault. It's been a festering wound inside me for all these years. You brought Mika here, and I wrongly assumed she was one of your clients."

"Ewww," she muttered, and Cain laughed softly.

His father stepped up to them. "I don't expect forgiveness." He shook his head. "I only want you to know that I am sorry." He raised his gaze to meet Cain's. "I'm proud of your strength and your success. I'm proud of my oldest son."

Mika stepped away from Cain. It was his decision, and she took the few paces to stand beside his mother, who wrapped an arm around her shoulders. Both men now had tears in their eyes. Well, crap. Now she did, too.

"Thank you, Papa." Cain nervously flicked a hand through his hair as another tear rolled down his cheek.

"Please, do not leave. Give us a chance. Give me a chance to heal the wounds I've inflicted on you," Cain's father asked.

Amos took the first step and gripped his son in a hug, and that's when a gasp of relief vaulted from Cain, and he hugged his father back. She and Leda were squeezing each other so tight they were cutting off blood vessels.

"Oooh, group hug!" Brandi squealed from the top of the stairs.

Abel stopped her from descending the stairs with the shake of his head.

Leda sniffled. "Breakfast is ready. Shall we?"

"I'm staaaarving," Brandi crooned.

Leda muttered under her breath, "God, I hope he doesn't marry her."

Mika chuckled. As the forgiveness fest broke up, Cain gripped her hand and yanked her outside. He closed the front door and glared at her.

Oh, boy. The tiles were very interesting. Wonder how long that took to install? A finger raised her chin, and she swallowed thickly.

"If I already didn't love you with all my heart and soul, I would now."

She blinked. Not what she expected. With a wrinkled brow, she said, "I know I stepped out of bounds, but I knew you wouldn't give it to him. You're both a bit stubborn. I'm sorry for getting involved in your family business."

"Sometimes it takes an outsider to make people see the error of their ways. I'd given up. My father had run away from the truth. You showed us we were both wrong."

"We can still leave if you want."

"Do you want to leave?" he asked, brushing a kiss on her mouth.

"I'm along for the ride. It's up to you, but I think you should stay as a sign of good faith." She shrugged. "And I wouldn't mind spending a few hours down on the beach today. The sun and saltwater are good for me."

Cain's eyes misted and his jaw went taut. "I love you, Mika. I tried hard not to, believing I didn't deserve you after the life I'd led. You are the most considerate woman I've ever known. Even if I only had one day of your affection, I'd consider myself a lucky man."

His dark features sucked her into the abyss of Cain. She hoped she would be able to find her way out before he turned her heart into a wasteland.

Chapter Twenty-one

The Victoria sky was a brilliant blue and the October afternoon crisp when they parked the car. Fall had arrived. He came to a stop in front of her cottage, and tension filled the air. They'd left as friends and come home lovers. She didn't want the shift to affect anything, but that was a lie. Cain dropped his hands into his lap and she jumped out before he could speak. The trunk lid popped open, and she gripped the handle of her luggage, but he interceded and took it out for her. Neither of them had said a word.

"Guess I have to pay the piper and step on the scale, then I'm going for a run," she said lightheartedly. "Breeze could probably use one, too. I'll come and get her."

"This feels awkward, doesn't it?" Cain asked, carrying her bag to the front door as she dug for her key.

"We'll adjust." She slipped the key into the lock. The living room had that vacant feeling as does any home when its inhabitants have been gone. Turning the heat up and the lights on would make it cozy again.

Cain drew her to the couch and urged her to sit with him. He clasped her hands in his. "You probably spent as much time as I did thinking about what would happen when we got home. I'm going to ask, even though I know what your answer will be. I want you to move in with me." He worked his cheek with his tongue, gazing at her.

She nodded. It was a long flight home, and her thoughts flitted between her moments in Greece and what would happen to their relationship when they were back in the real world. She expected this. "This is my home," she said, her gaze trailing around the room.

Cain took a deep breath. "And what would happen if I evicted you?" Brushing her fingers, he said, "Or better yet, what if I decided to move into the cottage."

She snorted. "Yeah, right, Mr. Chrome and Cold Architecture."

"To be honest, I hate it, too. It was pretty much that way when I moved in, but my being there didn't add the essence you do to this place. What am I supposed to do, sneak over here at night for a dalliance with my tenant, and then tip toe back to my place in the morning?"

She grinned at the thought. "Could be fun."

"Not fun," he answered with a serious expression.

"Let's not sweat over anything right now."

He leaned over to kiss her. "I'll go get changed, and we'll take Breeze for a run."

"Say hi to Sof for me!"

He raised a brow at her.

"How do you pay her, exactly?"

Cain turned away from her, shaking his head. "I'm not even going to answer that, and stop trying to pick a fight."

She deflated instantly. "Sorry."

"Mm-hmm."

Halfway through unpacking, her phone beeped with a text.

I love you. HB

She spit out a laugh and picked up her phone.

You should. YFL

???

She rolled her eyes.

Your Fair Lady.

A heart appeared on the next text.

****

A couple weeks slipped by. Work still sucked, and she trained hard for the marathon. Cain tip toeing back to his place in the morning made her laugh. He tried several more times to convince her to move into the main house, but she was adamantly against the idea. She really did love her little cottage more than his place. She bent over to tie the laces on her running shoes. Only another week before the race. Getting tense was not good for her, and she tried to ease her nerves with a breathing technique.

A text came in.

On a business call. I'll catch up.

She sent him a thumbs up.

Breeze, waited patiently by the door. "You ready to go, girl?"

The dog barked and turned in a circle. German Shepherds were big, fluffy babies. At least Breeze was. She had a huge bark, but she loved to cuddle.

They did three turns around the property first to warm up and stretch, then she ran down the trail toward the beach. Today she'd push herself. Remember her breathing. Ignore the burn.

Breeze ran ahead of her through the tide. Behind them was another jogger with a dog. She picked up the pace on the water-soaked shore, then she heard someone yelling.

Before she could turn, sharp teeth gnawed into the back of her thigh. Mika screeched in pain. Her blood froze with fear. The Rottweiler attacked again, his teeth sinking into her arm, and she yelled, trying to shake him off. The owner of the dog and Breeze arrived at the same time. Breeze jumped through the air and bit down on the other dog's neck. They rolled, snarling, embroiled in a vicious fight, teeth and yelps and growls.

The other owner, a woman, started screaming at her dog. The animals were killing each other.

Calling Breeze, Mika went for the first collar that became visible, and it was attached to the Rotti. She pulled hard and dragged it back.

"Breeze, down," she yelled, but her attention was off the Rotti, and it twisted. The dog dug its teeth into her wrist. She couldn't let go. All she could do was scream.

Then Cain was there. He wrenched the dog from her grip. It tried to bite him, but he used his weight to drive the Rotti's head into the sand. "Leash!" he yelled at the woman.

She ran up and quickly leashed the Rotti. The woman backed away and Cain let go. The dog lunged and snapped.

"Oh my God, I'm so sorry. He's new to our family. I had no idea."

Mika shook all over, the adrenaline pumping at high speed. Breeze lay on the sand, licking the blood off her leg.

Cain rounded on the woman. "That dog needs to be put down," he roared. Anger made him twice as big, and twice as scary. The woman's face drained to pale.

"Never mind," Mika said and bent down next to Breeze. She was bleeding from her neck and her back. She had bites everywhere, but so did the Rotti.

The gal began to cry. "I'm sorry. I'll pay for the vet bill."

"This is private property," Cain stormed. "Get off it."

The owner tugged on the leash, her dog barking frantically as she dragged him away.

Mika didn't feel the bites, only blood trailing down her leg, adrenaline still doing its job.

Cain hunched behind her. "Baby, we got to get you to a clinic. You need stitches."

"So does Breeze. Take her to the vet. I'll go to the clinic." Cain's expression twisted with indecision. "I'm okay." Breeze got up, but she began hopping, one leg in the air. Maybe the leg was broken. Cain picked her up and she yelped, sending Mika's heartbeat soaring with fear.

"I'll drop her off, and then come to the clinic. Wait for me there," Cain ordered.

Bleeding all over her car, Mika ignored the sting so she wouldn't freak out worse than she already was. She headed down the highway, her blood pooling under her thigh.

A half hour later she heard Cain.

"Where's Mika?" he demanded at the front desk.

"That's my overprotective boyfriend," she said to the doctor, who was finishing up with the stitches in her leg.

Cain burst through the door with a fierce expression.

"How's Breeze?" she asked.

"Getting stitched up like you," he said and forked his fingers through hers.

The doctor put gauze over her stitches, then cleaned the other bites. "I need to report this," he said. "Did you get the name of the owner?"

They shook their heads.

"I'll put a call in anyway. From what Mika says, it sounds like this dog needs to be euthanized."

"I don't know why it attacked," she said.

"You said you were running," the doc offered as he tossed the bloody pads into the garbage. "Obviously, it's aggressive and went after you, probably because you were running." The doc picked up a pen, wrote his notes on a sheet, then closed the folder. "The stitches need to be in for ten days, but you can take them out yourself. Just snip them next to the knot and pull."

"I'll do that," Cain answered. He helped her off the table.

The throbbing had begun, and she winced.

"Here," the doc scribbled on a prescription pad, "This is for the pain. Do you have any allergies?"

She shook her head.

That night, Cain made supper while she and Breeze sat on the couch. Everyone was okay. Breeze had a torn tendon the vet had stitched back together. "I still want to run the race, but today freaked me out," she said.

Cain brought a one-bowl wonder of a salad to the table. "I'll run with you. Breeze can't exercise until her wounds heal."

She gave Breeze a rub between her ears. "You came to my rescue, girl."

"Premium dog bones for the next week," Cain added. He pulled the kitchen chair out for her to sit. "And you, Miss Makris, are moving into the main house. You need someone looking after you, too."

"Nice try," she said and grinned up at him.

He settled across from her. Picking up his fork, he gave her a lingering look. "I know why you're doing this."

"No, you don't."

"You're keeping just enough distance between us to give yourself a safety net."

Okay, so he did know. Instead of answering, she filled her face with salad. When she finished chewing, she said, "Have you talked to your parents?"

"I hate when you change the subject, and yes, today actually. Dad's decided to become a contributor to the charity organization."

"That's great news."

Her handsome landlord shook his head. "I love you for what you did. I hope you know how much," he said, reaching across the table and covering her hand.

"Nothing compared to what you did for my mom."

They ate in silence, and she began to feel a little uncomfortable and a little guilty for refusing his request to move into the main house.

"You know, I was thinking about buying a new car," Cain said

She stopped chewing. "You have three. What do you need another one for? Thursday?"

Amidst a gulp of water, he laughed and choked it up, then shook his head. Cain dried his mouth before he said, "No, I don't need a Thursday car. I just thought we'd go check out a new one on the market. Kind of caught my eye."

Natasza Waters

She shrugged. "Sure."

"Did you leave a message for your boss?"

Mika pushed her bowl aside, not especially hungry. "What for?"

"You were attacked by a dog today. You're not going into work." He collected the bowls and rinsed them in the sink.

She didn't have a choice. "I could work from home, but Lt. Vickers is a battle-axe. I doubt she'll let that happen."

Cain filled the dishwasher and brought back two mugs of steaming tea. When he settled across from her, he stated, staring straight in her eyes, "I want you to quit."

The tea splashed against her lips and dripped over her fingers. "Well, the ocean is right there, I could always catch my dinner." She set her mug down and dried her fingers with a paper napkin. "Are you nuts?"

"I'm serious, Mika. You've come home plenty of times upset and angry from work. All because of this woman. It's not good for the P. In fact, it's the worst thing. Stress can bring on a flare." He paused, and then said, "Oh, shit. The attack. That must have scared the crap out of you." He looked around frantically. "You need a bath. No! You can't do that with the stitches. I know, I'll call in a masseuse for a massage." He reached for his phone.

Mika watched his emotions ramp into overdrive like she'd never seen before. "Cain."

336

His Perfect Imperfection

He ignored her. "Can I borrow your laptop? I'll find the best one in Victoria."

"Cain."

He stretched, gripped her laptop from the end table and shifted it to the kitchen table, then typed furiously.

"Cain!" She slammed her palm on the table. His eyes shot to her. "What's stressing me is you. What's wrong with you?"

"You don't need a job."

She sat back, getting a seed of an idea. "And if I don't have a job, than I'd be dependent on you, is that it?"

He shot out of the chair and behind the island to pace. "You can find something where you work from home. Be your own boss. Create your own company."

"Cain, would you stop pacing. It's not about the job, you're scared shitless my P is going to flare. And I don't blame you."

Ignoring her accusation, he said, "Isn't there something you've always wanted to do?"

Her heart warmed. "Yes, climb your abs like a sex crazed monkey. But I can check that off the list."

Rising from the chair, she winced. The dog had bitten right into the muscles and they smarted.

"I'm serious, Mika.

Cain was beside her instantly, and she pointed at the seat she vacated. "Please sit." Begrudgingly, he sat down. She took a stance behind him, placing her hands on his shoulders, rubbing her thumbs into the base of his neck. He groaned and his head dropped back, using her breasts as pillows.

"God, that feels good," he said, closing his eyes. "But you're the one that needs this."

"You first."

She worked his shoulders with her fingertips until she felt his muscles soften from rocks into...well...softer rocks. The man was ripped.

"I've lived my whole life with this enemy inside me. Even though I try to live a healthy lifestyle, it will flare when it wants." She continued to massage down his back, and he leaned forward. "Different things can trigger the disorder. Stress is one of them, but yoga helps, so does the running." Cain's arm stretched backward and around her leg, his palm working its way under her dress.

"My turn to make you relax."

He stood up, gazing into her eyes with that practiced look of a man who wants to devour a woman.

Seating her on the couch, he crouched at her feet. "Let me make things easier for you. Keep you happy." His lips brushed a gentle kiss on the inside of her knee. "And relaxed." His mouth found her other knee, and he licked the tender flesh.

Her pulse began to beat harder as his mouth continued to kiss its way up her thigh. His fingers reached her panties before his tongue. Her heart thumped madly as he rubbed his jaw against the inside of her thigh, and without much effort, slid her body closer.

"Cain?"

"Homeopathic remedy." With two fingers, he drew her thong down her legs and blew a warm breath over her aching sex.

Cain's idea of distraction a whole new level of wonderful. The man's tongue had a Master's degree in making a woman lose her mind. Mika forgot all about the dog bites.

Her pulse thumped, when Cain helped her stand, then slid her dress over her head and draped it across the armrest. There was something totally erotic about being naked in front of him while he was completely clothed.

His warm hands sent shivers through her body as his fingers skated across her skin.

After helping her sit on the couch, his hot mouth sucked her nipple while his thumb caressed her bundle of nerves. When his attention traveled back to her sex, he palmed her ass, and his tongue made her body unfurl with his sweet seduction. Cain never rushed. He seemed to love giving her pleasure. His tongue and fingers gently coaxed her into a sublime orgasm that had her gasping.

"Mm," he purred against her ear. "Relaxed?"

She loved threading her fingers through his soft hair. "I think so."

"Good. Now that I've got you in my web of control..." His phone landed in her other hand. "Call and leave a message for Vickers. You won't be in for a week. If you don't, I will. That's a promise."

At least he'd given up on the idea of her quitting. She dialed her office number and left a message on Lt. Battle-axe's phone, explaining the dog attack. When she'd finished, Cain swept her up and carried her across the yard. Naked!

"Just because I said I'd take a week off, doesn't mean I'll agree to everything you want."

"Door," he said, and she rolled her eyes and reached for the knob.

He carried her all the way up the stairs, then stood in the doorway of his bedroom. She looked around. In all the time she'd lived here, she'd never been in this room.

Jen had seen it. Jen had slept in his bed.

She tried to push back a catty grin, knowing Cain hadn't been here, but slept on her couch.

He stepped over to the bed and laid her down. "Half the time I know what you're thinking just by reading your expressions," he said.

Uh-oh. She adjusted the pillow behind her head and watched him shed his clothes. Mika would be a total hypocrite if she didn't admit she loved her Cain naked.

He rolled onto the bed.

She grinned at him. "You know, it's only eight o'clock."

Tingles flooded her body when his index finger traced the curve of her breast, then across her ribs, his eyes following the movements.

"Never in a million years would I sleep with Jen."

She cleared her throat and gazed at the ceiling, embarrassed he could read her so well. His bedroom had a tranquil feel. The walls were a comfortable moss green, with white baseboards and brown accents. The enormous sleigh bed made her feel small. The artwork hung in distinct focal points. Images of Greece and oil paintings of beautiful flowers warmed the room.

"Not the den of iniquity you thought it was, huh?" He kissed her shoulder then got up again and turned on the gas fireplace.

"You sure about that?" she asked, her eyes glued to his shaft as he returned to bed. Hard and erect, his cock pressed against his firm abs. Her heart began to bang again. Why did this man touch every hotspot inside her?

He rolled onto all fours. "You're injured and need tender loving care. So happens, I'm quite good at that." His forehead met hers, and he kissed her nose, then her cheek and slid to the edge of her lips. "When I heard you scream this afternoon, I lost my mind. I couldn't breathe. I couldn't get to you fast enough."

Her fingers itched to touch him, and he sucked in a slow breath as her hands strayed down his taut chest. She kissed him. "Definitely got my adrenaline running."

His voice low and seductive, he said, "I've got an idea."

"Idea?"

Cain's fingers thread her hair. "I'm hiring you."

Her mouth gaped open. "That is so naughty, Cain."

A smile twitched on his lips. "Full time caregiver for Breeze."

She chuckled and slapped his ass.

"What did you think I was hiring you for?" He broke out laughing.

He wrapped her against his chest and rolled her gently to his side. "Let me take care of you."

"I know you want that, but I can't lose my independence."

"I'm not trying to take away your independence." His brow furrowed. "I just want your life to be uncomplicated."

"Keeping my job isn't just for my security, it gives you the freedom to walk away when the time comes."

Her hand skimmed across his shoulders, tracing the bulges and valleys on his biceps. His fingers twined with hers, and he pulled them to his mouth and kissed her knuckles.

"Get some rest," he said and slid from the bed. He raised the blankets until she wiggled between the crisp, white sheets. The weight of his comforter cocooned her as he kissed her forehead.

He didn't sound angry. If anything, his expression hid any emotion. It reminded her of how he was when she'd first come to rent the cottage. Withdrawn. "Where are you going?"

"I'll be downstairs. Close your eyes."

The room was dark when she woke up. Cain hadn't returned. She rolled to look at the time. Ten o'clock. Carefully, she got out of bed and entered his walk-in closet. Wow, it was like a showpiece she'd seen in a magazine. His suits were lined up, his shirts in every color pressed and hanging neatly. She grabbed a pink one and slipped it on, turning up the sleeves as she made her way downstairs. The lights were off, and Cain sat in the darkness, naked, a glass in his hand.

She settled her rear on the stone coffee table and ignored the chill. He didn't say anything. She didn't say anything. They just stared at each other.

Finally, he brought the glass to his mouth and took a deep swallow, then lowered it to balance on his muscled thigh and said, "I'm not the empty man you think I am." His jaw flexed tight.

"I know you're not empty."

He tipped his glass, the liquid flowing to one side. Slowly, he tipped it the other way. "Did I ever tell you I have a Master's degree in Computer Engineering?"

"Cain, don't. You don't need to prove to me that you're worth something. I know who you are." The glass house was always cool and made her shiver.

He shook his head. "Why won't you trust me?"

She closed her eyes. "It's not about trust. It's about doing the right thing."

Natasza Waters

"And you get to determine that."

"Yes," she said with emphasis. "I've learned through experience that human beings have it wired into their DNA to reject the weak and accept the strong. Just as much as we are attracted to beauty, we are repulsed by the grotesque. An inner alarm system warns us something isn't normal. From there, our minds rationalize. If it's not a threat, we can accept it. If we are sickened by it, we want to distance ourselves. I can't tell you why we're made that way. I just know we are."

"Choice," he threw back at her. "You forgot conscious choice. My choice. My feelings. You've put a time limit on us based on how one man, a kid actually, acted like a fool, and you decided every man will be the same." He emptied his glass. "I have read almost every damn thing I could find on P. I've looked at the pictures. Yeah, I flinched sometimes, but it was because I felt for those people."

"I'm those people," she said, hoping he'd understand.

He shook his head. "I read their stories, felt the pain in their words." Cain scrubbed his jaw with his hand and placed the glass on the side table. He leaned forward, his gaze severe. "I'll make you this promise. If your remission ends. If your P comes back, I will consider the future, but," he said harshly, "it will be my god damn decision, and until that time, you will love me and I will love you as if it doesn't exist. That is the *only* promise I will give you. Do you accept it?"

344

She held her breath, her pulse pounding. His offer meant allowing him to settle in her heart, take a piece of it for his own, not push him away, and most of all, trust him to not tear her heart out when he chose to leave her. She blinked and released a ragged breath. Rising from the cold table, she slid onto his lap and curled her legs up, his expression still hard as rock and unreadable.

"We'd be living a lie, Cain." She smoothed the wrinkles on his forehead with her finger.

"Do you love me or not?"

"I do," she whispered. "That's why making promises is unwise."

He shook his head. "Do you accept my offer?"

Cain had a strong will, but wasn't usually overbearing. She recognized his subtle attempt to make her commit. "You're wearing blinders while asking me to make a decision I know is going to end in heartbreak."

The creases around his mouth deepened. His jaw rigid as carved rock as he waited for her answer.

Mika gnawed on her lip. "Do I have to sign in blood?"

He spit out a laugh and her heart warmed when his thick arms curled around her waist.

"I know this isn't easy for you, Mika, and I know you don't trust me, but you will."

She kissed his handsome face and nuzzled his cheek. "You drive a hard bargain, HB."

"I'm not finished yet."

She narrowed an eye at him.

"I happen to know you can apply for leave without pay for up to five years for health or family-related reasons. Tomorrow you're sending in your notification. Tomorrow is the last day you work for DND."

"How—"

He covered her lips. "That's the full deal. Take it or leave it, and if you leave it,"—he swallowed thickly—"you walk away from me now." His voice faltered in the middle of his offer, but ended with strength.

Did she actually mean that much to him? "You want me to be a kept woman?"

"Yes, I'm keeping you," he said, his gaze piercing her soul.

"You know what I mean."

"I do. Are you worried I'm not going to keep that beautiful ass of yours fed?"

She wiggled her butt, and he offered a reprimanding glare. "Deal?"

"No more suitcases to open? Maybe I should wait for a call from the banker."

"Stop it," he growled.

"You realize Jen is going to be green with envy. You're supposed to be her boy toy."

A gust of air escaped him. "Mika."

"All right, all right. If I say yes, do I get to finish what I started upstairs before?"

"For fuck's sake, woman." He palmed her cheeks.

"'Kay," she said, stilling her tongue.

"'Kay, what?"

"Man, you really know how to push a business deal into the corner."

"Yes, I do. 'Kay, what?"

She sat up straight and shook her shoulders loose. "I, Mika Maria Makris, agree to be Cain Dimitri Sallas' kept woman." She raised her hand and gave him the Girl Scout sign. "I promise to love him as if he'll never leave and break my heart." Her voice stuttered, and Cain's brows flexed. "I will believe that he loves me until he doesn't anymore." She blew out her breath and tried to resist the tears. Why was she crying? Simple, because she knew how this fairytale would end. She swiped the tear away. "I promise to be the best dog walker on the face of the planet."

Cain's firm lips pressed a sweet kiss against her mouth. "Did I mention the signing bonus?" he asked, his voice husky.

"No, I don't recall that."

He nibbled her neck and the spot behind her ear that made her squirm. His warm, large hand palmed her breast. How had he managed to undo the buttons on her shirt without her knowing it?

Who gives a shit?

"It's quite simple and very desirable." He nipped the pulse in her neck, his other hand fisting her hair and tugging lightly, revealing her throat. "I'm going to fuck you so deeply you'll see stars when you come. I don't want anything between us anymore. I want to bury myself in your moist heat and feel all of you. I need all of you because I love all of you."

Her blood thundered through her veins with the rugged alpha Greek male taking possession of her body and soul. Panting. Yes, she was panting—like a frickin' dog.

Chapter Twenty-two

Cain hovered over her like a drill sergeant as she filled in the leave without pay online forms. She'd finished her current assignment at work, but it was still scary, and she stalled before selecting the submit button.

His warm breath brushed past her ear. "Send it."

Mika hit the button, then swiveled in her chair to look up at him.

He raised a brow. "Now, you're all mine."

Yes, she was. For the first time since she'd left home, her well-being was in the hands of someone else. "I must point out, there was nothing in the deal about moving into this house." She pointed out the window. "I live there."

"Mika." His eyes widened with shock.

"Sorry, no addendums."

Cain folded his thick arms across his chest and glared at her. She smiled and shrugged.

"Time to go," he said holding his hand out to her.

They drove to the Nissan dealership after having lunch on the waterfront.

"Woo, that is pretty," she said, worried that came out a little too much like Brandi.

The salesman smiled. "Fast. Stylish. You'd look good in it."

"Oh, no, that's a little over my pay class," she said. "I'm just the dog walker. It's his car. Maybe."

Cain gave her a raised brow. "Let's go for a drive." They took the GT-R for a spin. Like a race car, it gripped the corners and handled like a dream. Of course the guy driving it was a dream, and that may have had something to do with it.

Cain rolled to the shoulder of the deserted road in Sooke. "Your turn," he said.

"Oh, no. I don't think so," she said, taking a good nip from her bottom lip.

"What's wrong? Whenever you do that you're hiding something."

"Am not," she spouted.

"Uh-huh." He got out.

She did, too. "Okay, fine. I don't know how to drive a stick."

He stalled at the front of the car. "Seriously?"

"Don't look so surprised."

"You'll use the paddles on the steering wheel. Get in. I'll show you."

Fifteen minutes later, they were cruising around the corners, and she noted Cain sat relaxed beside her. "You're awfully trusting."

"I don't have a heart monitor on."

She laughed. "This car is amazing."

"I agree. Let's head back."

350

While she wandered around the showroom, Cain spoke with the salesman. When he joined her and they walked out, she asked if he'd bought it.

"I told him I might be interested, but I'd think about it."

****

Sunday morning she woke to the sound of banging pots and pans coming from her kitchen. She'd warned Cain this would happen, and he escaped back to the main house around five in the morning. The girls did this every year to each other. When birthdays rolled around, they celebrated them together. She walked out of the bedroom to see Kate and Sarah in the kitchen making breakfast. The heavenly smell of coffee filled the air. She watched the girls unloading presents onto the table, and leaned on the counter. "Aren't you guys getting tired of birthday ambushes?"

"Nope," they all said together.

She saw a small box on the counter tied with a bow. "What's this?" she asked, picking it up and shaking it. Something shifted inside.

The girls gathered around.

"Not mine," Dinky said, and no one else fessed up.

Strange. She undid the bow and shimmied the top from the box. The girls all backed away grinning. "Is it a paint bomb or something?" she asked, popping the top and removing the paper hiding the contents. What the heck?

A set of keys sat in the box. The squeak of the screen door caught her attention, and she looked up to see Jen holding it open.

"Think those might belong to that," she said, pointing.

Her heart started to pound. The Nissan emblem on the keys gave her the first clue. "Oh my God," she blurted when she stepped outside and saw the GT-R sitting next to her cottage. "I'll be right back."

She stormed across the lawn and banged on his door with her fist. Course she had an audience of five women behind her when Cain opened it.

"Good morning." He nodded. "Morning, ladies." He was trying to cover a grin, but she was not happy.

"I gave you a pie for your birthday!" She didn't know why she was shouting.

His brows flexed. "It was a great pie."

She thrust her arm out, the keys dangling from her fingers. "I cannot accept this. That is a hundred thousand dollar car. Are you crazy?"

He scrubbed his chin and eyed the girls. "We'll be right back." He pulled her inside and shut the door. "Happy birthday."

"Don't happy birthday me. Take them." She swished the keys in the air.

"No."

"This is…I don't know… like blood money or sex money or…" He wouldn't take them, so she dropped the keys on the counter. "I get that you're comfortable and your family has money. That's good. Really good." She started to back up toward the door. "But a birthday present is a bouquet of flowers or a nice card. A gift certificate for Serious Coffee. Ya know?" Her heart twisted with his deflated expression.

Cain's gaze dropped, and he looked at the floor nodding.

The room became very quiet.

She held her breath, her heart pounding. She'd hurt him. She didn't want to hurt him.

He jerked his head. "I just thought…" He shrugged. "Your car is on its last legs. It's not even safe to drive. If you get into an accident, that old Toyota will crumble." He didn't look at her when he said, "I owe you so much."

"No, you don't! You don't owe me anything. My God, you, you paid two million dollars to allow my mother to live out her days in a safe place." He raised his head and looked very lonely all of a sudden. "Listen,"—she placed her fingers to her temples—"I don't want to be ungrateful. In fact, I feel terrible now. You just shouldn't be buying that kind of extravagant gift for me."

His jaw tightened. "Why can't I buy a car for the woman I love? Why?"

"Because," she drew the words out slowly. "It's a hundred—thousand—dollar—car." She was yelling again.

He leaned over, his eyes beginning to sizzle like steaks on the barbie. "I can afford it." He jerked back and crossed his arms. "You know what the problem is here. I'm wrapped around your bossy little finger, but guess what? You're keeping that car. You're driving that fucking car, and I'm having that piece of shit Toyota towed off my property, today!"

Her tongue got stuck in her mouth with his heartfelt balling out. She turned a look across her shoulder at her piece of shit sitting beside the Nissan. "So you expect me to drive around in Miss Sexy White-hot Fat-fenders and trash Old Tess?"

His tongue jammed in the bottom of his teeth, his chest expanding. "It's red." Cain smacked his palm against his forehead and broke out in laughter. "Come here."

She gave him a flutter of her eyelashes.

"Don't you dare give me Bambi. I want my spicy little kept woman."

She wrapped her arms around his neck. "I'm going to cry when Old Tess is gone."

"Okay, we'll give her a decent burial in the scrap yard, because that's where Old Tess is going. She's served you well. Now, I want your ass wrapped in leather with a good airbag." He kissed her, molding his thick arms around her shoulders. "Are the girls spending the day with you?"

"We usually do something," she said, her heart still breaking speed records. "It's a bit of a joke. Every year we try to do something silly for each other." She shrugged. "Usually ends in a few laughs."

A knock on the door interrupted her rambling, and she and Cain took a step apart. Dinky opened the door, and the other girls stuffed themselves in the doorway. "Breakfast is ready. Cain, you're invited, too."

"Thanks." He popped a quick smile. "I've got a call to make."

She let out an over-exaggerated sniff.

"Happy birthday," he said and leaned over, giving her a chaste kiss on the cheek. Then he smacked her ass when she turned to join the girls.

Breeze gave a little whine from the couch. There was a blanket on there now, and the dog watched her attentively. Mika scratched her head. "Try to talk him out of it."

****

"Start talking," Dinky demanded when they were back in the cottage. Dinky led her to the couch, and everyone else grabbed the floor or a piece of furniture to sit on and huddled around her.

Mika stuck her fingers in her thick hair and ruffled it. "What?" she said, scanning the faces she'd known since grade one, gaping at her.

The screen door nudged open, and Breeze padded in. She sat on her haunches, staring at Jen as if to say, "get outta my seat."

Jen squished over and Breeze jumped up, laying her head in Mika's lap.

"Yes, things have changed. We had an amazing time in Greece."

The girls leaned even closer.

"Don't stop there," Kate begged. "Please, please give us details."

"Details," they all chimed in, except for Jen, who smiled, but bowed her head.

"Is this going to bother you?" Mika asked, covering Jen's hand with hers.

Her friend smiled. "I feel terrible. I didn't realize you had feelings for him. I mean you've never let a guy get close to you. I was attracted to him, I…"

"I know you stayed overnight hoping he'd come back after his birthday party."

Jen squeezed her hand. "You haven't had a real shot at happy. You deserve this. You do. I just feel like a slut now."

Dinky's brows rose. "You are a slut."

"Oh, fuck you."

Dinky shrugged. "A nice slut."

"Gee, thanks." Jen crossed her legs and looked down at Breeze. "Maybe we should hang out," she said to the dog.

Breeze woofed back at her and they all laughed.

"Sooo," Sarah urged. "Spill. I want to hear this."

They'd always shared their juicy details. To them, it was almost ceremonial. Baptismal, for sure.

"Time for catch-up, friend," Dinky said. "You've been tight-lipped about your trip to Greece, but we know you well enough to see the dynamics have changed between you and your hotter-than-hell landlord."

"I don't have to explain to you guys what the problem is. You know what I'm scared of. I mean look at him. Do you honestly think a guy like that would stay with me?"

Jen growled. Actually growled. "When the fuck are you going to get a brain? A real man, a good man, will care about you no matter what happens to your skin. Does he know yet?"

"He does."

"I don't know Cain very well, but what's important is that I was wrong about him. In fact," she winced, "I may have intimated he was a shallow prick." Before everyone started freaking out, Jen lifted her hands in the air. "I was wrong. Completely wrong. He's a decent man."

Mika nodded. "He's even taken steps to fund a company looking for a cure."

The girls all smiled. "See," Kate said. "If he was an asshole, he wouldn't do that, would he?"

She bit her lip. "Up until very recently, Cain had another business. One that he made most of his money from," she hesitated. "This is in the vault, by the way."

They all nodded, eyes wide sensing something juicy.

In the vault was their most secret conversation place. When one of the girls put it in the vault, no one dared talk about it outside of their circle.

"Cain was a very expensive and very sought-after escort for wealthy women." She swallowed and blew out a breath. "His entire adult life has been spent making women feel good about themselves. A short-lived fantasy for a lot of money. Plenty of them, I'm sure, were quite beautiful, either naturally or surgically." She ran her fingers through Breeze's fur, finding comfort.

Jen groaned. "Well, that explains a lot."

Sitting on the other side of the coffee table, Dinky shifted to her knees. "You want us to believe, and more importantly, convince you that Cain's affection toward you isn't real, but a well-trained facet of his profession. Seriously? Do you believe that?" Dinky looked at the concerned faces huddled in a group. "I don't know about you guys, I've seen the way he looks at Mika. Cliché, yes, but even at the barbeque, he was watching you when you turned away. It was more than a fleeting look. More than curiosity. I think he loves you."

"So he says."

That's when the room exploded with what she was used to from her friends, all of them talking at the same time.

Jen shushed them all. "Mika, you have to ask yourself an important question here. Is he really the type of man to give you a pity fuck? What is it he wants from you? Do you have anything to offer him? Money? Prestige? If not, then you have to see the truth. Dinky is right, he just sees you and he wants you." She gave her a cuff on the shoulder. "The man just bought you a fucking car for your birthday, now snap out of it, you stupid bitch."

She blinked at her. All the heads bobbed.

Sarah grinned and chewed on her fingernail. "So, um, if he was an escort,"—she scratched her chin—"that would mean he's probably awesome in bed."

Mika coughed. "Well, it's not like I have much to compare to, but yeah, he's…"

The squealing and ribbing started before she could even finish.

"Oh my God, jackpot!" Sarah yelled. "He is sooo hot, Mika. Never, ever let him go. I'm happily married, but shit, girl, I'm gonna admit I was alone while Sam was outta town, and my vibrator and dirty dreams stole your boyfriend."

Everyone's mouth dropped open, and they all screamed again, then keeled over laughing.

When they calmed down, she said, "He made me make a promise to him last night."

"What?" Jen asked.

Five sets of unblinking eyes, wide and waiting. "He made me promise that I would love him and he would love me as if the

P will never come back. He wants me to move into that big, ugly house with him."

Jen smacked her again. "Big, ugly house? What the hell is the matter with you?"

"I love this cottage, but that's not all, and this is what scares me." The laughter was gone, all ears perked. "Today, I sent in my leave without pay request. Cain doesn't want me to stress about anything. I did it, but I know in here,"—she palmed her chest— "when the P comes back, he's going to break my heart into little pieces. How am I going to recover from that?"

The girls sat quietly for almost a whole minute.

"Nope," Dinky stated firmly. "No, I don't think he will. Guys like him, and I don't think there are many, when they decide on a girl, they're sure, and nothing can break that except us." Dinky blew her a kiss. "You would have to walk away from Cain, not the other way around. And I think you'd break his heart."

Sarah gathered the glasses from the counter, filling each with orange juice and champagne. "This is a special birthday. Your thirtieth, Mika. You're in remission. You have a man that many women would like to scratch your eyes out with jealousy over—except us." She paused and shot a look at Jen.

"He's poison to me now," Jen said, lifting her glass. "To Mika, our friend, the girl who taught us how to be brave no matter what life challenges us with."

They brought their glasses together. "Thanks, ladies."

Within twenty minutes, Cain knocked on the screen, and Jen jumped up to let him in. "Hey, buddy, come on in."

He slid past her with a crease of suspicion on his brow. "Safe to come in?" he asked, looking around the room.

Cain looked somewhat delicious in faded jeans, a pair of boots, white shirt, and his black leather jacket. Maybe she should kick the girls out and spend her birthday in bed.

The girls clucked over him, removed his jacket, sat him down, gave him coffee, gave him orange juice, and put a heaping plate of good food in front of him. The whole time he kept darting looks around. "Am I being sacrificed after breakfast? Tossed in a big volcano, maybe?"

The girls all laughed, but that's because all of them were half-way pissed on Mimosas.

"Definitely not," Dinky said. "We're just showing our appreciation."

Cain's brows disappeared under his bangs. "For?"

Jen rolled her big blues and placed a hand on her sultry hip. "For falling in love with our special girl, silly." She paused. "And I'm sorry for thinking you were a shallow jerk."

He stretched his neck and said, "You weren't wrong, just...people change."

Sarah slipped into the chair beside him. "We knew one day, someone would finally corral Mika, but he'd have to be someone amazing." She poked him in the shoulder. "That's you."

361

Natasza Waters

He nodded, a grin forming on his lips.

Mika heard a chorus of sighs when her handsome guy morphed into Mr. Holy-shit-on-a-stick-he's-hot. Jen wasn't the only slut in the room.

"Good. So the secrets out." He rose and yanked her into his arms. "That means I have allies." And he powered a kiss on her that sent her heart reeling. Whistles and catcalls filled her little cottage.

The sound of a truck backing up broke their kiss. "What's that? Buy me an RV, too?"

He laughed. "Nope, but you better hurry and say your good-byes."

"Oh, no," she screeched and ran for the door, the girls following.

They watched as the tow truck driver hooked up Tess. The girls saluted, then swept away imaginary tears.

Jen swaggered up to Old Tess and emptied a bottle of champagne on her hood. "You served us well, old girl," Jen sung out.

The tow truck driver was laughing by the time he was ready to pull Old Tess away. All her things had been emptied from the car and piled on the porch. Cain had been busy.

"How long did you have her?" he asked, as the whine of the winch pulled Tess's nose in the air.

"Dad gave her to me when I graduated. Twelve years. She's seen it all."

362

Dinky wrapped an arm around her shoulder, and the other girls huddled around. As the wrecker pulled Tess down the driveway, they all waved and blew kisses.

Jen circled Miss Sexy White-hot Fat-fenders. "I want to borrow your car," Jen said, leaning against the hood and posing. Two phones appeared in her friend's hands and snapped pictures.

"Not a fucking chance," Mika said. She'd had a few too many Mimosas herself. "You want my man. You want my car. Get your own, you fucking slut."

The girls bent over cackling when Jen gave her the finger.

"Holy shit," Cain muttered. "Women."

"Aw, she knows we don't mean it...much," Mika said, looking up at him.

Cain hooked his fingers in his jacket pockets and jerked his head. "So, what's the plan, ladies?"

"Male strippers," they shouted.

"No way. No." He cut a swathe through the air with his hand. "No. What the hell do you need that for? How about a fantastic lunch? You pick the place. I'll foot the bill. No strippers."

The girls stood there, only their eyeballs moved. Kate, who was one helluva marketing saleswoman could strike a killer deal. "Well," she purred. "We really had our hearts set on taking Mika downtown to see some raunchy moves."

Natasza Waters

Cain's hand slid across his chin. "What's so hot about what you can't have?"

Kate stepped away from the group, and they all smiled. "Oh-oh," someone muttered. "Showdown."

Kate walked in a crooked line as if she were toying with Cain, but knew the outcome was inevitable.

"Well, it is Mika's birthday so she should be the one to…have, as you say. Maybe the stripper should be someone more familiar."

Cain's eyes rounded. "No," he said, shaking his head. "No way."

"Aw, but Cain. You see, we six are very close. We share everything."

Cain's eyes slammed shut, and his head fell back. "You told them."

Mika pinched a cheesy smile. "It's in the vault."

His brow rippled. "I don't know what that means."

"Means," Kate said, "that no one shares what's in the vault on threat of exile and pain. Now, I'm guessing as a professional, you've danced once or twice before."

Cain's eyes strayed off toward the ocean, but he said nothing.

"Silence is an answer to the affirmative." Kate circled him. "If you don't want us to take Mika to a sleazy dive with hot guys and gallons of alcoholic beverages, you'll have to come up with something else."

Cain scratched his jaw. Mika was nearly pissing her pants. Was he actually considering this?

"We can promise you total and absolute discretion." Kate grinned, taking another turn around Cain.

"You women are absolutely lethal. Your husbands would fucking hang me from a tree."

Sarah jumped to her toes. "They'll never know. Ever, ever, ever."

Cain's gaze came to rest on Mika. She couldn't hold it in and doubled over laughing. The look he gave her just made her laugh harder.

"I must love you to fucking pieces," he growled.

The girls nearly went ape-shit, screaming and jumping up and down.

"Rules," he said harshly.

The girls froze and looked like sweet little angels.

"No touching. No full Monty, and if any of you tell your husbands about this, I'm taking Mika and we're moving out of the country. Got it?"

The squealing started again.

He shook his head in disgust. "Fifteen minutes. My place." He turned, and every set of eyes watched his tight ass walk away.

"Oh. My. God. Oh. My. God. Oh. My. God," Dinky gushed, gripping Kate by the shoulders. "Next time I want to sell sand to India, I'm calling you."

365

Natasza Waters

Kate blew on her fingertips. "I drive a hard bargain, girls, and I never lose."

Mika just shook her head, laughing. She knew it was in good fun, and truth be told, if she wanted her girlfriends to be green with envy, this was one surefire way to do it.

"Ladies," she called, and they gathered in a circle. "I have one request, since it's my boyfriend and my birthday. The second he's done, you girls are going home." She paused. "And then you can come back in two hours and pick me up for lunch."

Five sets of lower lips pouted, but then grew into wicked smiles.

"It's worth it," Sarah said. "Let's go."

Not much had changed since they were six years old. Life had steered each of them down a road with a few bumps and bruises, but they always had each other. Mika watched them head toward the house, a gaggling mass of giddy women. Crazy, beautiful friends. If the end of the world ever came, they'd be together to toast the finale. She ran to catch up.

Cain had them screaming their heads off, and all she could do was laugh. The man was a rock star, and he was her rock star. When Jen tried to break one of his rules, he swatted her fingers. He ended the dance by planting a big kiss on each of them and shooing them out the door.

Mika covered her blushing cheeks and shook her head at him. He grabbed her by the thighs and perched her snug against his hips.

"Now for the grand finale," he said, carrying her up the stairs. Stopping halfway, he set her on her feet and peeled her clothes off, leaving a trail of slow, sensual kisses across her body. He sat her down, and with both hands, parted her legs, and had her moaning his name within seconds. Only her palms and heels touched the stairs, her body arched, his mouth and tongue heaven.

Draped over Cain's arm, she bowed backward. He plunged inside her core, rocking her into ecstasy. Stars flickered behind her closed eyes. The delicious width of his hardness impaled her and they came apart at the same time.

After they'd cleaned up in the bathroom, he lay down on the bed and rolled her on top of him. "Happy birthday, beautiful."

She grinned sensing a trap. "I owe you big time now, don't I?"

He grinned. "Yes, you do, and it's going to be an addendum to our agreement."

"No way. I love my cottage."

His fingertips brushed lines up and down her back. "I want you to love this home, and I want you here with me. There's a number downstairs on the counter. It's an interior decorator. Call her, and because I love you so much, you don't have to move in here until the reno is finished."

He kissed each breast. Creating his own diversion, his eyes closed, teasing her nipples with his tongue.

"Why do you love me?" she asked, kinda surprised she'd voice what she'd wondered many times.

His blue eyes opened to gaze into hers. "Because it's an undeniable truth. An absolute awareness that no woman could make me happier than you. After the life I led, I want to protect that and you."

Mika's heart oozed to somewhere south of her belly. Lifting her hips, she rocked forward, easing Cain's thick cock into her core.

His groan traveled through her breast and into her spine. He rolled them over, stroking her with a sensual rock of his pelvis. His hand palmed the back of her neck, Cain's body rigid with muscle and sinew. The sight fired her blood and she met his every thrust.

She swooned with every kiss he'd ever given her. Possessive and giving at the same time.

"I love making you come, baby." Lust colored his husky timbre.

Her inner muscles clenched with need around his shaft, and his hips drove her into a frenzy of lust.

"God, you feel good." He kissed her again, his breathing coming in short gasps.

She loved this man, every ounce of him. Every wonderful, amazing cell of him.

Chapter Twenty-three

Cane answered his phone, recognizing the song attached to his brother's number. "Hey, what's going on?"

"You at home?"

"Yeah, why?"

"Pack a bag. The family business needs you. I'm stuck in St. Louis and Dad is in Austria. We've been after Taste of Grape for a couple years now. They're ready to make a deal, but it has to be now or we'll lose it."

"They're one of America's largest distributers."

"You got it. We've been aggressively courting them. If they pick up our ancient vine Mandilaria from our winery on the Island of Rhodes, the rest of the US will be scrambling to have the others. Dad wants your help. He knows you can pull this off."

Cain gripped his neck. "When?"

"Now. They want to see you at five this afternoon. We've set up the meeting at La Petite Grande, a restaurant in L.A. Dine them, entertain them, and get them to sign the contract. It's waiting in your email."

"Shit."

"What's wrong?"

"Mika is running the Goodlife Fitness Marathon tomorrow morning. I promised I'd be there. She's trained for months to do this."

"Are you running it with her?"

Cain stared down at the slip of paper on the counter. His heart clenched.

He and Mika had talked about how desensitized the world had become using cell phones and texting. The next morning, he'd taped a handwritten note to the coffeepot. *I'm going to love every moment of our lives together because you make it beautiful.*

A day later there was one waiting on his pillow when he left the cottage in the early hours of dawn and the sky was still dark. *My heart is still warm even if my arms aren't wrapped around you.*

Cain read the one lying on the counter. *Out in the garden pulling the annuals. Come roll around in the flowers with me. Love YFL*

"You still there?" Abel asked.

"No, I'm not running, but I want to be at the finish line for her."

"What time's the race?"

"She starts at seven-thirty. I think she's going to finish around two hours and ten minutes. She had to take a few days off after being attacked by the dog."

The line went dead. "What the hell happened?"

370

He relayed the story and what followed. As brothers, they shared just about everything. He admitted he was scared she was starting to draw away from him to protect herself in case her P returned, and about the promise she'd made to him.

Abel chuckled. "Why don't ya just marry the woman and be done with it. You're ruined for anyone else now."

"I'm planning on it. I want to blow her mind with the proposal. Don't know how I'm going to do that yet."

"Until then, get on a plane to L.A.," Abel said.

It meant a lot to Cain that his father had asked him to bring this deal down. How could he refuse him?

"I'll make it work. Talk to you later."

"Call me after the paperwork's been signed no matter what time it is."

Cain took the stairs two at a time. "What do you mean? You think these negotiations will go all night?"

"Not sure. I do know that Taste of Grape's executive office asked for you in particular. Maybe they've got wind of your charity company. Could be a homer for both, bro."

"That would be great! Talk to you soon."

He hung up, quickly packed a bag, and then made flight arrangements to L.A. He had an hour to get to the airport.

Yanking a couple suits off the rod, he cloaked them in his carrier, then ran back downstairs, dropped the bag on the couch,

Natasza Waters

and saw Mika kneeling over the garden bed surrounding the patio.

Holy shit, he almost forgot and ran back upstairs. He sprinted over to her place, hoping she didn't see him, and laid the package on her pillow with the note he'd quickly written on top, then ran back to the house.

He crept up and wrapped her in a bear hug. If he was a bear, she would be all the honey he needed. The October rain loomed in the heavy clouds overhead. He hoped it would hold until the end of the race tomorrow.

They had a big Canadian Thanksgiving dinner planned for all their friends on October twelfth. It was going to be a busy weekend and maybe one to celebrate, if he could bring this deal down for his family and make his dad proud.

"Hey," she said, pushing to her feet.

"Hi, sweetheart." He brushed a curl from her eye. "You look beautiful with your hands stuck in the dirt."

"Maybe I should become your full-time gardener."

"Nah, as much as I love seeing your beautiful ass in the air, I'd rather see it on my bed." He gave her a squeeze. "Sweetheart, I just got a call from Abel. Dad needs me to finish a deal. It's big. If I can get this company to sign on with us, the results will have a lucrative impact for years to come."

Her big brown eyes stared up at him. "When?"

He swallowed. "I have to go now. As in right now. I'm gonna make it back for the race tomorrow. I promise. I want to see you cross that finish line."

"Yeah, of course. Go."

"Nothing will stop me from being there. I don't know how long the meetings will run today, but at the very latest, I'll be on an early morning flight."

She nodded, her face lit with confidence in him. "Do it. Make 'em sign on the dotted line, tiger."

He kissed her lips and wanted to linger there forever, but he had to get on the road. He backed up a step and held her by the shoulders.

"I'll be with you every step of the way, cheering you on. Remember, don't run more than ten k today. Go to bed early tonight. No partying with that clutch of crazy hens you hang with."

She nodded. "I've got a doctor's appointment, and I need to go grocery shopping for Thanksgiving dinner." She snapped her fingers. "That reminds me, I have to go shoot the neighbor's turkey."

She said it so deadpan he cracked up. "I took the turkey out of the freezer last night and put it in the fridge in the utility room. That thing is frickin' enormous. Think we could feed Victoria with it."

Natasza Waters

She smiled at him. "I'm going to have great pleasure stuffing his butt."

Last night they'd been gasping with laughter watching Mr. Bean's Thanksgiving dinner on TV. "I love you, sweetheart. Wish me luck."

"You got it. I know you'll knock it out of the park." She lunged to her toes and kissed him again.

He backed away from her toward the house, but couldn't seem to take his eyes off her. She was wearing her favorite big, sloppy sweater and a pair of loose jeans. He'd have to steal those things when he got home and give them away. While he was at it, he was going to turf her fluffy pajamas. She'd been wearing them for three nights in a row. He figured she had her period, and not making love to her every night was killing him.

"Love you. See you tomorrow morning at the finish line."

The last look he got before he sped down the driveway was the love of his life standing on his front doorstep waving at him. He wasn't even gone yet, and all he wanted to do was come home.

****

As Cain's car disappeared through the tree line, Mika leaned her back against the front door. She glanced at her watch. Nine-thirty, she had to take a shower and get ready for her derm appointment. In her bathroom, she removed her clothes and turned on the water to just above tepid. Steaming hot showers were hard on her skin. She placed a foot on the toilet and palmed her shin, blowing out a deep breath.

"Why?" she said, but she knew why.

Three mornings ago, she saw the small patch of red skin. Being a psoriasis sufferer, she didn't have the luxury of turning circles in front of a mirror with pride. People like her looked into a mirror with fear in their bellies, and trepidation at what would be looking back.

She wanted to cry when she found the spot, searching frantically she found others. One on each elbow, and one beginning to grow on her right butt cheek. She hung her head, shaking it.

"Go away," she whispered, but P didn't listen, even though it was inside of her. No one could tell their own body not to rebel against itself. She'd quickly called her dermatologist and made an appointment. They told her to come in, and they'd make room.

She'd seen him all her life. Dr. Whittaker had just started his practice in Victoria when her parents brought her to see him when she was three. She couldn't say Whittaker at three so she called him Dr. Whitti, and it stuck.

Climbing in the shower, she grabbed her bar of organic goat's milk soap and lathered herself. During her remission, she'd splurged a little since Cain and she had become lovers, and bought a couple bars of scented soap. Now, depending on how bad things got, she'd be back to smelling clean but not pretty.

She reminded herself not to panic. Maybe this time it wouldn't get out of hand, but her hands shook as she laid her palms against the shower's tiled wall. Stress was her enemy. During the dog attack, her adrenaline and auto responses had hit a red line. There was no going backward to fix it. Only forward to wage another battle against her enemy within.

Sitting in the doctor's office, she read a magazine and glanced at the other patients around the room. There were all sorts of skin disorders. P and Eczema were brutal, but the people sitting with her could have skin cancer or Rosacea.

An older man sitting beside her said, "What ya in for?"

She chuckled. She loved old guys. They didn't worry about social graces. "I've got a lifetime membership with psoriasis."

He gave her a warm smile. "Me, too. Battled it all my life. After I retired, it eased up, but I still have to get a little of that witch doctor cream for my elbows and knees."

"Wish I could say the same. I'm on Humira."

"Did it work?" he asked, his eyes still bright in a face wrinkled with age.

"For a while, but I guess not for much longer."

"Coming back, eh?"

She nodded. "Unfortunately."

He patted her leg. "That which doesn't kill us, makes us stronger," he said. "My wife kept telling me that every time I'd flare."

Mika watched the light in his eyes die a little. "She's right."

"She was," he said and nodded. "I lost her last spring. Probably why my P is back again, worse than I've had in years."

"I'm sorry."

He shrugged and the John Deere ball cap he held in his hands flicked up and down once. "I miss her, but I don't linger on the fact that she's gone. I linger on the years we had. Fifty-two of them."

"Did she…was she ever bothered by the P?"

"No. She fussed over me. Made sure I ate right and didn't drink too much. I was the one that worried. I got it in some pretty nasty places, if you know what I mean."

She nodded. P didn't have the decency to stay away from the groin area, which made sexual relations a hardship, never mind the embarrassment.

"You married?" he asked.

"No, but since I've been in remission, I've found this really amazing guy." She looked down at her fingers and saw them linked so tight her knuckles were white.

The old guy gave her a warm smile. "If he's a good man and he loves you, he won't care."

A sarcastic laugh pecked at her tongue. Cain was a good man, and he'd had nothing but beautiful, perfect women. Now he'd have one of the most grotesque on the planet.

A nurse appeared by the hallway leading to the examination rooms. She looked over at her. "Mika, come on in."

"Good luck," she said to the old fellow.

"You, too!"

Fifteen minutes passed as she sat on the examination table with the gown on, swinging her legs. How many times had she sat here staring at the beige tiled floor? The door swung open with a *woosh*.

"Mika, how are you?"

She nodded. The words teetered on her tongue. "It's back."

Dr. Whitti gave her an empathetic look. Sheathing a pen in the pocket of his lab coat, he pulled the stethoscope hanging from his neck, coiled it and stuffed it in another pocket. "Okay, let's see."

She pulled up the gown and showed him the spots. "What happened here?" he asked.

"I was attacked by a Rottweiler. Six stitches on the back of my thigh, the rest are punctures."

Dr. Whitti looked at all the lesions that appeared worse in the brilliant light of the examination room. He sat down in the chair by his desk and pointed toward the chair next to it.

"Is there anything else that's happened?"

She nibbled on her lip and nodded. "Mom had a stroke. A bad one. She's in assisted living now."

A warm and aging hand covered hers. "I'm sorry to hear that, Mika. Sounds like you've really had a lot of stressors. Even the biologics can be hindered by that type of emotional trauma."

"There's one positive thing that happened." Whitti nodded for her to carry on. "I fell in love."

He smiled at her. "That's good. I bet he's an incredible man. Anything else?"

She nodded again and slowly looked up at him. "I stopped taking the Humira."

Dr. Whitti's brow buckled. "Why, Mika?"

****

Cain stepped into his suite at the Fairmont at two pm. He'd been delayed when he changed planes in Seattle, but he had plenty of time. He hung his suit and tossed his case on the bed. Abel had called him when he'd caught a cab at LAX.

He cracked his laptop open and settled back to read the summary Abel had sent him on the account with Taste of Grape. He would have it memorized by the time he stepped into the restaurant at five.

This account would have long-lasting ramifications for the family's business. His dad could have sent him to St. Louis to take Abel's place or even attended himself, but he gave it to Cain to bring this deal to a close. His father was holding out an olive

379

branch, and he wouldn't let him down. No matter what it took, he would accomplish this.

A few minutes shy of five o'clock he stepped out of the cab at La Petite Grande, a premier restaurant in the heart of L.A. The doorman opened the door for him and wished him a good evening.

"Thank you."

Taking a calming breath, he straightened his suit jacket, adjusted his tie, and walked up to the intricately designed host desk. "Good evening. I'm Cain Sallas."

A pretty woman with a fitted black dress and high heels nodded at him demurely. "Ms. Cartright is already waiting for you."

He stalled. "Excuse me?" His pulsed ticked up a notch.

"Ms. Cartright is at your table. She arrived only a moment before you. This way, please."

Abel hadn't mentioned the name of the executive because he wasn't sure which of five people would be attending.

La Petite Grande's dining room was ultra-chic, the tables spaced out for privacy, the lighting low for ambiance. Residing on prime real estate on Fifth Avenue, and room to breathe meant the price tag was extraordinarily high. He'd visited this restaurant before in his other profession, and he'd been here with Corrine Cartright. His pulse banged with warning.

A woman sat with her back to him, but there was no mistaking her. He prayed to all that was mighty the hostess

380

would keep walking, but she didn't. She stopped next to the table, and his stomach dove into a dark bottomless pit.

Corrine swirled in her chair and rose to her leggy five foot eleven height. "Cain," she said brightly and swung her arms around his neck.

He placed his fingertips on her waist and gave her a smile he hadn't used in a long time, the one that reached his lips, but shut down everything inside him.

"Corrine, what a surprise."

She held on for too long, then brushed her lips against his ear. "You still smell good enough to lick."

He swallowed thickly, holding the chair for the brunette to sit, then took a seat across from her, and undid his suit jacket.

They let the well-dressed server make her spiel about the chef's dinner specials. He glued his eyes on the girl while Corrine stared at him. *How the fuck could this happen?* She was in the wine industry too, but for another company. Her family were vintners, but not Taste of Grape.

Corrine had been a client, one that had started off hiring him once, but quickly became twice a year, then four times. It became very evident she wanted more, and he didn't. She was exotically beautiful with rich, dark hair, and she knew how to pleasure a man, but she was ruthless. That's what had got her to the top of her game.

Natasza Waters

Corrine had even offered to make herself an exclusive client. Pay for his time, so that he wouldn't see any other clients. That's when he'd ended their transactions.

He blinked when the girl announced the sommelier would bring their wine. His family's wine to be exact. Finally, he swayed his eyes to meet Corrine's.

"Cain, you look wonderful," she said.

"This is quite a surprise. I had no idea you were with Taste of Grape." He also wondered—no he knew—this was a setup.

Her gaze skated over him with desire. "My family took it over a year ago. My father asked me to head the company. I'd wet my feet in the industry, and he felt I was ready." She tilted her head, her leg shifting under the table to run slowly against his calf. "When your brother approached Taste, I was very prepared to hear what he had to say. I've always loved your family's wines."

He shifted and put some distance between him and her sensual play under the table. "I hope you love it enough to consider distributing Sallas Wineries and the ancient vine as an account."

Corrine folded her hand over his. "I am. I'm sure we can find a way to make that happen."

His heart grew cold. His pulse stopped. "Corrine, my interests have changed. I no longer run my other business."

An expression of relief washed across her face. "I'm very glad to hear you say that, Cain." She brushed his fingers with her

382

thumb. "I've missed you." The sommelier appeared and poured their wines. "Thank you." A deep shade of red colored her lips as they turned upward in a smile.

She lifted her glass for a toast. Cain gripped the stem so hard he threatened to crush it. *How the fuck was he going to handle this?* If she didn't get what she wanted, she'd flush the account down the toilet. The biggest goddamn opportunity his family had in years. They didn't need it to survive, but any business wanted to grow, become the best. This was their chance. His father trusted him. How could he let him down? He raised his glass and tipped it to hers.

"Corrine, it will be my pleasure to have a business arrangement with you again."

Her eyes narrowed ever so slightly. "It's what I look forward to as well, Cain. I know this is a great opportunity for your family. I'm sure you appreciate that as well." She touched her glass to his. "Iss Ighian," she toasted in Greek.

Darkness overcame him, his past rising up to shatter every light Mika had switched on in his life. Backed into a corner, there was no way out. Only who would lose the most. He closed his eyes, unable to hide the hurt.

He sat his glass on the table, wanting to crawl back into that dark place. Deceiving Mika or failing his father, those were his options.

Natasza Waters

"Cain, are you all right?" Corrine asked, her brow curling tight.

"Excuse me, I have to use the men's room."

He looked around the washroom when he entered. Seeing he was alone, he steadied himself on the counter and looked in the mirror. *Are you prepared to lose everything? Lose Mika?* He took a stuttering breath and jerked his head with disgust. His phone beeped with a text.

Did you make it there okay? Luv u.

He stared down at her words, a swirling storm of loss and regret eating him up.

He had no one else to blame. His past had brought him full circle even though he thought for sure he'd escaped. Soft jazz music piped through the bathroom, the beat matching his ebbing heart. He blinked away the mist collecting in his eyes and stared at himself.

"Mika," he whispered. "Nothing is more grotesque than the inside of my soul." She couldn't hide her disease, and he couldn't hide from his past.

He took a breath and typed a text back to her.

I'm an empty man without you.

He slipped the phone back in his pants pocket. He wasn't foolish enough to think that if he gave Corrine what she wanted, and got her signature on the account, that it would end there. He wouldn't be able to live with the deception. He'd never be able to look Mika in the eyes and ask for her trust.

A wave of pain swelled in his heart. This week he'd visited the jewelers and spent two hours designing the ring he wanted her to wear. Their future was in jeopardy because of his sins.

He turned on the tap and splashed cold water onto his face. He straightened himself, drying the droplets with a towel from the pile on the counter.

Corrine basked in the power position she knew she was in when he returned. "Everything all right?" she asked.

"Yes, shall we order dinner and talk about the account."

A hungry feline smile spread across her features. "Looking forward to negotiations."

He clenched his jaw, and with practiced grace, the lie rolled off his tongue with a low timbre. "As am I."

Chapter Twenty-four

Mika's eyes opened with a pop, and her heart pattered with excitement. Today, she'd run her very first marathon. She sat up and crossed her legs.

"Hey, you." She gave Breeze a scratch. "You are a bed hog, do you know that?"

Breeze lay corner to corner and, being a big shepherd, took up a lot of space. Her tongue slapped against Mika's cheek with a big morning lick. Great! Dog breath. "Kisses won't make it better."

Breeze gave a soft woof.

Mika finished her morning routine and checked her phone, while her hand held down the top on the Magic Bullet. Inside was a concoction to give her energy for the race. It was supposed to be a wonder drink, but it was blue. How the heck could anything blue taste good? Cain hadn't sent a text, and her heart dipped a little. She hoped he'd let her know he was on a flight back.

Yesterday afternoon she found his gift waiting for her. He'd bought her the Goodlife Marathon purple shirt, and she just happened to have a pair of purple running pants. She re-read his note twenty times since then. *I believe in you. I love you, and I'll be waiting for you at the finish line. HB.*

At seven-fifteen, she'd received her number and milled with hundreds of other runners. Cain had constantly reminded her this wasn't a race, but a marathon. Pace, rhythm, breathing, stop for water. Don't push until the last five k, and then do it in degrees. She stretched out and shook off the angst in her belly. Her gaze fell across the crowd. She hoped he'd made his plane, but if he'd missed it, she wouldn't be upset. The opportunity his father had offered him was more important than seeing her run the marathon.

As she loosened up, she tried not to think about the lesions that had sprung up. Dr. Whitti understood why she'd stopped the Humira, but warned her that more than likely it would come back aggressively. They would try to control it with creams, but she had to be prepared for the worst. A horn sounded, and she found herself in the middle of a throng of people.

She put her mind in what she called her running space. The horn blew again and her feet, along with many others, began to pad down Menzies. They would run south away from the inner harbor, and turn down Michigan, then left again on Government. The roadways were filled with cheering people. Family and friends called out, supporting their loved ones. The girls wanted to come and cheer her on, but she'd told them to stay home. There was really no point. After a couple "atta girls" she'd be gone, and they'd have to fight the traffic out of the city.

She ran past the Empress Hotel, the key landmark on the Victoria waterfront, sitting in all her noble glory, the vines covering her face, a deep autumn red.

Mika tried to keep herself from getting tangled up in the first two corners with the other runners who were in a tight pack. There weren't many hills on this marathon, only a gentle lift of seventy-five feet or so. She checked her watch when she ran through Beacon Park. By the time she reached Dallas Road, she was ahead of her normal time. Her breathing was good, and the stitches in her right thigh didn't hurt anymore. The cool day helped to keep her body temperature down.

Her legs burned, but nothing slowed her pace as she reached Richardson, the thirteen kilometer marker. Checking her watch again, she knew she was going to beat her best time. The course split at this point, and she turned right to follow the half marathon track.

She snagged her water as she passed by the station. She didn't need to stop, she needed to keep running.

The pack had thinned out. Many of the participants walked the course. Now, she was in the company of people like her, trained runners. She imagined Cain beside her, running through the forest surrounding their home, the leaves turning yellow and crunching under their feet as they padded through the trails. She loved running with him. His words always encouraging her to push harder.

He'd be proud of her, she knew he would. At kilometer sixteen she began to push. *Concentrate on your breathing, ignore the burn of muscles.* She was circling back toward Beacon Hill Park and the Ogden Point breakwater. She'd taken her last water break, cementing her vow to break her best time, and put her mind on the end of the race to finish in front of the Legislature Building adjacent to the Empress. Every foot fall, every breath counted, and then she heard Cain.

"Push it, sweetheart."

The sound of his voice juiced her adrenaline. She rounded the corner onto Belleville. The parliament building came into view.

Her target.

The end of the line.

Running toward one word—finish. She was breathing hard, her body exhausted.

"Mi-ka, I'm here. Run, baby, you're gonna break your time."

She looked around, but even her eyes were exhausted. All she saw was a blur of faces.

"Keep running!" Cain called out.

She stroked her arms and legs hard, every footfall a thud on the paved road. Cain broke from the crowd and into her view. She closed her eyes, and with one last burst of energy, she crossed the line and fell into Cain's arms.

A race committee member called out, "Congratulations to Mika Makris on her first half marathon."

Cain gripped her and kissed her cheeks. "Sweetheart, I am so goddamn proud of you. So proud of you."

She nodded and bent over, trying to catch her breath. Cain pulled her to the side of the roadway. His suit was rumpled, and he looked like he'd been up all night.

"When did you get here?"

"Just now. Thank God, the cops were busy somewhere else. I was nothin' but a blur down the highway."

She laughed. He gripped her so tightly she could barely breathe.

He palmed her cheeks and stared into her eyes. "Fuck, I love you so god damn much."

Her pulse at peak speed, couldn't pump any faster, but hearing his words made her smile. "I love you too."

"Next year, we'll run together," he said.

More people crossed the line and their names were announced over the speaker. She'd done it. Really done it.

"I need a bath," she spouted. "Actually." She concentrated on her breathing, inhaling and exhaling. "I need to fall down."

They arrived at home at the same time, and the second she was out of the car, Cain was all over her. Holding her. Kissing her.

"Wow, I'd hate to see what would happen if you had to go away for a week," she kidded.

He guided her into his house, and she flopped onto the bed, staring at the ceiling. Cain disappeared into the bathroom, and she heard the water pouring into the bathtub. When he returned, he was wearing his robe. Oh shit, if she got into the tub fast enough, he probably wouldn't notice her new spots.

"Up you go," he said, dragging her into a sitting position and peeling her shirt over her head.

"Think it's all right for me to soak with the stitches?"

"Think it should be knitted together well enough for that." He pulled her to her feet.

"How did the meeting go?"

Cain's hands stilled for a second. "Fine."

"Fine? That's all I get is fine? Did you make the deal?"

"If you get in the tub, I'll tell you all about it."

Cain dimmed the lights, and she was glad for that as she stepped into the tub big enough for four people. The warm water flowing around her legs drew out a sigh. He slid into the bath, his eyes almost pleading with her when he held out his hand to help her sit. She kneeled between his legs.

"Something's wrong, Cain. What is it?"

His gaze nearly shattered her, his dark blue eyes shiny as if they were misted with tears. His silky black hair fell around a shadowed rugged jaw. He looked tired. Sexy, but tired.

"I left here yesterday knowing I love you, but I learned that you own my heart. I'm just glad to be home."

He leaned forward and kissed her mouth with such tenderness her legs trembled. That or she'd just run a twenty-one km race, and they were about to buckle. She smiled at him. Today was a very special day.

Mika turned and Cain pulled her against his chest, his arms wrapping around her in a tight hug. She craned her neck, and he kissed her mouth, refusing to let it end.

"Cain?"

"Hmm," he said, nuzzling her neck.

"I feel like eating an entire elephant in one sitting."

He chuckled and bit her gently on the neck. "I feel like eating you."

Pow! Just like that, her hunger evaporated, replaced by desire.

"And after I'm done," he said, his palms cupping her breasts beneath the warm water and toying with her hardening nipples, "I'm taking you out for an early dinner. We're going to be cooking all day tomorrow."

"We? What's this *we* stuff?" She couldn't help but sigh with Cain's fingers sliding down her stomach to the heat between her thighs.

"I'm helping you. I'll be your kitchen slave and I-forgot-this-can-you-run-to-the-store retriever."

"The girls are all bringing something."

"Sure, but you're doing most of the work."

"Can we talk about food some other time?" she asked, reaching behind her to grip his hard shaft.

"Something particular you have in mind?" he teased.

A shot of regret passed through her, but she brushed it away for now. If her lesions kept growing, they only had so much time left. Shifting her view, she faced him and straddled his lap, looping her arms around his neck. He took the opportunity to pay close attention to her breasts as his strong hands massaged her butt. She kissed his forehead, his nose, then brushed his lips.

"Were you truly proud of me today?"

His beautiful eyes gazed into hers. "So proud. You beat your best time, and I wanted to be there for you when you crossed the line."

****

"Mika, you in here?" She'd just disappeared and that wasn't like her. Cain stuck his head in the cottage. Breeze sat on the couch. That was his first giveaway.

"In the bathroom," she called back.

"Hey, Cain!" Dinky yelled out.

Uh-huh. What were those two plotting now? "You two make me nervous."

They both appeared in the hallway. "Stitches are out," she said. "Dr. Dinky removed them."

"'Kay." He'd tried to do that yesterday, but she'd refused to let him near her.

Ten days had slipped by since he'd come home. Mika had only asked him cursory questions about his trip to L.A. When he told her he'd been successful at signing the account, she didn't dig. She had no reason to.

Thanksgiving dinner had been a hit. The food was great. Having their friends and the kids was fun, but the best part was when someone knocked on the door. Mika opened it to find Stevie, Kevin and Cash standing there yelling, "Surprise!"

Mika had burst into tears while the sisters hugged, then got mobbed by the rest of the crowd. It meant a lot to him to see Mika with her family. He'd bought them the tickets to fly out short notice and made Stevie swear she wouldn't tell Mika.

From the moment he got home, he'd put L.A. behind him.

Dodging Corrine's sexual innuendos and touches over dinner that night, he'd pushed on to business. He'd wished God would strike him down for what he had to do before she'd sign the contract. He'd prayed, but saw his future with Mika slipping into oblivion. God wasn't going to come thundering down from the heavens to help him. And then he was struck by an idea. God *could* help him! It was one fuck of a long shot, but he had nothing else. He began to drop religious references into their discussion. Slowly, but surely Corrine started to take note.

They were nearing the end of dinner. He'd tried to drag it out as long as possible, but she was getting impatient.

"Cain, you don't seem like the man I remember."

He smiled at Corrine warmly, although he was cold as hell inside. "That's because I'm not."

"Why did you close your business? I assumed you did very well." She smiled at him. "I was always satisfied."

He didn't leap into the reason. He looked around then back at Corrine, as if deliberating on telling her. "The reason was a personal choice, something I had to do. You're right, I was successful, but every time I saw a client I came away empty." He frowned and paused. "I started searching, looking for something to feel whole again."

Corinne listened attentively, the sexual light in her eyes dimming a little.

"I went home for a visit to Greece, and my mother begged me to go back to church. I'd always thought religion was a farce, but I joined her for mass, and I walked out of there feeling good about myself. I stayed for a couple months and kept going to mass. I confessed my sins to our Father, and we spoke many times. He made a lot of sense, and by the time I left Greece, I had made a decision."

Corinne leaned over the table with rapt attention.

"I'd given my body to so many women. Gave them pleasure, but it was empty pleasure. I walked away from that life, and I've made a conscious choice to abstain and live my life as a Christian."

She blinked. Her lips opened and then shut again.

"I know that's not what you wanted to hear, but I have to stand by my choice. I hope you can respect my decision, Corinne."

She sat back in the chair, her expression no longer heated with sexual desire, but stunned acceptance. "I think I do, Cain. I think I understand perfectly." She stared off into space for a moment, then nodded. "I do understand, and I respect you for it."

His heart galloped like a thoroughbred down the track. He'd rather live with this lie than to fail either his family or Mika.

"I'm truly sorry if I've disappointed you, Corinne, and I'll understand if you don't wish to do business with my family."

"No." She shook her head, reached for the contract and the pen. "Your family's wine is some of the best ancient vine in the world. Taste of Grape and Sallas Wineries will have a beneficial business partnership. She scribbled her signature on the paperwork then rose. "Can I give you a ride back to your hotel?"

"Thank you," he said, not believing he'd actually pulled this off. "I think I'll walk."

She leaned over, then stopped herself. He chuckled, meeting her halfway and kissed her cheek. "The best of luck, Corinne."

"Goodbye, Cain."

He watched her walk toward the entrance and did his damnedest not to do a football touchdown dance in the five-star world-class restaurant.

Cain had nearly shit himself when he'd called the airport. The Canadian Thanksgiving weekend had filled all the flights. He'd barely made it back to Victoria in time. With minutes to spare, he'd managed to see the woman of his dreams reach a goal she never thought she could reach, and he was there at the finish line, just as he'd promised.

Now, he had a new goal. The most important of his life.

Dinky and Mika sat down on the sofa, Breeze taking up most of the middle.

"Mika, I'm going to head into town. I'll see you ladies later." He leaned over the couch and kissed her.

"See ya, handsome," Dinky said, and they fist-bumped each other.

Parking in front of the jewelers, he watched the tourists meander past. Folks loved the downtown core of Victoria with its English flavor, fine dining and British accents. The cobblestone streets were filled with tourists. Even bundled up because of the moist air flowing in from the ocean, they still wore smiles. He ducked into a coffee bar and picked up a cappuccino.

When he walked into the jewelry store, the gracious sales clerk named Rita saw him and smiled.

"Mr. Sallas, welcome. One moment. I'll be right with you," she said, and turned her attention back to the customers in front of her.

Natasza Waters

There were only a few custom design jewelry shops in the Victoria area. This one had been rated as the best. He'd found them to be completely forthright and accommodating. He wandered around the store, viewing the beautiful pieces in their glass cases, a little impatient to see the special design he'd created for Mika.

"Mr. Sallas," Rita called as he approached a glass casement to browse.

He returned to the counter and she placed a velvet pad on the glass and opened a blue box to reveal the two rings he'd created. Beautiful. He hoped Mika would love them, because he'd put all his creativity and a little engineering into creating a one-of-a-kind engagement ring and wedding band. His phone rang, and he absently answered it.

"Hello?"

"Cain, hey."

He excused himself for a moment and walked away from the counter to stand by the front window. "Everything all right?"

"Bro, are you at home?"

"No, I'm downtown. Why?" Abel sounded tense.

"Shit, man I—am—sorry."

"For what?"

"Listen, I was talking with Corinne Cartright. She mentioned some crazy shit about religion and finding peace. I'm thinking maybe she was high or something. She said she needed to talk to you in person, and that she was in Victoria. She wasn't sure where you lived."

Cain's fingers gripped his neck. "You didn't tell her."

"Man, by the time I figured out you'd fed her a bunch of bullshit about abstaining from sex, I'd already made some stupid comment about you're probably overloading on it. I was kidding, but it went over like a lead brick. Do you two have history?"

"Fuck, yes," he spit out, anger welling in his guts. "She was one of my clients. I cut her off when she wanted more than a date. In L.A. I was cornered. It was either fail the family or fail Mika. I couldn't do either, so I told the woman I'd found God and was abstaining from sin. I had to do something. She's a spiteful bitch. She never would have signed the contract without me being part of it."

"Holy shit. Are you?"

"Am I what?"

"Abstaining from sex?"

"No, you idiot. When did this happen?"

"About an hour ago."

"I have to get home." He hung up on Abel and swung around. "Rita, I have to go. I'll be back."

"Certainly," she said and gave him a polite smile.

He jumped in his car and prayed to all that was holy, if there was any holy left for him, that he'd make it home before Corinne arrived.

****

Mika plucked a Kleenex from the tissue box on the kitchen counter. She and Dinky had a long conversation, and Mika showed her the toonie-sized lesions that spotted her entire body. Dinky listened and hugged her, telling her everything would be all right, suggesting she should just tell Cain.

Mika had tried a few times, but the words wouldn't come out.

Dinky promised to call later and gave her a hug goodbye.

Thirty minutes later the doorbell rang, and she didn't bother using the intercom, opening the door to see a very beautiful woman standing on the stoop, her rich, dark hair styled with a trained hand, and her dress a snug fit around a tall curvaceous body. Big blue eyes, with simple but effective makeup, looked up at her.

"Good afternoon, could you please tell Mr. Sallas, Corinne is here."

Mika hesitated. She spoke to her as if she were the hired help. "Cain isn't home right now. Was he expecting you?"

Corinne brushed by her without being invited. "Call him and tell him I'm here. I've tried several times, but the number I have has been disconnected. And get me a drink of ice water." Corinne sat down on the couch as if she owned the place.

Mika didn't know what to do. She followed Corinne into the living room and sat down in the leather chair. Breeze came to investigate and startled Corinne.

400

"Breeze, on your blanket."

Breeze trotted to her mat by the fireplace and dropped down with a huff.

"I'm sorry, how do you know Cain?"

Corinne put her aloof attention on her.

"Did he know you were coming? He didn't mention anything to me." She wondered if this was another Sofia.

"Aren't you the help? Who are you?" Corinne asked, her eyes narrowing.

Mika sat back in the chair and crossed her legs. "Well, you pushed your way into my home. I think maybe you should answer first."

"Your home?" she spat out. "Who are you?" she asked again.

Mika cleared her throat feeling a little intimidated under this woman's glare. "Yes, our home."

Corinne's steely gaze got even colder. "I'm Cain's business partner and his lover. Now, it's your turn."

"Lover?" she repeated. *Where in God's name would he find the time to do that when he's been here for months?* He'd had a few short trips for the web business, but…

Corinne cocked her head. "Did he not tell you he was in L.A. recently? Maybe we're both being deceived here."

Mika slowly stood up. "I'll get you that water."

401

Corinne stood as well and walked around, stopping to look out the back windows toward the ocean. "Cain did quite well for himself fucking women, didn't he?"

Mika brought the waters and set them on the stone table. "He did."

"You know what he does?" Corinne backtracked and scooped up the glass.

"What he did, you mean."

"Are you sure about that?" Corinne said, taking a deep swallow, then chuckled. "I'm sorry. I can see by your expression this is a shock. Cain is a master of deception." Her gaze swept around the room. "That's why he's so popular. He doesn't just fuck a woman, he makes her feel good about herself. It's an ingenious ruse. Each client actually believes they are the only one who matters when they're in his arms." She paused, her brow creasing. "You must realize, as do I, that Cain is an incredible man. He's generous and thoughtful. That's why he's so unique."

Generous. "Yes," Mika said. "He is generous."

Corrine's brow creased with concern. "Please, don't feel threatened by me. I'm a busy woman. There's no pecking order here just because Cain and I have been together for so long. I don't mind sharing him with you."

Mika remained silent. Suddenly, she wasn't sure of anything, only that Cain had gone to L.A.

Corrine set the glass down. "I assume you're his home base play toy."

Mika's anger began to burn in the pit of her stomach. He said he'd gone to Los Angeles to represent the family business. Had he lied to her?

"Are you trying to tell me, you were with Cain in L.A?"

"I don't have to try. I was." She smiled at her. "Like old times. We're both busy people, but we make room for each other. I'm an executive member of Taste of Grape, a company his family does business with. My and Cain's business is just a little more intimate."

"I see." She didn't. She didn't see any of this coming. Not a hint.

Cain's car raced down the driveway, coming to a grinding halt on the gravel in front of the house.

"Looks like Cain's home," Mika said, suddenly numb. "Excuse me."

She opened the patio door and walked out, not bothering to close it behind her.

****

Cain slammed on the brakes next to a white rental car parked in front of his house. Too late. He jumped out of the Jag. His heart deflated, seeing Corinne exit the front door. She stopped and glared at him.

"Religion, Cain, really? It was a good ploy, I must admit."

Natasza Waters

"Where's Mika?" he shouted, the talons of karma threatening to claw him back into the darkness.

Corrine offered a venomous smile. "I don't know, but tit for tat, Cain. Your happily-ever-after is done." She walked past him, a vengeful snarl on her features. She yanked the car door open. "I came in good faith. I believed you, Cain, but one manipulation is as good as the next."

His pulse drummed with fear. "What did you tell her?"

"Something you'll never be able to disprove, and with your history, I'd say whatever you thought you had with that woman is over."

He didn't bother sparing another glance at Corrine, bolting for the front door. "Mika!" He took the stairs two at a time and tore through every room, each one empty. "Mika!"

He ran through the open patio doors, searching the property, then his eyes turned to the cottage. When he reached it, his heart shattered on the ground. The front door was closed tight. He turned the handle, but it was locked.

"Mika, let me in," he demanded, banging on the door with his fist.

He ran around to the patio and peered in the window. Mika sat on the floor, her head leaning against the front door and her eyes closed.

"Mika, open the door." He slapped the glass with his palm. "Please, open the door."

She pushed herself to her feet and walked toward him, her expression blank. Her eyes dark and unemotional. She gripped the curtain, yanking it across the window, shutting him out. He bowed his head and backed away, bumping into the patio chair. With shaking legs, he sat down and put his head between his knees, trying to calm down. He'd give her time. Then they'd talk. He'd explain everything. Everything would be okay.

Everything would be fine.

Chapter Twenty-five

After the sun had sunk beneath the sea, music drew Mika to her front door. She stepped onto her stoop, wrapping her sweater tightly around her shoulders. Only a small light shone from the glass house perched on the cliff.

Cain's silhouette sat at his piano.

At first there were only random notes, the sound of keys being prodded with uncertain fingers, but as she stood there, the evening air filled with the most beautiful song she'd ever heard. Bittersweet and exquisite, the notes painted a picture with sound. She leaned against the post and listened to the story he played for her.

Every keystroke reached her heart as the notes tumbled together with love. His broad shoulders swayed with the ballad. She hadn't spoken to him in three days, and now he reached out to her another way.

Song after song spoke to her heart, and she cried for both him and herself. She never strayed any closer. When the sound of the ocean replaced the sweet notes, she picked up her phone and texted him.

That was beautiful.

Right away, he texted back.

Please, let me talk to you.

You just did. Goodnight, Cain.

406

For weeks she'd managed to avoid Cain. Mika slid her pants over her legs where the lesions had begun to knit together into a large patch from knee to ankle. Each time she bent her elbow, she winced as the cracks in the thick plaque re-opened.

The cream Dr. Whitti had prescribed managed to soothe, but not heal. The enemy within was in full attack mode. More lesions had sprouted on her arms. A fist-sized spot covered her right butt cheek and another sat at the top of her ass. Fast and furious, the P waged war.

She'd started wearing her long sleeved shirts and loose clothes again. With a bite of regret, she packed her new clothes, all of them sleeveless and form fitting, into what she called her hope box. She hoped one day she could wear them again, but a bleak despair filled her heart, as did acceptance.

Mika had sequestered herself in the cottage. Cain came to her door so often, she'd lost count. Her cell was filled with texts she didn't answer. She read his emails and wrote back, telling him everything was fine, while the beautiful Corinne flashed for the hundredth time in her mind. She couldn't help seeing them entwined in each other's arms.

Housebound, she was sick to death of breathing the same air. With a quick look around and no sign of Cain, she ventured outside to sit in the early December sun. Bundled up in a jacket against the moist and cold, she placed a chair at the edge of the patio to look out over the sea.

Inside, her emotions churned but between her heart and her head, there was a valve that cut off those emotions and made her numb. They weren't really terminated, just redirected, her disease feeding on her regret and growing stronger.

The time had come to move on. Readjust. Control her environment.

She heard a footstep crunch on the gravel walkway behind her.

He placed a chair in front of her. "Please, don't run away from me."

Breeze padded up and placed her chin on her leg. "Hi, girl." She bit back the tears, and a stuttered breath escaped her.

Cain lunged forward as if he wanted to hold her, and she put out her gloved hand to stop him. "Don't. I'm okay. I just miss this furry girl."

He slowly sat down and ran both hands through his hair. Deep creases around his eyes made him look older than his thirty-five years. He looked tired, and she probably didn't look much better.

"But you don't miss me." He swallowed deeply.

She gazed at him, shielded by her sadness. "Time to rewind, my friend."

Cain jerked his head in refusal. "No, I will not pretend that I don't love you."

She rallied up her balls—girls had them, too—when needed. "Listen, Hooker Boy, I'm a little late on my rent, but I'll leave it for you to pick up. I'm back to work on Monday."

"I did not sleep with her, Mika. Whatever she told you was a lie. She's spiteful and vengeful."

Mika licked her dry lips. "She said she was your lover and that you were together in L.A."

"My client, not my lover," he said, barely above a whisper. "I stopped our business arrangement a year ago. She wanted more, and I didn't. She's a powerful woman, and I had no idea her family had taken over Taste of Grape. When I showed up in L.A., I realized I'd been set up. If I didn't sleep with her, she wouldn't sign the contract and I'd fail my father. If I did, it meant deceiving you. So I made up a bullshit lie, and said because of my past I had found God, and was abstaining from sex." He ran his hand through his hair, raising his eyes to look at her from beneath his bangs. "She bought it, and I thought that was the end of it. I don't know why she showed up here or what she wanted. Abel told her where we lived, not realizing Corrine and I had a past. That's the truth, Mika. I might have lied to her, but I had no choice. I couldn't forsake you or my family."

She listened quietly. "That must have been a terrible no-win spot to be in. If it's true."

Cain let out a gust of air and knelt in front of her. "It's true." He curled his hands into fists on her knees. "I know you have every reason not to believe me, but I swear to God it's true."

"Think you've probably pissed off God already." She didn't know what to think, but she'd had enough of mentally flagellating herself.

He ran his hands down her coat sleeves. "It's cold out here. Why don't we go inside?"

She shook her head. "I need some fresh air to clean out the cobwebs."

"I'm going to make us some tea, okay?"

"Sure."

She ventured inside after a few minutes just as Cain filled two mugs with boiling water. The smell of mandarin oranges rose with the steam. He picked up the mugs and brought them to her little kitchen table.

"Thank you," she said when he set hers down.

Cain took a quick sip of the hot brew.

"Your dad must be happy with the Taste of Grape contract"

"He is, but I told him the whole story. The same as I just told you. At first he was shocked, but then he thought it was kinda comical. He said it was Karma, but he turned the account over to Abel to manage, which is what I was going to ask him to do anyway." He sat down at the table. "Whatever Corrine said to you was a calculated attempt to hurt us. To leave a trail of destruction and doubt."

Mika shrugged. "She said plenty. Anyways, Lt. Battle-axe has an assignment ready for me the second I get back to work. Sure wish she'd retire."

"Mika, you don't have to go back to work." Cain's brows shot together. "Nothing's changed. Nothing between us has changed."

He said it so emphatically that if her P wasn't running rampant across her body, she might actually have agreed. "I'm going to grab a nap. The girls are coming to pick me up later. We're going to a movie. It's Jen's turn to choose, and she picked some chick flick. I hate those things."

Cain shifted into the chair adjacent to her. "I should have told you what happened in L.A. as soon as I got home, but I didn't want you to stress over it."

She pulled her hands away from his, but he chased them and gripped her gloved fingers. "Are you cold?" he asked, about to pull her gloves off, but she quickly retracted her hands.

"A little. Just need a nap." She should just tell him and be done with it but instead, she rose and stepped to the door. "Thanks for explaining, Cain."

He pushed himself up from the table as if he were an old man. "Why don't we go out to dinner tomorrow night?"

"I think I'm just going to hang around here."

"Do you want to go for a run this afternoon?"

"I'm finished running. At least for a while." She held the door, putting her attention on the floor, hoping he'd take a hint. "I'll come by later and get my things."

"Mika," he choked out her name. "Don't do this."

She shooed him with her hand, and he stepped onto the porch. "I told you when we were in Greece that I would be your friend forever, and I meant it." She closed the door and leaned her forehead against the cool wood for a minute before she lay down to catch up on some much needed sleep.

****

Cain drove his sports car over the speed limit. He headed toward the Malahat, passing cars on the double lines and blind corners. The pressure kept spiraling higher in his chest. He missed her smile, fiery retorts, and teasing tongue. He wanted to hold her, but Mika evaded him every time he reached out to her.

He'd given her three days of space before he'd attempted to see her again. He didn't understand why Mika wouldn't forgive him until he stood outside the door of her cottage a few minutes ago.

The girls were over for breakfast, and he needed his allies to talk some sense into her. He was going to bare his soul, and hope like hell they believed him. The cottage sounded like a hen house of clucking women.

Standing on the stoop, he heard Dinky ask if she should call him for breakfast. Sarah made a joke and said maybe he'd dance for them again. He smiled and shook his head. Suddenly, the room became very quiet.

"Oh, shit, Mika. What's wrong?" Dinky exclaimed. "Intervention, girls."

He peeked around the corner and saw Mika on the couch crying against Dinky's shoulder. The other girls giving each other confused looks.

"What happened?" Dinky asked.

Mika explained it didn't work out between them. When the gals asked why, she said she believed one day he'd wake up and open the doors to his escort business again. The girls chimed in with, "bullshit." Listening to Mika, he heard the regret in her voice.

"We're friends," she said to her girls. "We'll always be friends."

"But you love him," Kate said.

"I do, but so do other women."

Mika told them exactly what Corinne had said. He wanted to kill that rich scheming bitch.

Through her tears, Mika said, "Maybe the business trips he took were to see her or other clients. I don't know. There's no way to know. Corinne said they were together in L.A. You should have seen her. She looked like she walked right out of a magazine of the most beautiful women in the world. Why would she lie to me?"

"Why do you think?" Jen spouted. "You're here with him, and she's jealous as shit."

Mika buried her face in her hands. "I should have never gone to Greece. I should have treated him like every other guy. We'd still be happy." Jumping to her feet, she stormed into the kitchen. As if warding off her heart, she swished her hand through the air. "I'm just gonna pretend it never happened."

"Aren't you forgetting about somebody else's feelings, Mika?" Cyn asked, and wrapped an arm around her shoulders. "I bet if we banged on Cain's door, we'd find one very unhappy man in that house."

Mika shook her head. "I'm sure the next woman who hires him will put everything back into balance." Tears fell down her cheeks. "It won't take long."

Because of Corrine, she thought he'd been playing her all this time. In her eyes, he was still an escort, and he'd never amount to anything else.

Anger at himself and at her made him press harder on the gas pedal. Shutting down the business and putting all his efforts into the charity site had been for her. To prove to her he was a man she could be proud of. He wanted to be the man she could always turn to and rely on.

Reaching the other side of the Malahat, he took a sharp turn into a gas station and threw it into park beside the air gauge to answer his phone.

"Mr. Sallas, this is Mr. Klein's personal secretary. He'd like to speak to you if you have a moment."

Releasing his seat belt, he waited for more bad news. Klein had been one of the two money men he'd gone after to purchase the website.

"Yes, put him through," he said and switched the phone to speaker in the car.

When he disconnected from the twenty minute call Cain sat very still. Klein had offered him a dollar value he couldn't refuse and promised to keep the lab searching for the cure to P as the core recipient.

He'd done it. He'd created, gathered, nurtured and then sold a web-based business so enormous it would hit the money mags for sure.

His heart race. Cain knew what he needed, and it wasn't money or prestige. He could be a pauper tilling the land like his namesake. Bear the scorn of his father. Accept what he'd done and move past it, but he could not, would not, live his life without Mika.

****

He waited until Mika arrived home that afternoon. As soon as she parked the car, he hit the door running, swiping the bouquet of flowers from the kitchen counter on his way. Breeze barked and took chase.

"Come on, girl. Let's do this."

415

When he opened the screen door to the cottage, Mika was setting down an armful of flattened boxes. "Hi," she said, clasping her hands behind her back.

"Hey, I was waiting for you to get home." The girls had picked her up, and they'd been gone all afternoon. "Shopping?"

She nodded jerkily. "Mm-hmm. Shopping malls are decked out with pounds and pounds of ho ho ho." She put the kitchen island between herself and him.

"I have some good news and wanted to share it with you first." He walked toward her, but she stiffened, and he stopped.

"What good news?"

Ignoring the invisible wall she placed between them, he forged on. "I did it. I found the primary benefactor and buyer for the web business."

She smiled. "That's great!"

"Mika, we're set. I turned it over for seven hundred and fifty million dollars."

Her face slackened and her eyes widened. "What?"

He rounded the island, and she backed up against the fridge. It was a milestone for both of them. "It was because of you, Mika." He advanced, putting both hands on the fridge, leaning toward her. "We're going to celebrate. Pack a bag, and let's take a flight out of here tonight. Send your boss an e-mail and tell her you quit for good." She went from happy, to fascinated, to scared, and settled on sad within five seconds. "Hey." He palmed her cheek. "I mean it. I want to travel the four corners of the world with you. We'll stay as long as you want or as short as you want. I just think we should start off in a place with warm saltwater and a lot of privacy." When he bent to kiss her, she slid under his arm.

"I am...so happy and proud of you, Cain. I can't even imagine what kind of savvy it takes to accomplish what you did."

With his palms on the fridge, he stared down at the floor. He might as well tear out his heart and shove it in the freezer. Without turning, he asked, "What are those boxes for?"

She drew a folded piece of paper off the kitchen table and held it out to him in her gloved hand. Why the gloves? The cottage was warm.

"What's this?"

She remained silent as he opened it. One month's notice. She was giving him her one month's notice. He stared down at the printed note as if he was holding a grenade about to detonate in his hand. His mind whirled, but there were no answers.

"Why?"

"It's my tenancy notice. I'm moving out."

Fear made him raise his voice. Hurt made it worse. "I can see that. I'm asking you why? The only answer is this is some kind of joke, and you're going to tell me you're moving back into the house with me."

She shook her head. "I've got to start packing," she said, looking around. "I don't know how I managed to buy more crap."

He was across the room, forcing her up against the table. "Tell me what's going on in that head of yours."

"I can't go with you," she said in a raspy voice, and then cleared her throat.

"I would never open the escort business again, Mika. Never." He stepped back, devastated and confused. "We love each other."

She dropped her gaze. "I do love you, but so do women like Corrine, and I'm sure there are others. Now get going. I have work to do."

He shook his head, his heart rampaging. "Biggest milestone of my life. I wanted to share it with you. It's because of you."

Anger, resentment, but mostly abandonment made him withdraw. That dark place that had consumed him until the day she knocked on his door, began to creep across his consciousness. He had to think this out. Mika stood still as a statue, her expression empty of emotion.

He bolted through the patio door of his house and straight up the stairs. The half packed suitcase on his bed, and the small velvet box that lay on top of his clothes, taunted him. His past had come back to steal his future. Was this about Corinne or something else? He looked out the window, hoping the sea could offer an answer.

****

Mika stepped out of the cool bathwater. She'd bet it was half saltwater by now as she flicked the lever to empty the tub. Turning, her eyes slowly rose to the mirror. Her breath stuttered with a leftover sob as the marred person in the glass stared back at her. "So fast this time."

Lesions had formed under her breasts and across her torso. The worst had now arrived, the ones on her hands. The ones she couldn't hide.

The bathroom door slammed against the wall and Cain filled the space. "I have to know..."

There she stood, in all her naked, grotesque glory in front of him. The towel hung eight feet away, no hope of hiding and saving her embarrassment. Her bottom lip quivered, and she closed her eyes tightly, ice crackling down her spine.

Shame.

"Cain, have we not talked about tenant-landlord privacy?" Oh, God, save her. She couldn't look at him. She wouldn't look at him and see the disgust in his eyes. He didn't make a sound, and her heart twisted into a tight little knot. "Please," she whispered, the word coming out like a gust of wind. "Please, leave."

Instead of hearing the door close, she felt Cain's arms wrap around her. "Look at me, Mika."

She shook her head and bowed it.

"Then you can listen. Without talking to me, you've judged and sentenced me to a man who only sees skin deep. Did you do that to me? Did you judge me for what I was, the unacceptable profession in the minds of the self-righteous?"

After talking with Dinky and her friends, Mika realized she was using Corrine as an excuse. She believed Cain, but it didn't matter. In fact, the timing was perfect. She shook her head.

"I know you didn't because you saw who I was and still wanted to be my friend and my lover. We are the same. For the next fifty years, I'll walk proudly beside you. I'll still love you no matter how bad it gets."

"Open your eyes, Cain. Look at what you'd have to live with."

"I see you," he said, staring at her. "And I love all of you. I've told you that so many times. You are part of my life, the best part. I would literally give up everything I have, except you."

Slowly, big tears slipped from her eyes and splashed on her chest. "I can't let you do that."

"None of this was about Corinne. Your P returned, and you're putting yourself behind prison bars again." His gaze followed his finger as it gently circled one of her lesions. "Tell me what I have to do to make you trust me."

She thrust his hand away. "Look at me!" she screeched in her panic, her brows crushed together. "I'm covered in lesions and bloody cracks. It's only going to get worse." She began to shake and her chest squeezed so tight she could barely breathe.

420

"Grotesque is an understatement." Her voice cracked just like her skin. "All your life you've had beautiful women, Cain."

He shook his head. "I never had them. I never wanted them, but I want you."

"Liar!" She ripped the towel from the bar and wrapped it around her mottled body. "No sane person could love this!" she yelled. "Children who don't understand, point their fingers because they know it's abnormal. People who should know better, but don't, see me on a beach, and their expressions curl with disgust as if I'll poison the water like a leper. Men are repulsed by it. So—don't—lie—to—me!"

Cain's expression became raw with shock, and he took a step back.

The stupid tears didn't know when to quit, and she covered her face, but mostly from shame. "Cain..." Her chest heaved. "You won't lose me, but don't come back until you're ready to make a commitment to be my friend, and *only* my friend." She dropped her hands and glared at him. "I told you this day would come. It's hard. I know it's hard. I should have never let my heart walk through those bars. I belong behind them."

He jerked his head, his eyes darting toward the mirror. "I don't give a shit about your skin."

"You've seen the pictures, but you don't understand. I leave a trail of scales behind me. Dust balls look more like snowflakes covered with dead skin. These lesions will cover every limb.

421

Twenty-four hours a day I'm sticky with creams. They stain my clothes. My blood is smudged on the sheets." She laughed but it came out like someone halfway bound by hysterics. "That," she shouted, "is the reality."

The drip of water from the faucet sounded as loud as a church bell when it struck the porcelain tub. Slowly, he turned his gaze back to her. His striking features were a palette of pain and confusion, but she also saw acceptance and Mika breathed with relief even though her heart shattered.

"It's you that doesn't understand. You think you can gross me out or frighten me? There was nothing inside of this,"—he fisted his chest—"until I loved you, and it will be empty again because I don't want it back unless I have you."

"Cain, you are a strikingly handsome man and I am deeply scarred. You will never convince me that you could be happy living a life with me. Give it time, and you'll realize I'm doing what's best for both of us."

He shook his head. "You're not. All you see is what's in that mirror and condemning us to walk through this life without each other." He clamped his jaw. "If you could feel what I'm feeling, you'd run into my arms and never leave."

Standing in the bathroom, Cain gone, and doubt filling the space he left behind, she sat on the edge of the tub and closed her eyes. If only she could open them and see nothing but perfect skin. The enemy living inside her had won another battle, but it was truly for the best.

His Perfect Imperfection

With time, everything healed, except her.

Chapter Twenty-six

Not much had changed in the office since Mika had been gone. Lt. Vickers didn't disappoint, riding her ass all day. In a strange way, it brought comfort. Earning three thousand dollars a month, she planned on giving Cain back some money for her mom out of each pay check. Because of that, she quietly accepted Vickers diatribe on how she needed to tighten up the project she'd been given. Losing herself within her work helped. When four o'clock came, she grabbed her bag and walked out as numb as when she'd walked in.

Mika stopped at the nursing station of the Golden Years. "Hi, Andie," she greeted. She'd come to know all the staff, but she especially liked Andie.

Finishing an entry in a big binder, she raised her head. "Hi, Mika. Your mom's doing okay today," she said with a smile. "Cain's a little late, think you'll catch him in there."

"Cain?" Her brows pinched together.

Andie turned her wrist to check her watch. "Usually he comes in at around one o'clock, but he's late today."

"How many times has he come?"

Andie shrugged. "Lots. Every other day." She gave her an odd look, as if she should know that. "He sits with her for an hour then leaves."

"Thanks." She walked down the corridor to her mother's room. The door was open a crack, and she peeked in. Cain sat beside her bed, her mother's eyes open and staring up at the ceiling. It still broke her heart to see her this way, but Mika had gotten used to the vacant stare.

Cain cupped her mom's hand in his, pressing it against his cheek. "I wish you could talk some sense into your daughter," he said. "Mika loves me, but she's so afraid to trust her own heart." He gently brushed the hair from her mother's forehead. "I'm lost without her. I feel like I'm walking through a wasteland far emptier than the one she drew me from. How the hell am I supposed to live my life without my mate?" His words choked to a stop, and Mika realized he was crying, his shoulders jerking with sobs. Cain raised his face, his expression twisted with emotion. "I love your daughter. I want her beside me forever because she's perfect. In my eyes she's perfection."

Mika backed away from the door and hurried down the hall. Driving home, she kept wiping away the tears as they continued to fall. When she got to the cottage, she wrapped herself in a blanket, cocooned by Cain's words. Why would he forsake his life and a chance at happiness to be with her instead?

The room was dark when she opened her eyes again, but she wasn't alone. A wet nose pressed against hers. Unfurling her arm from the blanket, she ran her fingers through Breeze's soft fur.

"Hi, girl." Something hung from her collar, and she undid the ribbon, rolled around a piece of paper.

Meet me tonight. Eight o'clock. The corner of Belleville and Menzies. You asked for a commitment, and I'm ready. Bundle up. It's cold outside.

Cain.

Mika parked her car and gazed across the Victoria waterfront. The Empress Hotel sat majestically decked out with Christmas lights. Couples snuggled together as they walked down the sidewalks. Large candy canes hung from the five-globed lamp posts lining the street. The dry arctic air pushing in from the north, smelled as if it might snow tonight.

She rounded the corner and saw Cain standing on the sidewalk by a horse-drawn carriage. He watched her approach, his handsome features twisting her heart when a small smile curved his lips. Cain's strong physique and confidence surrounded him. She missed everything they had, and it broke her heart that she caused him any pain.

"Hi," he said, staring down at her, his eyes unreadable.

"Hey. What's this all about?"

His warm hand cupped her jaw. "I thought that maybe my best friend needed me. She's hurting right now, and I need to tell her something important."

She bit her bottom lip, trying not to cry. Cain opened the door to the carriage. The driver looked ahead with the reins hanging loosely in his hands. She nodded and Cain helped her inside. Sitting beside her, he pulled a large blanket over them. With a quick look over his shoulder, the driver made a little sound, and the four large horses began to pull, the *clip clop* of their hooves echoing in the crisp air.

Under the blanket, Cain slid his hand over hers. She always wore gloves to hide her hideous skin. Cain pinched the leather and removed the gloves. When she resisted, he gently clenched her wrist then thread his fingers with hers.

"I went to visit your mom today. When I'm with her, it reminds me that no matter what's around the corner for us in this life, there are certain things we get to choose and other things we just have to accept because they're unchangeable. Sometimes, they're the same thing."

Cain's handsome face angled toward her, and the desire to kiss him yanked at her heart.

"I can't make you trust me. All I can do is tell you the truth, which I have always done." He drew her closer and tucked his chin against her head. "I never believed I could fall in love. How could I, considering what I did. My clients..." He paused, his jaw clenching. "My clients paid me to make them feel special, make love to them and fulfill a fantasy. I never made love to any of them because I wasn't in love. I don't know if you'll ever understand this, but flesh is just flesh when you're fucking it. The act means nothing. It has no value. There's no depth or emotion other than lust. When you showed up on my front

427

doorstep, you drew me from a dark place with your smile. Your eyes were so shiny, they sparkled. I could see your soul. An incredible, beautiful soul." He took in a quick gasp of air, and his head turned away from her.

She didn't want him to stop talking, so she wrapped her arm around his waist and held him tight.

"Just after you'd moved in, I left to see a client. I was standing out on the balcony in the middle of the Fijian Sea looking at the heavens filled with stars, and I reached for my phone. I needed to hear your voice. It was a balmy night in paradise, but I was cold until you picked up. That was only a short time after knowing you. I made an excuse and came home early because you were here, and I was too far away.

"I waited impatiently for four-thirty every day, when I knew I'd have an excuse to spend an hour with you and we'd run. For the longest time, I didn't want to admit I was falling in love. I didn't deserve you after what I'd done, but even when you knew what I was, you didn't criticize me. You accepted me. Somehow, you put an invisible marker at the point we met and didn't look back. Love, Mika, is more than skin deep. It has nothing to do with flesh and everything to do with what the heart desires." Cain drew away and looked straight in her eyes. "I have never had, nor will I ever have, a desire as deep as I have for you. I need you in my life because I want to give you the best moments in yours. My passion comes from my heart, and has nothing to do with your skin. You asked me for a commitment, and I intend to keep it. My heart is reaching out and asking if you will be my wife and partner for as long as we live."

Tiny snowflakes began to fall and Mika looked into the night sky. "Have you considered you're doing this to pay a penance?"

Cain unfurled his hand, revealing an open velvet box. The diamonds caught the lights and twinkled like stars. "You mean a hundred different things to me, but don't you ever call yourself that again or so help me God, I'll spank your ass red." The corners of his eyes creased. "You can stall all you want, because I have enough money to pay this gentlemen to keep going for the next sixty years. But I'd prefer you admit you love me and accept me with all my faults, so I can put this ring on your finger, and tell the Wyatts and Bens of the world that we will grow old together."

Of all the scenarios and all the dreams she'd ever had, none of them dared to hope the most handsome, honorable man she'd ever met, would propose to her this way. He waited, his brow taut, his eyes hopeful.

"This isn't real."

He twirled his finger in a curl of her hair. "This is as real as it gets. I'm going to take care of you, and you're going to take care of me. That's what people do when they love each other." He paused, then raised his brow. "So stop pissin' around. Let me put this ring on your finger because it's never coming off."

429

Her lips twitched. "If I say yes, I won't be able to call you Hooker Boy anymore."

A grin slipped across his delicious mouth. "No, but Hot Buns works." He brushed a kiss across her lips.

She tried to deepen it, but he pulled away.

"Now, now, my fair lady. I haven't heard what I want to hear."

She gave him a bashful look and mustered up a fine British accent. "It is to say, our paths should have never crossed, but now my heart is in your palm. Do not crush it if I say yes."

Cain raised her hand, the lesions red and angry looking. Her brows flicked with worry, expecting to see disgust in his eyes as he slipped the ring onto her finger.

Cain spoke in his mother tongue. When she queried him with her gaze, he said it again. "Never in my life could I destroy something so brave and beautiful to me."

After the world's longest kiss, he pulled his cell and video messaged someone.

"What are you doing?" she asked.

Dinky answered. *What the heck?*

He held the phone in the air. "She said, yes!"

The cheering and screeches from all their friends came through the tiny speaker.

"Then get your asses home, we're ready to celebrate," Dinky yelled back.

"Be there soon." He disconnected and grinned as if he'd swallowed a large furry beast. "There was plan A and plan B." His grin widened, showing his perfect white teeth.

"And plan B?"

"Intervention. All our friends are waiting back at the house. Kate was up first." He kissed her gently with a sensual promise, then nuzzled her nose. "You didn't stand a chance."

She laughed. "That's not fair."

"It was a ten to one decision. Your friends love you and I love you. None of us was going to let you walk away without a fight."

****

"Bye!" Mika yelled as all their friends poured out the door, waving.

The guys hooted something about consummating the engagement. She swallowed nervously at that one.

Dinky walked backward. "I'm coming over tomorrow morning for coffee, and I'm bringing all my wedding magazines." She blew her a kiss, then jumped on Jeff for a piggyback ride to the car. Jen winked at them and wrapped her arm around her newest boyfriend. A good-looking man, but a little standoffish. Hopefully, he'd warm up. If he stayed with Jen, he'd just earned himself ten new friends.

She closed the door and scanned the mess. "I'm going to clean this up." Cain's arm shot out and caught her by the waist.

Natasza Waters

"Oh, no you don't. If you don't think I know what you're doing, guess again." He curled her into a bear hug. She wiggled, but there wasn't much wiggle room.

"I don't want to look at this mess tomorrow morning."

He placed a slow kiss on her lips. "Get." Another kiss. "Up." Another kiss. "Stairs."

Usually his kisses worked to soothe her, but instead her heart raged with fear. "We should talk about this."

Nudging her, he backed her up toward the stairs. She took the first four, then plunked her butt down.

His chin dropped, and he shook his head.

"Talk," she ordered.

"Fine," he said sharply and muscled her into his arms, carrying her the rest of the way, dropping her unceremoniously on his large bed. He backed up, opening the buttons on his shirt. "Start talking. You've got about ten seconds to say what you want to say."

She laughed nervously, but this was no laughing matter. "Stop."

He wasn't listening and kicked off his boots, then hooked his fingers in the waistband of his jeans. Why the hell did this man have to have such an extraordinarily hot body? A speckled trail of dark hair on a firm stomach led to his belt. His jeans sat low on his hips, revealing the sexy indents that she knew was called the Adonis belt. How appropriate for the Greek god that

432

he was. She wanted to touch him, but she didn't want him to touch her.

"Nothing? Good," he said when she didn't immediately make her argument.

She jumped up. "Stop. I—I can't, Cain. I should have taken more time to think this through." She didn't expect to look up and see a very angry man staring back at her. Her stomach flopped over at the intensity of his glare. "Please, I understand why you're mad." She raised her hand and couldn't believe how much her fingers shook—not a little, but a lot.

He gripped her arms tightly. "Mika, this is the last time I will ever say this, because this is the last time you will ever feel ashamed in front of me." He leaned over, inches from her face.

The Greek was coming out again, and Greeks weren't known to be passive fighters. When they were riled, and Cain was definitely riled, their tempers flared. His chest flexed with deep breaths. With molded pecs and bronze skin, he was perfection and although intimidated, she was also feeling the burn of desire.

Her gaze flashed to his. "How? How do you do it? I couldn't." She shook her head. "I can barely stand to look at myself. How…how?"

Cain stripped his pants off and stood before her, his hard, carved body making her wet. "You're being stupid."

She blinked. "Pardon me!"

"Take off your clothes." When she resisted, the intense blue of his eyes snapped. "Now," he said, his voice a low, dangerous timbre. "Slowly."

She kept her attention on him. One tiny glint of disgust, and she knew she would run, but as she peeled each piece off, Cain's shaft became harder. He stood with his muscled legs a little apart, his hands draped at his sides. Her heart beat like a thunderstorm as she stepped out of her pants. Slowly, he gripped his erection.

"Does this look like a man who isn't turned on by the woman he desires?" One step brought them toe to toe, and he gently pinched her chin and raised her head. "You are more than your skin. Months ago, you asked me if I would be honest with you."

She nodded.

"Then I will. I fell in love with a real woman. Your body is a vessel, but your soul is the essence of who you are. What shines through your eyes is what I see." His palm flattened against the mottled skin on her stomach, and she took a nervous breath. "During our life together, this will come and go, but you will always remain the woman I put before all others." He brushed a curl from her cheek. "In sickness and in health, I will never break my commitment to you. It hurts me to think you're in pain, but I will not allow you to be embarrassed about something you can't change. I told you that night when you made your promise to me, that it would be my choice if the P ever returned. You agreed."

He palmed her cheeks, and his mouth powered onto hers, weakening her knees. With an arm around her waist, he laid her down, the cool sheets making her shiver. The desire in his eyes and the coiled tension in his body, spoke to her.

"My choice will forever be you." His mouth brushed the words on her lips. "That's my truth. What is yours?"

His shadowed jaw begged to be touched, and she ran her thumb along the edge, her breath shallow and uneven. "I choose to be brave."

The world and all its many faults, all its challenges, tumbled away when he made them one, and all she saw was love.

Chapter Twenty-seven

Sitting on the expansive balcony outside their room at his parents' villa overlooking the Mediterranean, they sipped on their morning coffee. "Should we bring the gang to Greece for the wedding?" she asked.

Cain tipped a little milk in his coffee and added some to hers. "We could have it here. Mom and Dad would love it, but they'd also be inviting the world. We've got about two hundred relatives alone."

"Two hundred?"

"That doesn't include friends and business acquaintances. The Greeks take marriage very seriously."

"As in forever?" she asked quietly.

His eyes darted to her and he rose, drawing on her hand, leading her back to bed.

"Forever is too short."

They'd only been in Greece for two weeks, but she went swimming in the sea and lay out in the sun every day. It helped immensely. The lesions had backed off. Not to mention his mother had piled home remedies on her by the bucketful. There was another reason for the P sliding into remission that Cain didn't know about but once again, it wouldn't last.

His hand strayed inside her robe and up her body, pushing the terry cloth from her shoulders, kissing her skin.

"As you know, I'm a professional when it comes to allowing a woman to embrace her sexuality," he whispered against her ear, his tongue grazing the tip sending tremors through her.

"Apparently, I get freebies." She sighed.

He chuckled. The warmth of Cain's large hands cupped her breast. "A lifetime membership for one."

Laying her down, he hovered above her, his robe coming apart to reveal a body women had paid a lot of money to simply touch once, but would never touch again. With his tanned, ripped chest exposed for her fingers' pleasure, she followed the swell and valleys down to the rope of muscle leading to his erect shaft.

"What about a family? We haven't talked about that," she murmured as his mouth roamed down her belly, making her tremble. "Did you know a lot of women go into remission when they're pregnant?"

"Have you taken your pills in the last two weeks?"

She could play along. "No, I can't find them."

"Huh," he said against her belly button. "Oh, well." His tongue slashed across her hip, taunting her with promised pleasure. "Guess we'll just have to take a chance."

Pretending to be a little miffed, even if she wasn't, she said, "Hey, family planning is supposed to be a two-way convo, Hooker Boy. What did you do with my pills?" He stood up and let his robe fall to the floor. The possessive look in his eyes jumpstarted her heart.

"They accidentally fell in the toilet."

"And did you accidentally flush them?" she asked, the edge of one lip lifting with a grin.

"Totally accidental," he murmured, his fingers slid down his pecs, ending with a slow, sexy stroke of his shaft.

She rolled her shoulder. "Guess it doesn't matter. Your little swimmers are probably on vacation after all those years of racing to the finish line with nowhere to go."

His chest shuddered as he burst out laughing, but the heat in his eyes roared into a flash fire. Stroking a sensual path up her thighs, her nerves hitched as his hands passed over a couple of lesions. A small part of her was still very scared that one day she'd see regret.

"Don't do that." His voice was warm and reassuring as his finger gently followed the sway of her thigh with a whisper touch.

"What?"

"My beautiful fiancée, I only see us." His palm made her skin sizzle with need. "There's nothing I want more than to kiss your swollen belly with our first child growing inside you."

She almost broke out laughing as he kissed her belly. To her it was obvious as night and day, but to Cain who had turned himself inside out to prove he loved her for who she was, not what she looked like, didn't say a word about the little bump she now had.

"Cain, those pills you flushed are years old."

He stilled, sensing her thoughts as he always did, before she said them.

"I wasn't on the pill in September. We used a condom, remember? Then we kinda didn't use anything."

His eyes slowly rose to meet hers. "Yes."

"There's a reason I stopped the Humira."

He blinked. "Yes."

"I'm not going to get pregnant, Cain." She placed her gaze on her tummy and offered an impish smile.

His eyes snapped to her stomach, then slammed shut. A gust of warm breath kissed her cheek. He blinked and blinked again. "We're pregnant?" he finally said.

Her brow arched. "I love how men always say 'we,' but they're not the ones hurling in the toilet and getting fat ankles." She paused. "That's why I stopped taking the injections."

He slapped a hand against his forehead. "We're pregnant?"

"Is there something wrong with my dialect?" she asked, grinning at him, pretty sure he was happy about it.

Cain leapt from the bed and aimed for the door. "I have to share this with the family."

"Whoa!" she yelled. "Pants."

He stopped, turned. "Right."

She curled her legs under her, chuckling. "You just gonna ditch me?"

"No. Shit, what am I thinking?" He stopped and stared at her. "I'm going to be a father. We're going to be parents." He sat on the edge of the bed and put his head between his knees. "Holy shit."

She rubbed his shoulder. "You'll be a wonderful father, but go ahead and have a little freak-out session."

Slowly his panic turned into a mixture of awe and love. "You." He reached his toned arm out and brushed her chin with his thumb. "You have given me every happy moment I've ever known, and now you're giving us a child to love."

She cocked her head slowly as if looking at a unique science experiment. "You kinda helped," she said, winking at him. Cain crawled over her, stopping to kiss her stomach, then found his way to her lips. As he'd once said, making love was a dance not a sprint. He never loved her in a rush.

"You are everything that's important in my life, Mika."

She sucked in her breath, her blood heating when he gently thrust into her body, but a tease wasn't far from her tongue. "You can do better than that, Hooker Boy."

He grinned. "Indeed, I can."

Cain accepted the challenge and proved to her how exceptional he was.

****

Mika stood at the floor-to-ceiling windows, looking out across the ocean while the coffee finished perking. Cain's morning paper with the bold heading of *Victoria Times Colonist* fluttered in the wind as he sat reading it on the patio. She collected three plates and the cutlery, then nudged the patio door open to feel the warmth of the May morning. Setting the table, she said, "That army sergeant of a wedding planner will be here today."

He grinned, folded the paper, and dropped it on the table. "You need her help."

"I only needed her help because there's three hundred frickin' people invited."

"I'm going to be back and forth from the airport five times today," he said. "Mom and Dad come in first around noon." His arm curled around her ass, and he gently pulled her closer, smiling up at her, his eyes hidden behind his ridiculously expensive shades. "Go ahead and say it, I know you've been dying to."

She rolled her lips together and shook her head. He'd been trying to get her to say it for months. She chuckled, but resisted!

Cain kissed her enormous belly. "You can't keep it in."

"Hey, you want the coffee?" Abel asked, hanging out the patio doors.

"Yes, please," she shouted back.

441

Cain's house, now theirs, would be full of family by tonight. The wedding was a week away, and she wished it were next Monday already. Abel brought the coffee urn and poured. He remained standing as he drank his brew. "Hey, is that somebody in your cottage?" he asked.

Cain grumbled.

"Oh, stop," she drawled. "Yes, we rented it out. Your brother didn't want to, but I insisted."

"And where am I supposed to sleep when you're pissed at me and kick me out?" Cain asked, gently rubbing her stomach.

Jerking her thumb toward the house, she said, "Oh, I don't know, how about one of the other forty bedrooms in there?"

He gave her a narrowed eye. "There aren't forty bedrooms."

"Nearly." She bounced her brows at Abel.

Abel gazed at them. "Bro, if you keep rubbing her stomach like that, the kid's gonna come out all shiny."

She choked on her orange juice, and Cain's shoulders shook with laughter. "I want coffee," she whined, setting down her glass.

"Just another couple weeks, sweetheart," Cain said, picking up his cup and taking a long swallow, sighing with delight to rub it in.

Abel sat down at the table and shook his head. "You know you're gonna pay for teasing Mika like this, tenfold."

"Counting on it, Uncle Abel."

Abel swept his shades from the top of his head and pinned them on his face. "Mom and Dad are gonna freak. Don't know how you kept the baby a secret from them."

"Great timing. We got pregnant while we were visiting in September, and then we went back for Christmas to tell them we were getting married, but decided to keep it a secret for a while, but I think Mom knew."

"Why didn't you wait another month so you didn't have to waddle down the aisle?" Abel asked her.

She tsked. "Blame Mr. Old-fashioned here. He wanted us to be married before the baby came."

"And she didn't want to get married in the winter," Cain added. "So, she gets to waddle down the aisle."

Mika nudged him and rolled her eyes.

"What do ya think, bro? Boy or girl?" Abel asked.

"Girl," Cain spouted, as she said, "Boy."

Abel laughed. "Just do me a favor and don't call him Enoch."

They both groaned.

Cain's brother shrugged. "Whatever is baking in there, there'll be no hiding that next week."

"You referring to my..." She paused for effect. "Big, Fat Greek Wedding!"

"Haaaaaa, I knew it had to come out." Cain laughed. "She's been dying to say it for months."

Natasza Waters

Cain dragged her onto his lap and wrapped his arms around her big tummy. "So how come you didn't bring Bambi, I mean Brandi?" she asked.

Abel shrugged half-heartedly. "She's not the one. We broke up soon after we got back from Greece."

She and Cain remained silent.

Abel fiddled with his fork. "Kind of tired of the scene, to be honest. No end to the line of Bambis. They eventually find out about the family and the business, and start pushing for a ring." He spit out a caustic laugh. "They want move in and take them shopping, their finger poised over the number of the most expensive stylists and dressmakers." He shrugged again and looked out toward the water.

Cain cleared his throat and shot her a look. "Don't tell them who you are."

Abel's head jerked with surprise. "Why?"

"You want someone real? Make sure she wants you first for who you are, not your assets." Cain shrugged. "You've always put too much importance on a woman's beauty."

Abel gazed across the lawn, soon to be filled with white-covered tables, awnings, and a gazillion chairs. His cup stopped halfway to his lips.

"Excuse me, Mika, Cain. I'm sorry to bother you guys."

She and Cain swiveled. "Morning, Hailey, what's up?" Cain asked.

"Um, I can't get any warm water to come out of the taps."
She blushed and darted a quick look toward Abel. Then again,
Hailey always blushed. A sweet girl and straight-laced as could
be. In her final year at UVIC, majoring in Biology, she intended
on returning to Saskatchewan where her family lived.

The poor girl had a bad case of home sickness. Mika and the
girls had taken her out a few times, but whenever a guy—and
there were lots attracted to her sweetness—came close, she shied
away. Hailey had been raised on a farm with a very religious
family. One night they'd managed to get her to down a couple
drinks, and she admitted she had wholesome values and would
never break them until married.

"Uh, hi. I'm, Abel."

She gave him a brief smile. "Hailey."

"I'm ah, Cain's brother. The poor one."

Mika groaned inwardly and bit her top lip.

"Maybe I can take a look at your problem."

"That would be great, thank you." She clasped her hands
together and turned a shy look at them. "Thank you for inviting
me to your wedding."

"I'm the best man," Abel said, rising to his feet, never taking
his eyes off Hailey. "Where's your family?"

"Just outside of Saskatoon."

"Well, whether you want to or not, you're going to meet all
of ours. All two hundred of them."

"Really?" she sputtered. "That many? And they're all coming?"

"Yeah, Greeks really take marriage seriously. They're mostly farmers." He prompted her to start slowly meandering back toward the cottage.

"I thought Mika said Cain's family were vintners."

"Umm, well yeah, we farm grapes. So, is your boyfriend coming to the wedding?"

She shook her head and her blonde locks waved like sheaves of wheat in the sunshine.

"I don't really have a date either, um..." He cranked his head to look at them, and they both gave him a thumbs-up. "Sorry, I'm usually a lot better at this."

A loud snort erupted from Cain, and Mika swatted him. "Shh."

Behind his back, Abel gave his brother the finger, and they both burst out laughing at Abel's big, fat lie.

Mika watched Cain's brother stroll beside Hailey back toward the cottage. "Err, didn't you say Abel can't even change a tire?"

Cain blinked and nodded, rising to his feet, stabilizing her heavy load. It had to be a boy. "Yup. Think I better go, too, or he might blow up the cottage if he pisses around with the pilot light."

While Cain had been blessed with a technical mind as well as business sense, Abel was the entrepreneur who couldn't change his own oil. "I'll keep breakfast warm till you're finished. Why don't you invite Hailey?"

Cain wrapped his arms around her. They watched Abel and their tenant for a few seconds, and she snuggled against her soon-to-be husband's safe embrace. "She's not a Brandi. She's smart but really shy."

"Did you see the look on his face? Kinda reminded me of…me when you knocked on my door."

She shaded her eyes with her hand. "Was it lust at first sight?"

He chuckled. "No. I expected a young woman with a full face of makeup and her hair done in a preppy twist, and there you were, kneeling on the ground giving Breeze a pet in your loose clothes and ponytail. I remember when you looked up at me. It felt like my world shifted and someone turned on the lights."

"Huh. I thought you were hot."

Cain's brilliant white smile cracked the morning shadow on his striking features. He turned her so he could look directly in her eyes, their baby wedged between them. "You know what I like the best?"

She shook her head.

"I fell in love with my sexy best friend, and next week, she's going to be my sexy wife."

Poor Cain had put up with her swinging emotions during the pregnancy, but the tears that welled in her eyes were from pure joy. She rested her head against his powerful chest as they saw Abel and Hailey reach the porch.

"You know, there might be something magical about that cottage," she said.

"I'm certain of it, and I hope there's some left for my brother. I know he acts like an egomaniac and a pompous ass sometimes, but truth is, he's a down-to-earth kind of man," Cain murmured before pressing a deep kiss on her lips.

"Go help him, I'd hate to see that building go up in flames."

Cain put it into a jog across the property.

She groaned and rubbed her belly, blowing out a big breath. There was nothing *fake* about the next contraction that hit her. "Oh, shiiit."

Breeze jumped to her feet and started to bark with a high-pitched warning. She barked so fiercely Cain stopped and turned to look at what she was raising a fuss over.

Mika felt something pop. "Oh, double shit," she said, steadying herself with the table.

"Mika?" Cain was beside her, gripping her arm. "What's wrong?"

She blew out a breath. "I don't think my dress is going to fit," she hissed, and then the water gushed out of her and splattered on the stone tiles.

Abel and Hailey came to a stop after running full tilt across the lawn.

"Hailey, go upstairs. In our bedroom closet there's a bag." Cain pulled his keys and threw them at Abel. "Get the SUV. Come on, sweetheart." He steadied her with one strong arm. "You ready for this?"

Men! They said the stupidest shit sometimes. "No, honey, I like carrying around a baby elephant."

Epilogue

Cain was in utter awe when they placed their son in his arms. The look in his eyes made her fall in love with him all over again.

"Our son." Cain cradled him gently, then placed him close to her breast, brushing it with his thumb.

"Look, honey," she whispered. "He's a boob man just like his father." Her son didn't need much prompting before he began to feed. He was perfect, even though he was a little early. He had dark hair and huge, deep blue eyes.

Cain's shoulders rocked with a laugh, and he peeked at the pretty nurse who grinned at him. While their son suckled her breast, Cain kissed her hand and then her lips. "Nice try getting out of the wedding, but it's still on, even if I have to carry you down the aisle."

She chuckled. Tired but happy. "Wouldn't dream of it."

"You ready for a little company?"

"As in how many?"

"Well, there was enough that the hospital thought maybe a plague had broken out. I told them we're Greek." He chuckled. "They didn't get it."

"Are they still waiting out there?"

He nodded. "They're not going anywhere, but Mama and Papa said they get precedence since they're the grandparents."

Cain walked to the door of her private room and opened it. He nodded. "Yeah, come on."

Leda's hands clutched her chest when she and Amos walked in the room. "Μια ευλογία."

She looked for a translation from Cain, but his father offered it instead as he and Leda held hands beside her bed. "It means, my blessing. I have not seen a more beautiful sight since I laid eyes on my first son. You bring us pride, Mika. May I hold my grandson?"

Alexander had finished feeding and had his little burp. She offered him to her soon-to-be father-in-law.

Leda was beaming, tears in her eyes. "He is so beautiful."

Cain squeezed her hand, and the warmth in his smile was real. He held no ill will against his father, forgiveness absolute. Alexander's forehead wrinkled as his little pink mouth wiggled. "We think that's a smile," she said to Amos. "He knows he's in safe hands."

Leda kissed his forehead. "He has Cain's eyes."

Amos' dark features softened, and he smiled down at his grandson. "Sallas men are handsome, intelligent and strong. You, Alexander, will be the strongest of all."

Cain's elbows were perched on her bed, his chin balanced on his fist, and he nodded. "His middle name will be Damon, in honor of Mika's father."

Amos nodded. "It is right."

"And his second middle name will be Amos," she added with a smile.

Amos's throat flexed with a deep swallow and he blinked quickly. His gaze landed on Cain. They watched as his brow furrowed, but it wasn't from anger, it was to stop the tears that shone in his eyes.

"I love you both, very much," he choked out and swept a tear from his aging cheek.

****

Five days later, she walked down the aisle toward the most breathtakingly handsome man in the world. Dinky, Sarah, Cyn, Kate, and Jen stood waiting. In the front row, Leda held Alexander, who slept in his grandmother's arms. Stevie, Cash, and Kevin sat beside Cain's parents. One seat remained empty but for a vase filled with white roses. It had been Jen's idea to acknowledge Mika's mom this way.

With a quick alteration, Mika walked proudly in a wedding dress hemmed above her knees that flowed into a long train behind her toward the man who made her braver than she already was because his support and his love never wavered.

After saying their "I dos" she was surprised when Cain left her side and disappeared around a temporary folding screen.

The minister announced, "If you would all remain seated. Cain would like to present his wife with a special gift."

Her eyes, as well as everyone else's, swung toward the screen which was removed and revealed Cain's grand piano sitting on the deep, green lawn.

"Mika?" Abel said, reaching a hand out to her. "Your husband requests your presence." He led her down the aisle, and she nestled on the polished wood bench beside him.

Cain embraced her in his arms. "You asked me once to play for you."

She held the stems of her flowers so tightly, she worried the heads would pop off. "You did. I heard you that night."

"But those were dark moments for me, and this," he said, raising the lid, the brilliant white keys gleaming under the afternoon sun, "this is my joy. It's called, *Song of the Heart* and I chose it because you have owned mine since the day I first saw you."

A Kleenex was tucked into her hand by Dinky as she passed by, joined by the rest of the wedding party, who surrounded the piano.

With gifted hands, her husband played from his beautiful heart. As Cain's fingers stroked the keys, even the gulls stopped to listen. Although she tried to catch every tear, one managed to fall just as his hand passed underneath. As the drop splashed onto his tanned skin, he smiled and closed his eyes. His soul sang to her and with each note, there was love.

****

453

The party waged on late into the night. Greeks certainly had endurance. From outside, the murmur of voices and laugher filtered into their bedroom. She and Cain lay on their sides, propped on an elbow facing each other, their son sleeping between them.

"How was the visit with your mom this morning?" Cain asked.

"Leda insisted on coming along to pay her respects. She wasn't unnerved at all. She held my mom's hand and talked to her as if they were having a two-way conversation. Leda told her how beautiful their grandson was, and how happy she was to have all of us as part of her family. It made me cry."

"I wish both of your parents could have been with us today, but I know a part of them was," he said, looking down at their son.

Neither of them could stop staring at Alexander. He was so tiny, but he commanded both her and Cain.

"He's you and me," Cain said, smiling warmly. "I never thought I could feel a love so powerful or protective."

He brushed her cheek with the tops of his fingers. She grinned, seeing the extra-wide wedding band she'd bought for him. She wasn't insecure, noooo, not her, but it was quite possible it was large enough to view from another planet.

"I believe everyone who is willing to be loved, will find love."

Cain smiled at her. "Who taught you that?"

She shrugged. "This guy I met."

He nodded and his handsome smile widened. "Just some guy?"

"Mmm, tall, dark and handsome. He's pretty amazing. I think you'd like him."

"Should I be jealous?" he asked with a playful timbre.

She rolled her eyes, pretending to think it over. "I married him today. Apparently, he's crazy about me."

Cain placed an enduring tender kiss on her lips. "He is."

A wet nose snuffled along the edge of the bed, and they both chuckled. No one could get Breeze more than two feet away from Alexander since they'd brought him home. She tapped the bed, and one very large German Shepherd wore her happy face as she settled between them and gracefully rested her chin on her paws, her nose touching Alexander's feet.

Mika kissed her husband. "I love you, Cain Sallas, and because of you, everything I cherish the most is right here. My very own family."

Cain's eyes misted as he kissed her palm. She didn't need words to read the depth of his love. She could clearly see she was her husband's perfect imperfection.

The End

Natasza Waters

Message from Natasza

His Perfect Imperfection is a work seeded and nurtured from the heart. This novel, although nested in fiction, reflects the hard truths about Psoriasis, a disorder affecting twelve million people. This is a rare but honest look through Mika's eyes of what sufferers endure publically and the private psychological battle in many cases.

The arc of this story is uncomplicated. Love is blind. Beauty is in the eye of the beholder. When struck by cupid's arrow, love is hardly what we expect. It's more than we can hope for. For people with P, our skin may be grotesque at times throughout our lives, but we are unique, not flawed. If someone is brave enough to see past the disease and still love us, we must be brave enough to accept their truth.

To listen to the story song list visit
http://voicebetweenthelines.com/music-inspiring-my-writing

About the Author

I'm blessed to live on the beautiful west coast of British Columbia. After finishing my education, life took a drastic twist. I spent thirty-four years working with the Coast Guard.

Writing my first book in 2011 was more of a lark than a passion. Yet, one book turned into several. Military, contemporary, and paranormal romance is where you'll find my name. Receiving three literary awards for Code Name: Ghost, Code Name: Luminous, and His Perfect Imperfection was a wonderful acknowledgment and keeps me hunkered over the keyboard. When you open one of my novels you'll always find a cup of romance with a twist of steam.

If you'd like to catch up on other novels I've written visit my author's page on Amazon or BookBub and click the follow button. They'll notify you when I have a new release.

Other books by Natasza

SEALed with a Weekend
Twila's Tempest
Unquenchable Cravings: Gamble on Love
His Perfect Imperfection
Committed to Chase
Legend of Spiralling Cedars

A Warrior's Challenge Series
Code Name: Ghost – Book One
Code Name: Kayla's Fire – Book Two
Code Name: Nina's Choice – Book Three
Code Name: Luminous – Book Four
Code Name: Forever & Ever – Book Five
Code Name: Redemption – Book Six
Code Name: War of Stones – Book Seven

A Warrior's Passion Series
Cricket Under Fire – Book One
Dixie Under Siege – Book Two

Vyro Creek Series
Arizona Lightning
Arizona Thunder